D0468565

ROWAN'S DESIGNER COLLECTION

SUMMER & WINTER

KNITTING

ROWAN'S DESIGNER COLLECTION

SUMMER & WINTER

KNITTING

STEPHEN SHEARD

THE WESTMINSTER TRADING CORPORATION
Amherst, New Hampshire

Also available from Westminster Trading:
DESIGNER KNITTING by HUGH EHRMAN
DESIGNER NEEDLEPOINT by HUGH EHRMAN
BIG AND LITTLE SWEATER BOOK by SASHA KAGAN

First published in 1987 by Century Hutchinson Ltd,
Brookmount House, 62-65 Chandos Place, Covent Garden,
London WC2N 4NW

Published in the United States of America by
The Westminster Trading Corporation
5 Northern Boulevard,
Amherst, New Hampshire 03031

Library of Congress Cataloging-in-Publication Data

Sheard, Stephen.
Summer & Winter Knitting.

Includes index.
1. Knitting——Patterns. I. Title.

TT820.S48 1987 746.9'2 87-14783
ISBN 0-938953-02-8

First American Edition: September 1987
10 9 8 7 6 5 4 3 2 1

Photography by Tony Boase and Eamonn J. McCabe
Designed by Patrick McLeavey and Sue Storey
Additional text by Karen Elder
Styling by Kimberley Watson and Julia Fletcher (Classics),
Caroline Baker, Anne Drummond and Tracey Jacob (Moderns)
Manufactured in Italy

Opposite the title page *Christopher Fischer's Sun-Bleached. See page 133.*

Pages 10-11 *Susan Duckworth's Butterfly Floral Sweater. See page 78.*

Pages 80-81 *Bodymap's Ruched Panel Cardigan and Frilled Dress. See pages 150-55.*

Note The patterns in this book are not to be knitted for resale.

DEDICATION

To the British Designer Knitters,
without whom this book would not have been possible.

CONTENTS

THE MODERNS

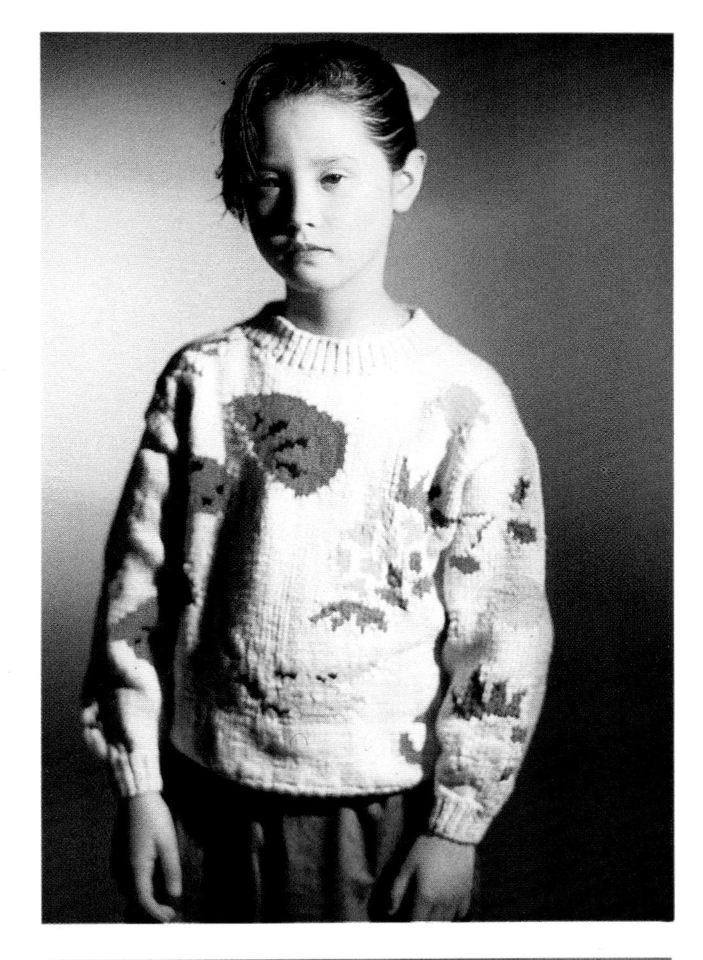

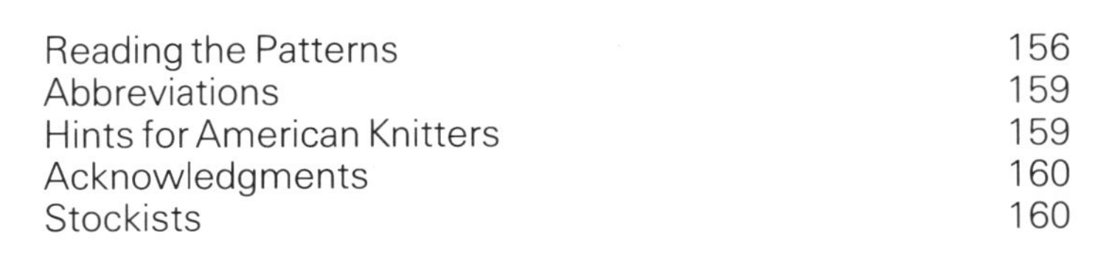

*Yarn kits are obtainable for these patterns. See page 160 for details.

INTRODUCTION

This book brings together the work of the most interesting and creative designer knitters in Britain. Over the past ten years they have revolutionized knitwear design and injected enthusiasm and excitement into a mundane market. The sharing of their designs with so many home knitters has fostered a new approach to knitting which has parallels with the Arts and Crafts Movement of the 1880s. Many of these talented designers built on their knowledge of traditional knitting skills to create innovative hand-made garments that often sell for ten times the price of mass-produced knitwear. Many were educated in the optimism of the 1960s and 1970s, and one of the few ways in which they could express their life-style was the emerging crafts movement of the time. Knitting, pottery, jewellery, weaving and many other crafts became popular, and by the natural survival process of any business, the best grew and prospered.

It has been argued that because the Industrial Revolution began in Britain as early as 200 years ago, much of the traditional craft heritage was lost, whereas countries which industrialized late managed to save a good deal of their craft and folk traditions. The fact that thousands of small, and not so small, craft businesses are thriving in Britain would tend to disprove this theory.

Designer knitwear is one of the areas where some of the best designers have flourished. There is no need for expensive capital equipment to transform design into a marketable product, so the designers have become knitters and manufacturers, adding on marketing, selling and administrative skills. This is one field where Britain leads the world. Designer knitters have been able to keep the chain of ideas through to product short, so that none of the usual compromises apply.

There is so much creativity in Britain today. We have more design colleges than many other European countries yet we fail to make the link between design and manufacturing, and many designers do not get the chance to put their ideas into practice. This is largely because of our generally conservative manufacturing industry which in the past has been lacking in imagination and fantasy. In other countries the factories would be producing the results of their designers' talents. Italy leads Europe in design and our colleges

Right *Kaffe Fassett's rich and sumptuous Carpet Jacket, a beautiful example of the wonderful work being done in Britain today.*

Above *Tucked away in a secluded valley in the Yorkshire Pennines, Green Lane Mill is the home of Rowan Yarns.*

train designers whose skills are widely acknowledged there. In an increasingly segmented market there are valuable lessons to be learned for manufacturing industry. The Victorian days of our own mill, which was then devoted entirely to weaving white gaberdine cloth for piece-dyeing with 50 men and women labouring under a clerk and the master, are thankfully gone. But many textile units, even today, yearn for the long runs of one quality and one design. These days are gone for ever in the Western world.

An increasingly discerning public is now searching for material goods which express individual life-styles rather than the processed formulas of mass production. This presents a major problem to the conglomerate approach to advertising and production. That the designer knitter can survive and prosper, producing hand-made articles in an automated age, is a credit to the producer and consumer. We have a long way to go, but there is plenty of room in the market place between the admirable efforts of Next and those of Yves Saint Laurent. It would be good to see more design in this country that pleases the spirit and without the dead hand of mass production and compromise. The designer knitters have given us a lead.

I set up Rowan Yarns with a friend in 1978 for many of the reasons mentioned above. It became clear that the new designer knitters needed yarns that were not readily available. The 'fashion yarns' in hand knitting were based on light, airy, fancy effects in easy-care synthetics. Tremendous effort goes into designing such yarns for maximum impact and minimum knitting time. The hand-knitting spinners have had great success in finding a look that is sufficiently different to factory-produced garments to form an alternative fashion statement, which is necessary if hand knitting is to move from knitting for economy to knitting for pleasure. It is also necessary for spinners to gain added value if they are to survive and prosper in a textile industry that is seen by many as the domain of the Third World.

However, designer knitters found it hard to get beyond this type of yarn as it inevitably dominated the design of a garment, and industrial yarns were generally in limited colour palettes and in synthetic fibres, often too fine for hand knitting, and only available in large quantities. What the designers needed were reasonably small quantities of natural fibre yarns of a fairly smooth linear construction in wide colour palettes. The yarn construction should not dominate the designers' skills, it should complement them, and their individual personality should come through as strongly as possible, as the designers in this book show.

The designers span the entire range of taste and fashion, from Kaffe Fassett through to Bodymap. Ten designers are broadly classic in their approach, and ten are broadly modern. Some, like Artwork and Sarah Dallas, have a strong feeling for fashion and may think of themselves as having little in common with the more craft-based designers. But they all share a strength in knitwear design, and this is the link. Some, like Christopher Fischer and Carrie White, are machine-knitwear designers, and their complex designs translate well into hand knitting.

There are photographs of 40 patterns, and a number of secondary pictures of other designs which are not available as patterns. These are intended to show the range of the designers' skills. The equal emphasis in the book on summer cottons and winter wools is a reflection of the new interest in lighter garments and the resurgence in good cottons for knitwear that may be worn all year round. The yarn weights cover the whole range, from fine four-ply soft cottons and Botany wools that allow designers maximum pattern and colour expression, through to the chunkies in rich wool tweeds. The yarns for some of the more complex designs are available as kits (see page 160), but are also available in good yarn shops in a number of countries (see page 160).

I hope this book will be, above all, a creative challenge, as well as a visual feast, to all those hand-knitters who enjoy spending their leisure time creating garments of real value and individuality.

Stephen Sheard

THE CLASSICS THE CLASSICS THE CLASSICS THE CLASSICS

KAFFE FASSETT

After visiting Kaffe Fassett the world outside seems a different place. He is so good at putting across the excitement and delight that colour and yarn afford him, and he opens the eyes of all who come into his realm. When he first picked up his knitting pins over 20 years ago what he saw was an opportunity to create fabric, colour combinations and shape, all under the control of his own two hands. The results were so startling that the rich, the royal and the famous have sought him out ever since, commissioning one-off pieces that they will treasure all their lives.

However, it is not only those privileged few who can be the proud owners of a Kaffe Fassett piece, for he and Rowan yarns have collaborated for several years, producing kits of his fabulous designs, containing all the necessary colours, weights and textures.

Kaffe has worked with Rowan since its early days in the late 70s. His suggestions for a colour range for Rowan Chenille were an immediate success, and provided the basis for several of the colour ranges for which they are now renowned, particularly among knitting designers.

Kaffe need not go far for his inspiration for with his painter's eye he sees colour and pattern in everything around him. He adores Oriental pots and rugs, but the studio is lined with more everyday ephemera – little snippets from magazines, picture books, decorated objects from old fans and umbrellas to floral tiles and sweet papers. In his hands the mundane can take on an exotic character that most of us would have missed.

★ ★ ★

WINDOWS COAT

Winter

KITS Certain shades in this design use only a proportion of the weights stated in the pattern. A yarn kit is available which has sufficient yarn to complete the garment and so will work out to be more economical. See page 160 for details.

SIZE

To fit one size up to 111cm (44in) bust

MATERIALS

500g Rowanspun Tweed in caper 762 (A); 300g in caviar 760 (B); 100g each in tea 752 (C), cedar 759 (D), tobacco 751 (E), damson 755 (F), confetti 758 (G), iris 757 (H) and paprika 754 (J)
100g Chunky Tweed each in tudor brown 712 (L), china blue 702 (M), blue lovat 705 (N), indian red 711 (Q), turkish pink 708 (R) and blue days 703 (S)
75g Light Tweed each in atlantic 223 (T) and midnight 224 (b); 50g each in lakeland 222 (U), lavender 213 (W), cherrymix 216 (X) and autumn 205 (a); 25g each in grey 209 (V), rosemix 215 (Y) and earth 206 (Z)
50g Classic Tweed in grey/grey 453 (c), heather grey 454 (d) and chestnut 457 (e)
150g Designer Double Knitting in airforce 65 (f); 50g each in purple 99 (g), grey 61 (h), amethyst 501 (i), red brown 71 (j), mist 118 (m), beige fleck 82F (n), brown fleck 77F (q), black fleck 62F (r) and royal fleck 56F (s)
25g Lightweight Double Knitting in gold 72 (l)
100g Bright Tweed each in viola 722 (t), nelson 723 (u), nautilus 727 (v) and mocha 725 (w)

Equivalent yarn Aran-weight
1 each 5mm (US8) and 6mm (US10) circular needles 100cm (40in) long
1 pair 5mm (US8) needles

NOTE The finer yarns are used in combination. For example, 'fi' means 1 strand each of yarns f and i; 'TTT' means 3 strands of yarn T; 'Tab' means 1 strand each of yarns T, a and b, and so on.

SPECIAL NOTE The 'outline' stitches separating each block of colour are worked throughout in yarn A. Carry yarn A across back of work from one block to next, always working to end of row to give an even texture, and 'weaving-in' where necessary every 3 stitches.
Each individual block of colour is worked using separate lengths of yarn or combinations of yarn, and yarns from adjacent blocks are then linked by twisting them together on wrong side to avoid gaps. In order to make work as neat as possible treat outline yarn (A) and yarn from block just worked as one, then twist yarn for next block round both of these together.

TENSION

16 sts and 20 rows to 10cm (4in) over patt on 6mm (US10) needle.

BACK, FRONTS AND SLEEVES (one piece)

Beg at lower edge back, using 6mm (US10) needle and yarn A, cast on 150 sts. Beg colour patt from chart 1 on page 14, work in st st throughout, beg with a K row. Work 150 rows from chart, marking each end of 100th and 130th rows for pockets.

Shape sleeves

Next row With yarn A, cast on 34 sts, work across these sts in patt from chart 2 on page 15 as foll: K1A, 14 Fa, 1A, 13bbb, 1A, 4Tf; cont in patt from 151st row of chart 1 as set to end of row, now using spare yarn A cast on 34 sts on to left-hand needle, cont in patt across these sts from chart 3 on page 15 as foll: K15C, 1A, 17L, 1A. 218 sts.
Cont in patt on all 218 sts, foll charts 1, 2 and 3 until 198 patt rows in all have been worked, ending with a WS row.

Divide for neck and fronts

199th row Patt 101 sts, turn, leaving rem sts on a spare needle and cont on these sts only for first side of neck.
200th row Cast off 6 sts, patt to end (from this point read charts from top to bottom for fronts, beg with 200th row again, and reading even-numbered rows as K rows, and odd-numbered rows as P rows). 95 sts.
Dec 1 st at neck edge on foll alt row. 94 sts.
Work 6 rows straight, ending at neck edge.

Shape front neck

Keeping chart patt correct, inc 1 st at neck edge on next and foll alt row. Work 1 row. Cast on 2 sts at beg of next row, 4 sts at beg of foll alt row and 7 sts at beg of next alt row. 109 sts.
Now work straight until front sleeve matches back sleeve from shoulder line, ending at sleeve edge.

Right and pages 15-16 *The sumptuous Windows Coat is worked in more than 40 colours. It can be worn as a casual garment or as an elegant evening coat.*

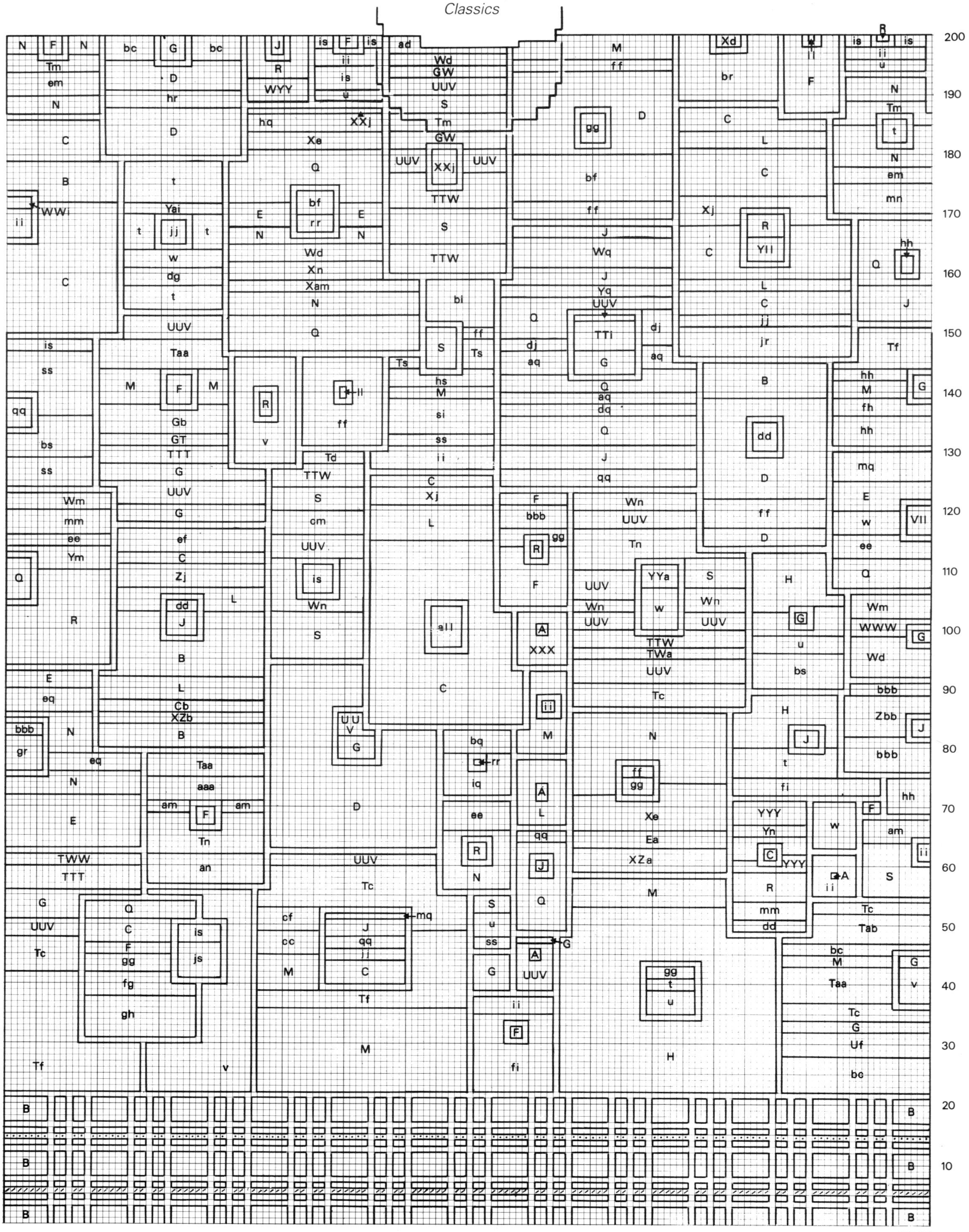

N F N bc G bc J is F is ad M Xd R is is 200
Tm R ii Wd ff ii
em D is GW br u
WYY u UUV F
N hr S N 190
hq XXj Tm D C Tm
C D Xe GW gg L t
UUV XXj UUV 180
B t Q C N
bf em
bf TTW mn
ii WWi Yai E rr E ff Xj R 170
t jj t N N S J
w Wd Wq C YII hh
dg Xn TTW J Q
C Xam Yq L 160
t N bi UUV C J
UUV Q ff Q dj jj
is Q S Ts dj TTi jr Tf 150
Taa Ts aq G aq
ss M F M hs Q B hh
R II M aq M G 140
qq Gb v ff si dq fh
GT ss Q dd hh
bs TTT Td ii J
ss G TTW C qq 130 mq
Wm UUV S Xj F Wn D E
mm G cm L bbb UUV ff 120
ee ef UUV R gg Tn D w VII
Ym C ee
Q Zj is UUV YYa S H 110 Q
L F Wn w Wn
R dd Wn all UUV UUV G Wm
J S A TTW u WWW
B XXX TWa bs G 100 Wd
E UUV
eq L C Tc 90 bbb
bbb N Cb ii H Zbb
gr XZb UU N J
B V M t 80 bbb
eq Taa G bq
N aaa rr ff fi
E iq gg
am F am D ee A Xe YYY 70 hh
Tn L Yn w am F
TWW an qq Ea ii
TTT UUV R XZa C YYY 60
N J A S
G Q Tc ii R
UUV C is cf mq S M mm Tc 50
Tc F js cc J u G dd Tab
gg qq ss A UUV bc G
fg M jj G gg Taa v 40
gh C Tf t
u Tc
ii F H G
M Uf 30
Tf v fi bc
B B 20
B B 10
B B

CHART 1

KEY

[•] = qq

[/] = s

Work Outline sts in A throughout

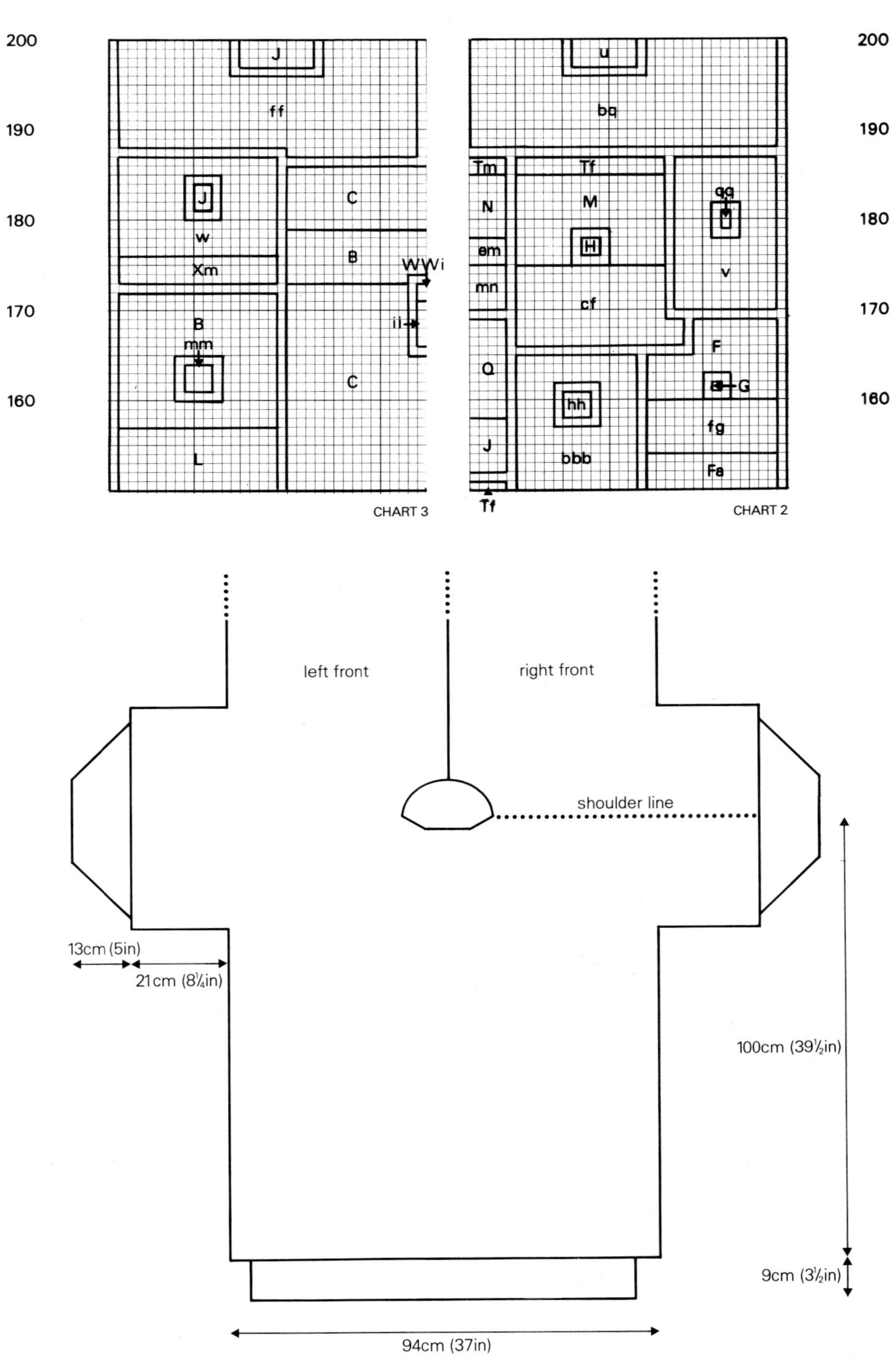

Next row With yarn A, cast off 34 sts, patt to end. 75 sts.
Now work straight until front matches back to 1st chart row, marking same rows for pockets. Work 1 row in yarn B.
Leave these sts on a spare needle.
With RS of work facing, return to sts on first spare needle, rejoin yarn to next st, cast off 16 sts, patt to end. 101 sts.
Next row Patt to neck edge.
Next row Cast off 6 sts, patt to end. 95 sts.
Complete second side of neck and front to match first side, reversing shapings.

LEFT POCKET LINING

With RS of work facing, using 5mm (US8) needles and yarn B, K up 25 sts between pocket markers on left back side edge.
Next row Cast on 8 sts, P to end. 33 sts.
Cont in st st, work 3 rows straight, then dec 1 st at end of next and every foll P row until 20 sts rem. Cast off.

RIGHT POCKET LINING

Work as given for left pocket lining, K up sts along right back side edge, and reversing shaping.

POCKET EDGINGS (alike)

With RS of work facing, using 5mm (US8) needles and yarn B, K up 25 sts between pocket markers on fronts.
K 1 row for foldline.
Work 4 rows in st st, beg with a K row.
Cast off loosely.

CUFFS

With RS of work facing, using 5mm (US8) needles and yarns Db, K up 52 sts evenly along sleeve edge.
Work in striped K1, P1 rib as foll:
1st-4th rows With yarns Db, work in rib.
5th row With yarns bs, rib 5, P2 tog, (rib 8, P2 tog) to last 5 sts, rib 5. 47 sts.
6th row With yarns bs, rib to end.
7th-8th rows With yarn B, work in rib.
9th row With yarns Fb, rib to end.
10th row With yarns Fb, rib 4, K2 tog, (rib 7, K2 tog) to last 5 sts, rib 5. 42 sts.
11th row With yarns FX, rib to end.
12th-13th rows With yarns CX, work in rib.
14th row With yarn J, rib to end.
15th row With yarn v, rib 4, K2 tog tbl, (rib 6, K2 tog tbl) to last 4 sts, rib 4. 37 sts.
16th row With yarn v, rib to end.
17th row With yarns ff, rib to end.
18th-19th rows With yarns Zff, work in rib.
20th row With yarns Zff, rib 3, P2 tog, (rib 5, P2 tog) to last 4 sts, rib 4. 32 sts.
21st-22nd rows With yarns CZ, work in rib.
23rd row With yarn Q, rib to end.
24th row With yarns XXX, rib to end.
With yarns XXX, cast off evenly in rib.

TO MAKE UP

Use yarn f for sewing up.
Join sleeve and side seams above and below pocket openings using backstitch seams.
Fold pocket edgings on to WS and catch down using yarn j. Catch down pocket linings on to WS of fronts.

Welt
With RS of work facing, using 5mm (US8) circular needle and yarn B, K up 151 sts evenly along bottom edge as foll:
K up row (K2 tog) 37 times, K1 across 75 sts on stitch holder at left front edge, K up 75 sts evenly along lower edge back, K1, (K2 tog) 37 times across 75 sts on stitch holder at right front edge. 151 sts.
Work 16 rows in K1, P1 rib using yarns as for 9th-24th rows of cuff.
With yarns XXX, cast off evenly in rib.

Front edgings (alike)
With RS of work facing, using 5mm (US8) circular needle and yarn B, K up 170 sts evenly (3 sts for every 4 row ends on rib and 6 sts for every 7 row ends on main piece) along front edge.
K 1 row to form foldline.
Work 10 rows in st st, beg with a K row.
Cast off loosely and evenly.
Fold front edgings on to WS and catch down.

Collar
With RS of work facing, using 5mm (US8) needles and yarns BZ, K up 90 sts evenly around neck edge.
Work in K1, P1 rib, working (3 rows in yarns BZ, 1 row in XXX, 3 rows in ff) twice, then 3 rows in BZ and 1 row in XXX, *at the same time* shape collar on 6th, 12th and 18th rows as foll:
6th row Rib 2, (K2 tog tbl, rib 10) to last 4 sts, K2 tog tbl, rib 2. 82 sts.
12th row Rib 2, (K2 tog, rib 9) to last 3 sts, K2 tog, rib 1. 74 sts.
18th row Rib 1, (P2 tog, rib 8) to last 3 sts P2 tog, P1. 66 sts.
With yarns XXX, cast off evenly in rib.

★ ★

CLOUDS BATWING

Summer

SIZE

To fit one size up to 101cm (40in) bust

MATERIALS

250g Sea Breeze Soft Cotton in turkish plum 529 (A)

250g Salad Days Knobbly Cotton in linen 562 (B)

Equivalent yarn four-ply

1 each 3mm (US2) and 3¾mm (US5) circular needles approximately 100cm (40in) long

2.50mm (USC) crochet hook

TENSION

25 sts and 31 rows to 10cm (4in) over patt on 3¾mm (US5) needles.

BACK, FRONT AND SLEEVES (one piece)

Beg at lower back edge, using 3mm (US2) needle and yarn A, cast on 150 sts.

Work 7 rows st st, beg with a K row.

K next row to form foldline.

Change to 3¾mm (US5) needle and beg colour patt from chart; work in st st throughout beg with a K row, rep 50 patt sts 3 times across row, strand contrast colours loosely across back of work over not more than 3 sts at a time, spreading sts to their correct width to keep them elastic.

Work 90 rows straight, end with a WS row.

Shape sleeves

Keeping chart patt correct, cast on 3 sts at beg of next 48 rows. 294 sts.

Now cast on 6 sts at beg of next 2 rows. 306 sts.

Work straight until 176 patt rows in all have been worked, ending with a WS row.

Divide for back neck

Next row Patt 139 sts, cast off 28 sts, patt to end.

Next row Patt to neck edge, turn, leaving rem sts on a spare needle and cont on these sts only for first side of back neck. 139 sts.

Cast off 7 sts at beg of next row and 5 sts at beg of foll alt row. 127 sts.

Work 3 rows straight, ending at neck edge.

Shape front neck

Inc 1 st at neck edge on next and 2 foll alt rows. 130 sts.

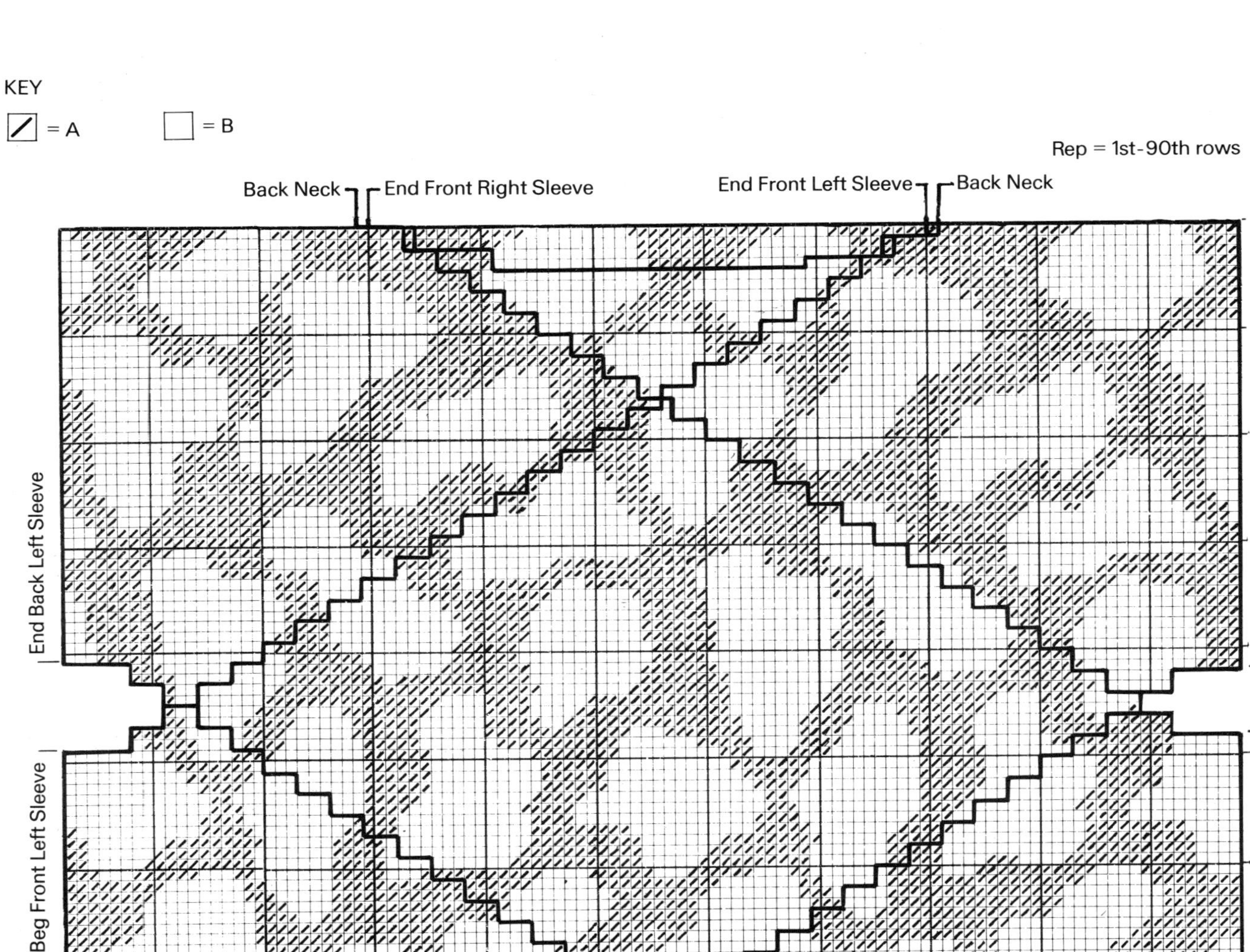

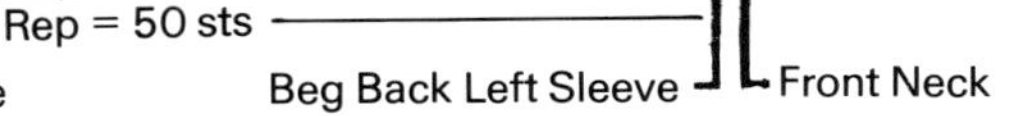

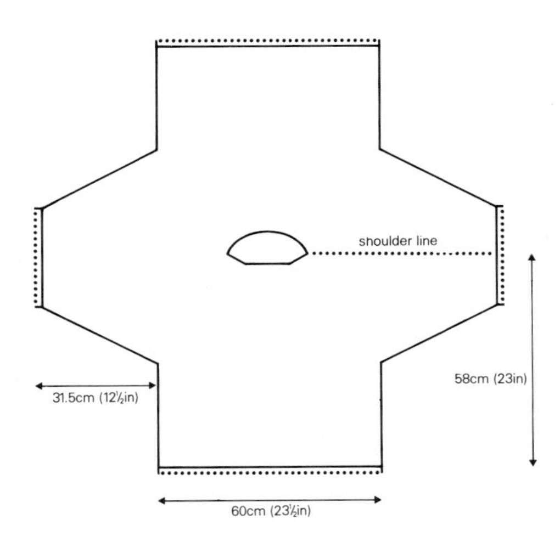

Work 1 row. Now cast on 2 sts at neck edge on next and foll 2 alt rows, then 3 sts at neck edge of next alt row and 4 sts at same edge on foll alt row. 143 sts.
Work 1 row. Leave these sts on a spare needle.
With WS of work facing, return to sts on first spare needle, rejoin yarn to next st and complete second side of neck to match first, reversing shapings and ending at sleeve edge.
Next row (21st row of 3rd patt rep) Patt across 143 sts of right side front neck, cast on 20 sts, patt across 143 sts of left side front neck to join both sides. 306 sts.
Now work straight until 221 rows in chart patt have been worked, ending on 41st chart row.

Shape sleeves
Cast off 6 sts at beg of next 2 rows, then 3 sts at beg of foll 48 rows. 150 sts.
Work 89 rows straight (4 complete patt reps have been worked).
Change to 3mm (US2) needle.
With A, K 2 rows to form foldline.
Work 7 rows in st st beg with a K row.
Cast off loosely purlwise.

TO MAKE UP

Sleeve edgings
With RS of work facing, using 3mm (US2) needle and yarn A, K up 70 sts evenly along sleeve edge, picking up 5 sts for every 6 row ends.
K 1 row to form foldline.
Work 6 rows in st st, beg with a K row.
Cast off loosely and evenly.
Join side and sleeve seams using backstitch seams.
Fold hems on to WS and slipstitch loosely in place.

Neck edging
With RS of work facing, using 2.50mm (USC) crochet hook and yarn A, work 2 rows double crochet evenly around neck edge.
Fasten off.

Right *Kaffe Fassett's Clouds Batwing in, unusually for him, only two colours. The yarns are both cotton – one soft and smooth, the other slightly textured.*

ZOË HUNT

Zoë Hunt has knitted for as long as she can remember, always creating her own designs, approaching them line by line which she says gives her a feeling of security. 'You can only be in one place at a time', unlike in painting or embroidery where the brush or the needle are free to move around. She wanted to make knitting her livelihood, but employing knitters and producing collections has never attracted her. She met Kaffe Fassett on a couple of occasions, and in a desperate moment rang him and asked for a job. That was over a decade ago, and the collaboration has been fruitful for both ever since.

Commissions for one-off clothes from Kaffe Fassett are often large, complicated and exotic. Zoë is a formidable knitter and has the rare talent of being able to interpret Kaffe's designs and make them a reality. The details of combinations of yarns for colour and touch, the exact scale of a flower or shape must be worked out with the needles, not just on paper. The sheer weight of some of the garments make them difficult enough to handle, but Zoë manages this effortlessly as she adds another 12 colours to the row she is working on.

Zoë continues to design in her own right, working to commission and for books. She has a particular skill in pattern writing, producing immaculate charts and instructions, and uses this talent too in her work with Kaffe. She admits to being influenced by the Fassett school, and this is surely inevitable and nothing to be ashamed of. The combination of these two design personalities can be stunning. But she also produces knitwear that is only Zoë Hunt – soft and feminine in a style that is elegant and sophisticated, as well as colourful. It is a rare mixture.

★ ★ ★

MOSAIC SLIPOVER

Summer

SIZE

To fit one size up to 96cm (38in) bust/chest

MATERIALS

100g Sea Breeze Soft Cotton in ecru 522 (A); 50g each in wheat 523 (B), smoke 527 (C) and pine forest 538 (D)

150g Salad Days Knobbly Cotton in linen 562 (F); 50g each in ecru 561 (E) and grey 565 (G)

50g Fine Cotton Chenille each in mole 380 (H), bran 381 (J), steel 382 (L) and shark 378 (M)

100g Handknit Double Knitting Cotton in taupe 253 (N)

Equivalent yarn double knitting

1 pair each 3¾mm (US5) and 4½mm (US7) needles

NOTE The finer yarns (A-G) are used in combination. For example, 'BE' means one strand each of yarns B and E, 'DD' means 2 strands of yarn D, and so on.

SPECIAL NOTE The 'outline' sts separating each 'tile' are worked in colours shown at edge of chart. Carry these yarns across back of work from 1 'tile' to next, always spreading sts to correct width to keep them elastic, and 'weaving-in' where necessary every 3 sts. Each individual 'tile' is worked using separate lengths of yarn or combinations of yarn, and the yarns from adjacent 'tiles' are then linked by twisting them tog on WS to avoid gaps. In order to make work as neat as possible, treat 'outline' colours and those from tile just worked as one, then twist colours for next tile round both of these tog.

TENSION

22½ sts and 26 rows to 10cm (4in) over patt on 4½mm (US7) needles.

BACK

Using 3¾mm (US5) needles and yarns AF, cast on 100 sts.

Work 19 rows in K1, P1 rib as foll: 2 rows in CC, 1 row each in N, AF, DD, FF, BE, 2 rows in CG, 1 row in AF, 2 rows each in N, DD, 1 row each in AF, GG, BE, N, DD.

Next row With yarns AF, rib 5, (make 1, rib 6) 15 times, make 1, rib 5. 116 sts.

Change to 4½mm (US7) needles and beg colour patt from chart on page 22. Work in st st beg with a K row until 80 chart rows have been completed, thus ending with a WS row. **

Shape armholes

Cast off 6 sts at beg of next 2 rows, then 2 sts at beg of foll 6 rows. Now dec 1 st at each end of next and foll 5 alt rows. 80 sts.

Work straight until 140 rows in all have been worked from chart, thus ending with a WS row.

Shape shoulders

Cast off 7 sts at beg of next 6 rows. 38 sts. Leave these sts on a stitch holder.

FRONT

Work as given for back to **.

Shape armholes

Cast off 8 sts at beg of next 2 rows and 2 sts at beg of foll 2 rows. 96 sts.

Divide for neck

Next row Cast off 2 sts, patt 44 sts including st used to cast off, K2 tog, K2 tog tbl, patt to end of row. 92 sts.

Next row Cast off 2 sts, patt 45 sts including st used to cast off, turn, leaving rem sts on a spare needle and cont on these sts only for first side of neck.

Now dec 1 st at armhole edge on next and foll 5 alt rows, *at the same time* cont to

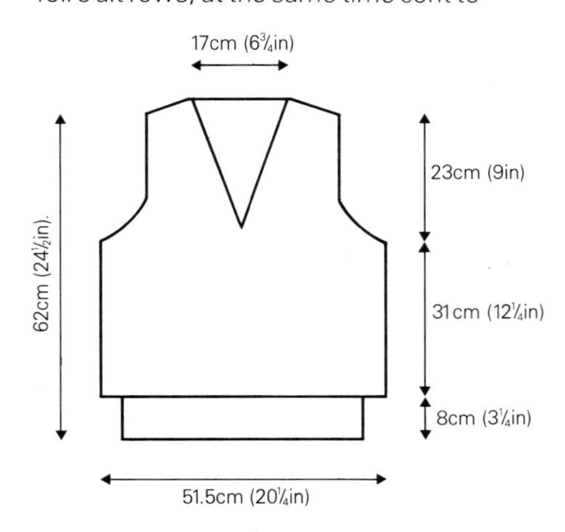

Right *Spanish architect Gaudi's famous broken-tile walls were the inspiration for Zoë Hunt's brilliant slipover.*

shape neck by dec 1 st at neck edge as set on 2nd and every foll 3rd row until 21 sts rem, working neck edge sts in outline colour. Work 2 rows straight, ending at armhole edge.

Shape shoulder

Cast off 7 sts at beg of next and foll alt row. 7 sts.

Work 1 row. Cast off.

With WS of work facing, return to sts on spare needle, rejoin yarn to next st, patt to end of row. 45 sts. Now complete second side of neck to match first side, reversing shapings and working K2 tog at neck edge instead of K2 tog tbl.

TO MAKE UP

Join left shoulder using a backstitch seam.

Neckband

With RS of work facing, using 3¾mm (US5) needles and yarns CG, K 38 sts from stitch holder at back neck, K up 61 sts down left front neck and 61 sts up right front neck. 160 sts. Work in K1, P1 rib as foll:

1st row (WS) With yarns AF, rib 59, P2 tog, P2 tog tbl, rib to end.

2nd row With yarns FF, rib 96, K2 tog tbl, K2 tog, rib to end.

3rd row With yarns DD, rib 57, P2 tog, P2 tog tbl, rib to end.

Cont to dec at front neck on every row as set, work 1 row each in yarns BE, N, CC and AF. With yarns AF, cast off evenly in rib, dec at centre front as before.

Join right shoulder and neckband seam.

Armhole edgings

With RS of work facing, using 3¾mm (US5) needles and yarn N, K up 128 sts evenly along armhole edge.

1st row (WS) With yarns DD, P to end.

2nd row With yarns AF, K to end.

3rd row With yarns AF, K to form foldline.

With yarns AF, work 4 rows in st st, beg with a K row. Cast off loosely.

Join side seams and armhole edgings. Fold edgings on to WS and slipstitch down.

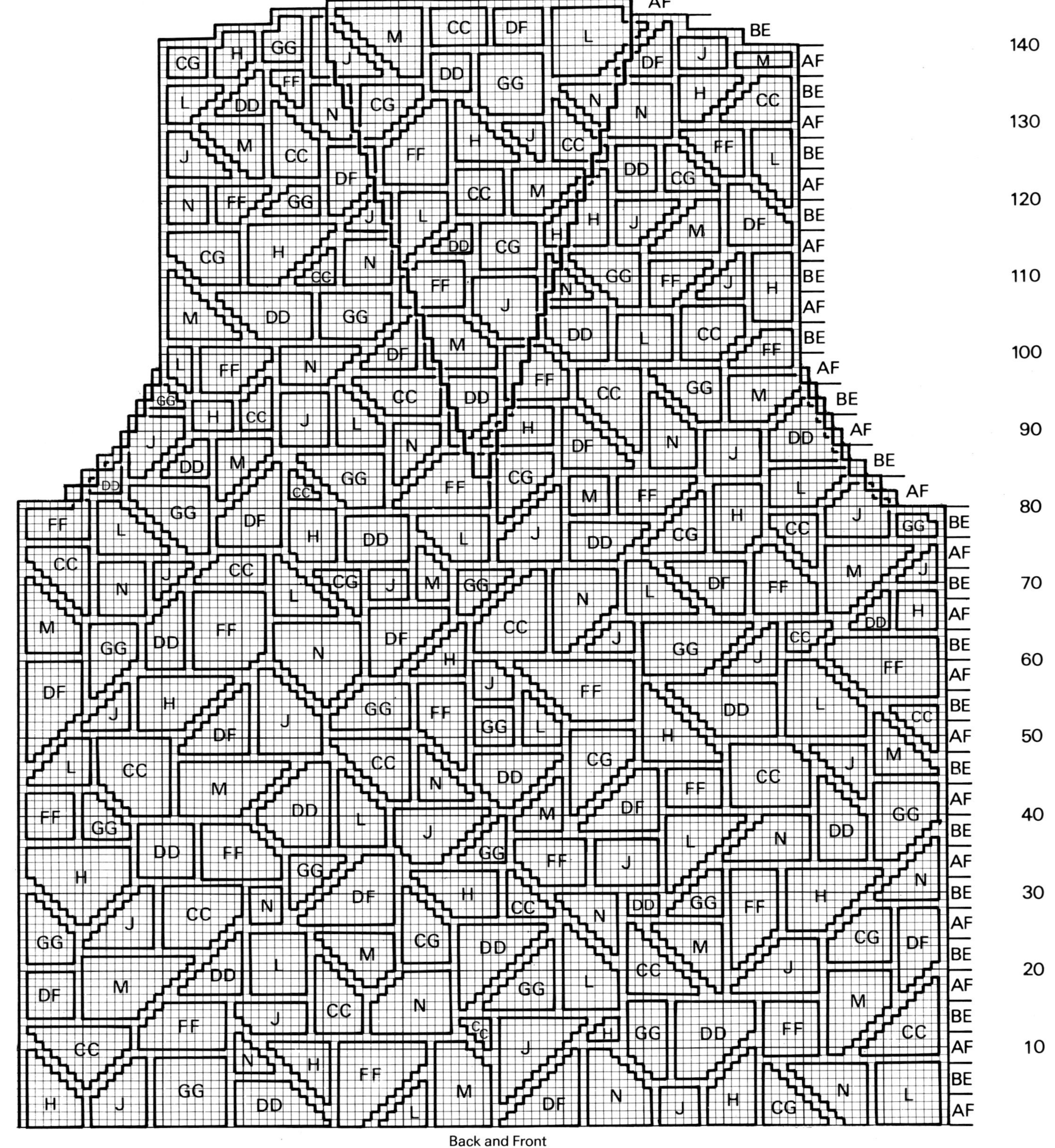

Back and Front

Above *The Mosaic Slipover is a marvellous example of Zoë Hunt's ingenious use of geometrics and her subtle blending of soft pastel shades. The same features are evident in many of her designs including this baggy V-neck (actually designed for her husband) which she made in a mixture of mohair and tweed yarns.*

★ ★ ★

MOSAIC SWEATER

Winter

KITS A yarn kit is available for this design. *See page 160 for details.*

SIZE

To fit one size up to 96cm (38in) bust.

MATERIALS

75g Lightweight Double Knitting each in navy 108 (A), sky 55 (E) and periwinkle 501 (F); 50g each in sea blue 53 (B), royal 57 (C), turquoise 125 (G), bright purple 126 (J), lavender 127 (L) and mauve 611 (M); 25g in light royal 56 (D) and purple 99 (H)
50g Fine Fleck Yarn in pink 410 (Q); 25g each in beige 82 (N), lavender 611 (R) and royal 56 (S)
50g Botany Wool each in brown 616 (U) and beige 82 (V); 25g each in royal 56 (T) and taupe 102 (W)
Equivalent yarn double knitting
1 each 3¾mm (US5) and 4½mm (US7) circular needles 100cm (40in) long
1 2.50mm (USC) crochet hook

NOTE The finer yarns (N-W) are used in combination. For example, 'NU' means one strand each of yarns N and U, 'QW' means one strand each of yarns Q and W, and so on.

SPECIAL NOTE The 'outline' sts separating each 'tile' are worked in colours shown at edge of chart. Carry these yarns across back of work from one 'tile' to next, always spreading sts to correct width to keep them elastic and 'weaving-in' where necessary every 3 sts. Each individual 'tile' is worked using separate lengths of yarn or combination of yarn, and the yarns from adjacent 'tiles' are then linked by twisting them together on wrong side to avoid gaps. In order to make work as neat as possible treat 'outline' colours and those from 'tile' just worked as one, then twist colours for next 'tile' round both of these together.

TENSION

23sts and 26 rows to 10cm (4in) over patt on 4½mm (US7) needles.

FRONT, BACK AND SLEEVES

Beg at lower front edge, using 3¾mm (US5) needle and yarns NU, cast on 92 sts. Work 19 rows in K1, P1 rib as foll: 1 row each in C, H, RU, ST, QR, G, B, NV, J, F, QV, E, RU, A, G, NV, ST, L, UW.
Next row With yarns RU, (rib 1, make 1) twice, (rib 2, make 1) 43 times, (rib 1, make 1) 3 times, rib 1. 140 sts.
Change to 4½mm (US7) needle and beg colour patt from chart 1. Work in st st, beg with a K row, until 38 chart rows have been completed, thus ending with a WS row.
Shape sleeves
Keeping chart 1 patt correct and working from chart 2 for left sleeve and chart 3 for right sleeve, cast on 5 sts at beg of every row until there are 340 sts.
Now work straight until 96 rows in all have been worked from charts, thus ending with a WS row.
Divide for front neck
Next row Patt 158 sts, cast off centre 24 sts, patt to end of row.
Next row Patt to neck edge, turn, leaving second group of sts on a spare needle and work on these sts only for first side of front neck. 158 sts.
** Keeping patt correct, but working neck edge sts in outline colour, cast off 4 sts at beg of next row, 3 sts at beg of foll 2 alt rows and 2 sts at beg of next 2 alt rows, then dec 1 st at neck edge on foll 3 alt rows. 141 sts.
Now work straight until 115 rows in all have been worked from charts. (The 115th row marks the shoulder line.)
Now reverse patt by turning charts upside

Right *Zoë's mosaic theme translated into winter wools in a mixture of intense blues and purples.*

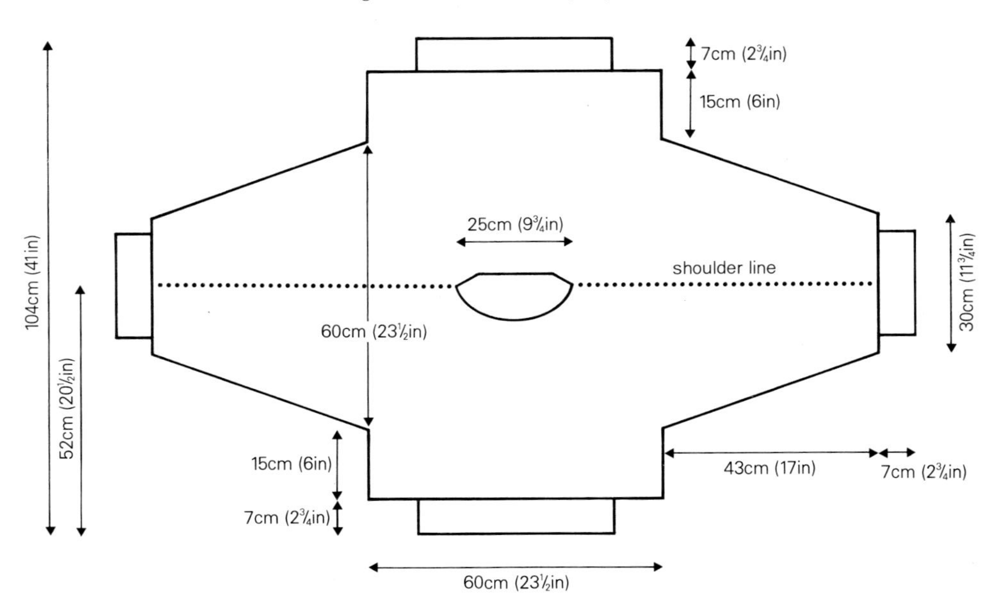

upside down and working back from 114th-1st rows (the first 5 reversed rows are shown).

Next row Patt 114th chart row.**

Shape back neck

Keeping reversed chart patt correct, cast on 5 sts at neck edge on next row and 7 sts at neck edge on foll alt row. 153 sts.

Work 1 row.

Leave these sts on a spare needle.

With WS of work facing, return to sts on first spare needle, rejoin yarn to next st and work as given for first side from ** to **.

Shape back neck

Work as given for first side of neck. 153 sts.

Join right and left sides

Next row Keeping reversed patt correct, patt to end of row, turn and cast on 34 sts, turn and patt across second side sts on spare needle. 340 sts.

Now cont to work back, reversing chart patt and shaping until 115th-1st rows of chart have been completed. 140 sts.

Change to 3¾mm (US5) needle.

Next row With yarns RU, (P2 tog) twice, (P1, P2 tog) 44 times, (P2 tog) twice. 92 sts.

Work 19 rows in K1, P1 rib, reversing colour sequence given for front rib.

Next row With yarns NU, rib to end.

Cast off evenly in rib.

TO MAKE UP

Cuffs

With RS of work facing, using 3¾mm (US5) needle and yarns UW, K up 52 sts evenly along sleeve edge.

Work 19 rows in K1, P1 rib, reversing colour sequence given for front rib.

Next row With yarns NU, rib to end.

Cast off evenly in rib.

Neck edging

Using 2.50mm (USC) crochet hook and yarns RU, work 1 row double crochet round neck edge, then work 1 row in yarn F.

Fasten off.

Join side and sleeve seams.

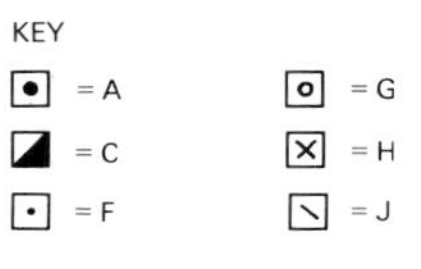

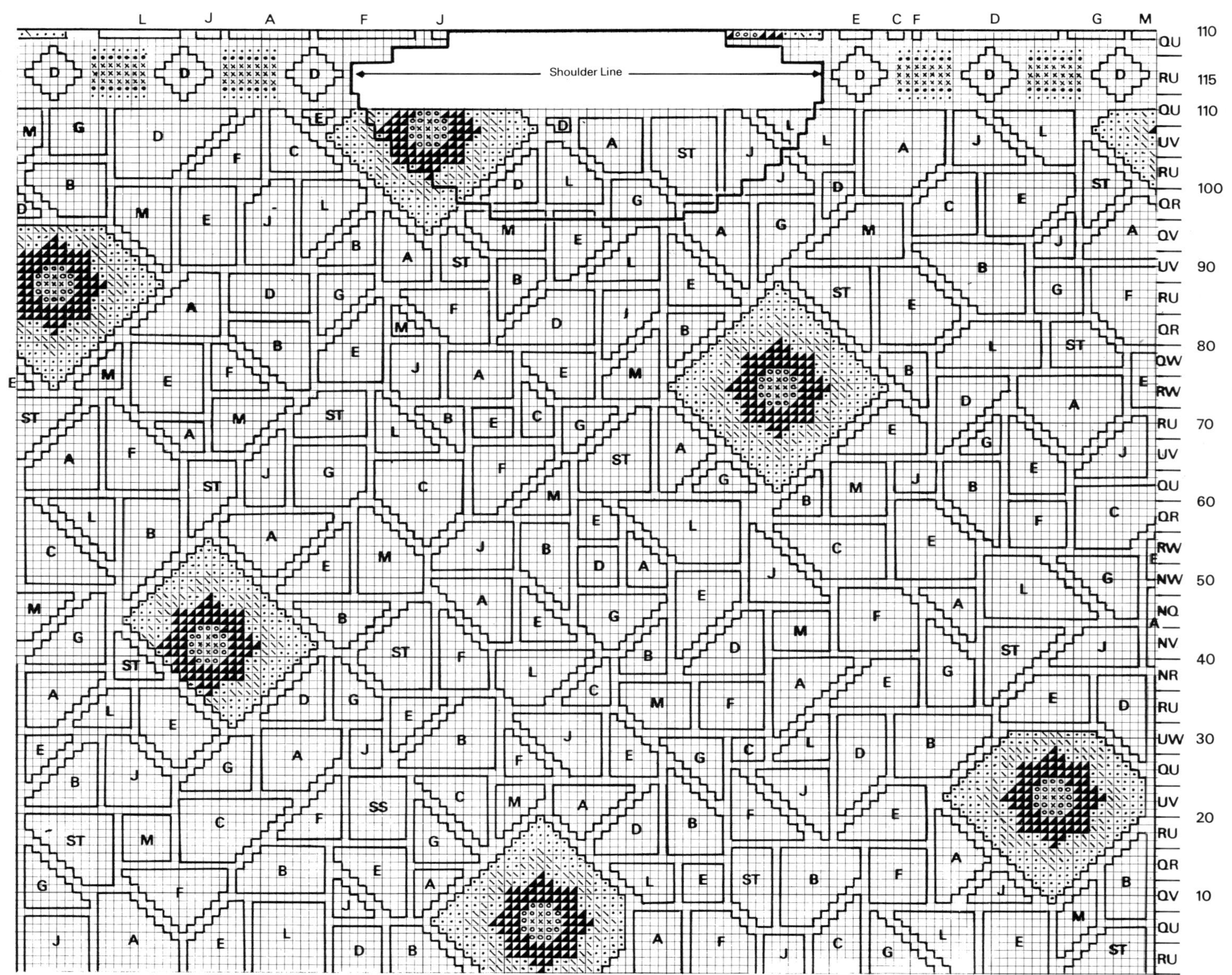

CHART 1

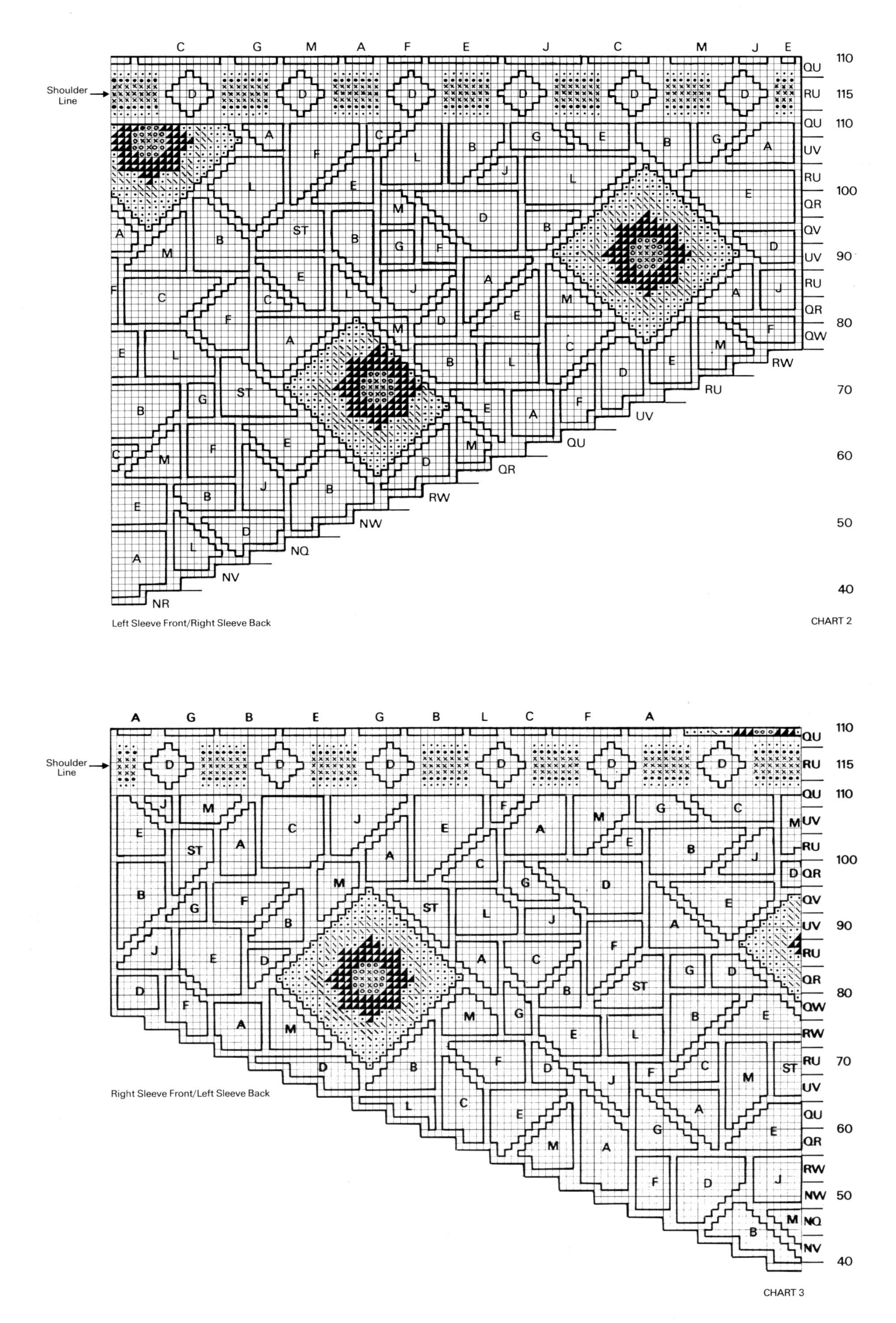
Shoulder Line
Left Sleeve Front/Right Sleeve Back
CHART 2
Shoulder Line
Right Sleeve Front/Left Sleeve Back
CHART 3

SASHA KAGAN

Sasha Kagan is a natural sharer, and through the colourful knitwear she designs and produces she shares her art. American fashion buyers soon discovered her in her rural retreat. Sasha rather likes the thought of her sweaters selling in sophisticated American stores and appearing in glossy publications, while she can savour the wholesome life amongst the trees and country lanes. Her first samples were things out of her own wardrobe that shops responded to when a friend offered to take them round on a trip to London. Handling colours, drawing the shapes, and visualizing the end result come easily to Sasha. She was a fiddle fingers as a child; her mother was a lampshade-maker, and together they knitted and made things constantly. She claims that many of her designs are inspired by her mother's *Stitchcraft* magazines. They may have been a starting point, but her colour combinations and lively motifs are surely way beyond the dreams of early post-war needlework.

★ ★

FISHES

Summer

SIZE

To fit one size up to 96cm (38in) bust

MATERIALS

150g Sea Breeze Soft Cotton each in polka 530 (C) and bermuda 539 (E); 100g each in black 526 (A) and sienna 535 (B); 50g in bleached 521 (D)

Equivalent yarn four-ply

1 pair each 2¾mm (US2) and 3¼mm (US3) needles

1 set four double-pointed 2¾mm (US2) needles

TENSION

28 sts and 36 rows to 10cm (4in) over st st on 3¼mm (US3) needles.

BACK

Using 2¾mm (US2) needles and yarn A, cast on 170 sts.

Work in K2, P2 rib as foll:

1st row (RS) (K2A, P2B) to last 2 sts, K2A.

2nd row (P2A, K2B) to last 2 sts, P2A.

Rep these 2 rows until rib measures 5cm (2in) from cast-on edge, inc 1 st at end of last row. 171 sts.

Change to 3¼mm (US3) needles and beg colour patt from chart, working in st st throughout, beg with a K row, using small separate balls of yarn for each colour area, twisting yarns tog on WS at colour joins to avoid holes, rep 1st-100th rows until back measures 33cm (13in) from cast-on edge, ending with a WS row.

Shape armholes

Cast off 9 sts at beg of next 2 rows. 153 sts. **

Now work straight until back measures 26.5cm (10½in) from beg of armhole shaping, ending with a WS row.

Shape shoulders

With yarn E, cast off 17 sts at beg of next 6 rows.

Leave rem 51 sts on a stitch holder.

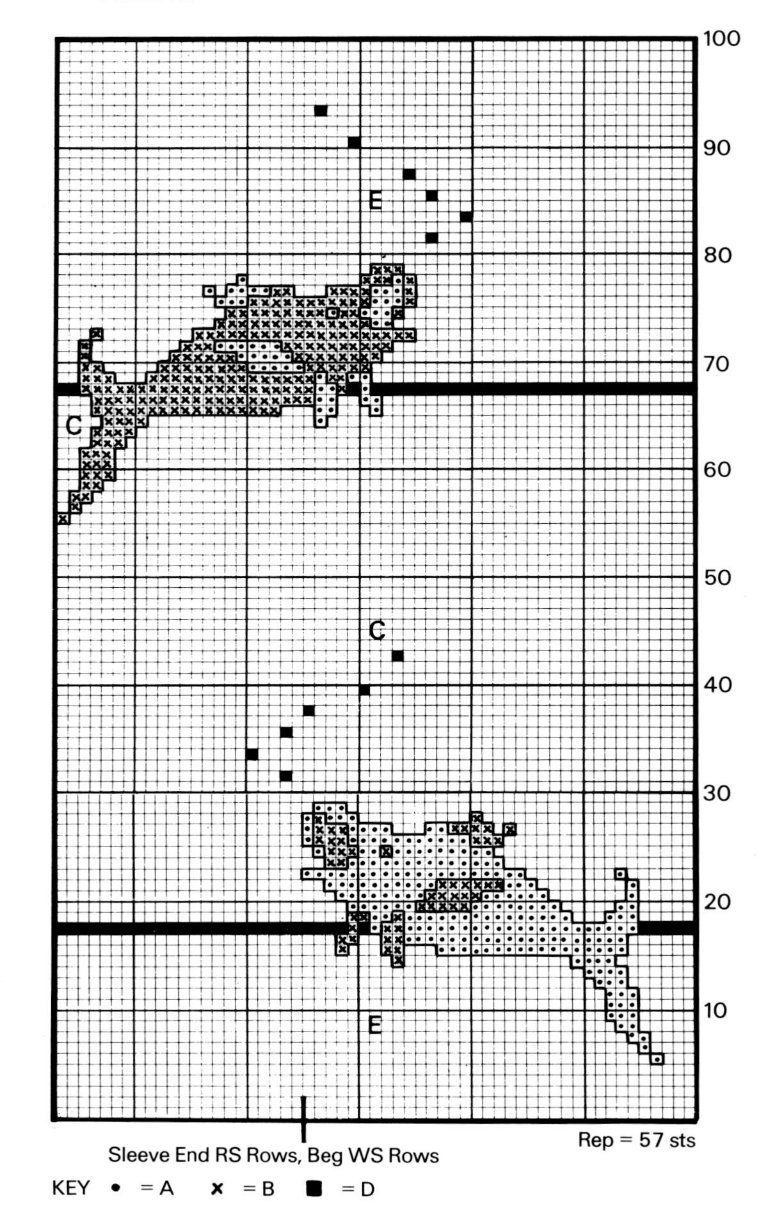

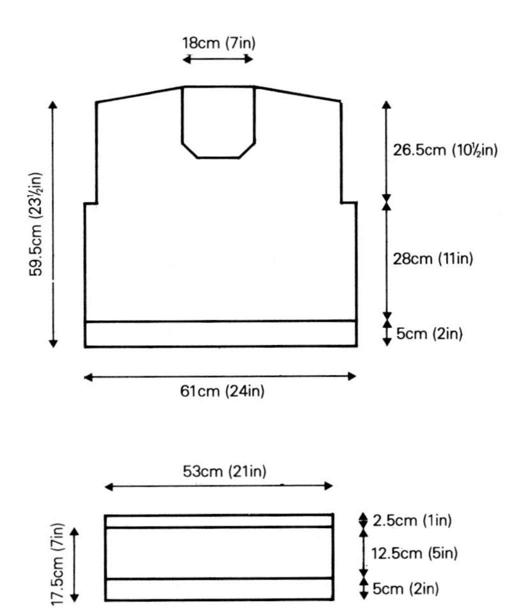

FRONT

Work as given for back to **. Work straight until front measures 10cm (4in) from beg of armhole, end with WS row.

Divide for neck

Next row Patt 60 sts, turn, leaving rem sts on a spare needle and cont on these sts only for first side of neck.

Dec 1 st at neck edge on next 9 rows. 51 sts. Now work straight until front matches back to shoulder, ending at armhole edge.

Shape shoulder

With yarn E, cast off 17 sts at beg of next and foll alt row. 17 sts. Work 1 row. Cast off. With RS facing, return to sts on spare needle, rejoin yarn, cast off centre 33 sts, patt to end. 60 sts. Complete second side of neck to match first reversing shapings.

SLEEVES

Using 2¾mm (US2) needles and yarn A, cast on 148 sts. Work in K2, P2 rib as foll:

1st row (RS) (K2A, P2B) to end.

2nd row (K2B, P2A) to end.

Rep these rows until work measures 5cm (2in), inc 1 st at end of last row. 149 sts. Change to 3¼mm (US3) needles and work in chart patt, end RS rows and beg WS rows at sleeve marker, work 1st-45th rows, dec 1 st at end of last row. 148 sts. Change to yarns A and B, and work 2.5cm (1in) K2, P2 rib as before. Cast off in rib in A.

TO MAKE UP

Join both shoulders using a backstitch seam.

Neckband

With RS of work facing, using double-pointed 2¾mm (US2) needles and yarn A, K up 60 sts down left side front neck, 33 sts across centre front, 60 sts up right side front neck and K 51 sts from back neck stitch holder. 204 sts.

Work 2.5cm (1in) in K2, P2 rib in A and B as given for 1st row of sleeve (work in rounds). Cast off evenly in rib in A.

Set in sleeve joining last few rows of sleeve to cast-off sts at underarm. Join side and sleeve seams.

Right *Sasha Kagan's Fishes Sweater.*

★ ★

Winter

SIZE

Sweater and Cardigan
To fit one size up to 96cm (38in) bust
Child's Sweater
To fit one size up to 66cm (26in) chest

MATERIALS

Sweater
350g Designer Double Knitting in grey fleck 64F (A); 250g in black 62 (B); 100g in white 1 (C); 50g each in yellow 13 (D) and mauve 127 (E)
Cardigan
450g in black fleck 62F (A); 200g in purple 501 (B); 100g each in green 90 (D) and pink 96 (E); 50g in yellow 13 (C)
Child's sweater
200g in black fleck 62F (A); 100g in green 90 (D); 50g each in purple 501 (B), yellow 13 (C) and pink 96 (E)
Equivalent yarn double knitting
1 pair each 3¼mm (US3) and 4mm (US6) needles
Set of four double-pointed 3¼mm (US3) needles (adult's sweater)
One 3¼mm (US3) circular needle 100cm (40in) long (cardigan)
4 buttons (cardigan)

TENSION

22 sts and 27 rows to 10cm (4in) over patt on 4mm (US6) needles.

SWEATER

BACK

Using 3¼mm (US3) needles and yarn B, cast on 120 sts.
Work in twisted K1, P1 rib as foll:
1st row (RS) (K1 tbl, P1 tbl) to end.
Rep this row until work measures 7.5cm (3in) from cast-on edge.
Change to 4mm (US6) needles and work in colour patt from chart as foll (carry yarn A across the back of the work but use small separate balls of contrast colours for each motif):
1st row (RS) *K8A, 1C, 11A; rep from * to end.
2nd row * P10A, 3C, 7A; rep from * to end.
These 2 rows establish the position of chart patt.
Cont in patt as set, work in st st and foll colour sequence table for changes in contrast colours until 100 rows in all have been worked in chart patt, ending with a WS row.
Shape armholes
Keeping chart patt correct, cast off 10 sts at beg of next 2 rows. 100 sts. **
Work 58 rows straight (160 rows in all have been worked in chart patt).
Change to yarn B and work 10 rows in twisted K1, P1 rib, ending with a WS row.
Shape shoulders
Cont in rib, cast off 11 sts at beg of next 4 rows and 10 sts at beg of foll 2 rows.
Leave rem 36 sts on a stitch holder.

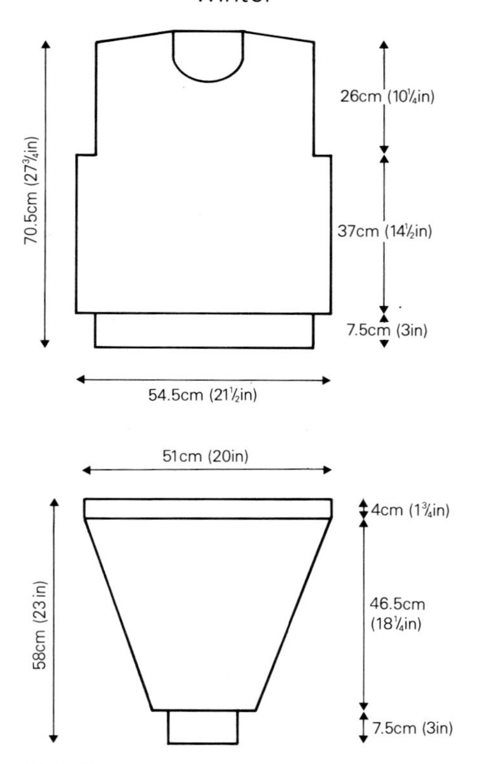

FRONT

Work as given for back to **.
Work 44 rows straight, end with a WS row.
Divide for neck
Next row Patt 42 sts, turn, leaving rem sts on a spare needle and cont on these sts only for first side of neck.
Dec 1 st at neck edge of next 10 rows. 32 sts. Work 3 rows straight.
Change to yarn B and work 10 rows in twisted K1, P1 rib ending at armhole edge.
Shape shoulder
Cast off 11 sts at beg of next and foll alt row. Work 1 row. Cast off rem 10 sts.
With RS of work facing, return to sts on spare needle, rejoin yarn to next st, cast off 16 sts, patt to end. 42 sts. Complete second side of neck to match first, reversing shapings and working 1 more row in twisted rib before shoulder shaping.

SLEEVES

Using 3¼mm (US3) needles and B, cast on 50 sts. Work 7.5cm (3in) in twisted rib.
Change to 4mm (US6) needles and A. Work 4 rows in st st beg with a K row. Cont in st st, commence chart patt.
1st row (RS) K5A, *8A, 1C, 11A; rep from * to last 5 sts, 5A.
2nd row P5A, * 10A, 3C, 7A; rep from * to last 5 sts, 5A.
These 2 rows establish the chart patt.
Cont in patt as set, foll colour sequence table for changes in contrast colours, *at the same time* inc 1 st at each end of next and every 3rd row until there are 68 sts, then every 4th row until there are 112 sts, working extra sts into patt.
Work straight until 120 rows have been worked in chart patt, ending with a WS row. With yarn A, work 2 rows in st st.
Change to yarn B and work 10 rows in twisted K1, P1 rib. Cast off in rib.

TO MAKE UP

Join both shoulder seams.
Neckband
With RS of work facing, using four double-pointed 3¼mm (US3) needles and yarn B, beg at left shoulder seam, K up 27 sts down left side of front neck, 16 sts across centre front neck and 27 sts up right side of front neck, then K 36 sts from stitch holder at back neck. 106 sts. Work 10 rounds in twisted K1, P1 rib, as given for back. Cast off in rib.
Set sleeve in flat, joining last few rows of sleeve to cast-off sts at underarm.
Join side and sleeve seams.

Right *The adult's Scotty Sweater.*

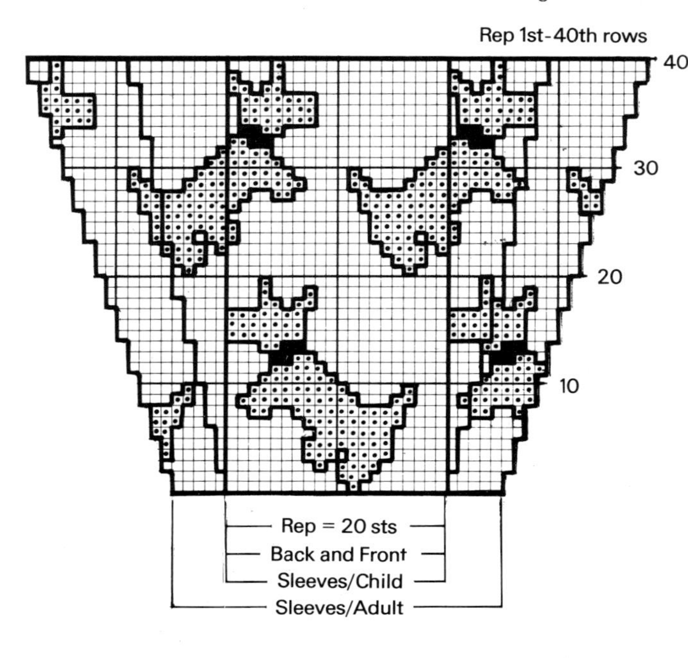

Colour sequence table

Adult's Sweater

Rows	□	⊡	■
1-20	A	C	D
21-40	A	B	E

Rep 1st-40th rows

Cardigan and child's sweater

Rows	□	⊡	■
1-20	A	E	B
21-40	A	D	E
41-60	A	C	D
61-80	A	B	C

Rep 1st-80th rows

CARDIGAN

BACK
Work as given for sweater back foll colour sequence table for changes in contrast colours.

POCKET LININGS (make 2)
Using 4mm (US6) needles and yarn A, cast on 25 sts.
Work 7cm (2¾in) in st st, beg with a K row.
Leave these sts on a stitch holder.

LEFT FRONT
Using 3¼mm (US3) needles and yarn B, cast on 60 sts.
Work 7.5cm (3in) in twisted K1, P1 rib as given for sweater back.
Change to 4mm (US6) and work in colour patt from chart as given for sweater back, but foll colour sequence table for cardigan.
Work 20 rows in chart patt, ending with a WS row.
Place pocket lining
Next row Patt 10 sts, sl next 25 sts on to a stitch holder, now patt across 25 sts of pocket lining, patt to end of row.
Patt 39 rows, ending at side edge.
Shape neck
Dec 1 st at neck edge on next and every foll 5th row until 52 sts rem.
Work 4 rows straight (100 rows in all have been worked in chart patt), ending at side edge.
Shape armhole
Next row Cast off 10 sts, patt to last 2 sts, K2 tog. 41 sts.
Keeping armhole edge straight, cont to dec 1 st at neck edge on every foll 6th row until 32 sts rem.
Now work straight until front matches back to beg of twisted rib, ending with a WS row.
Change to yarn B and work 10 rows in twisted K1, P1 rib, ending at armhole edge.

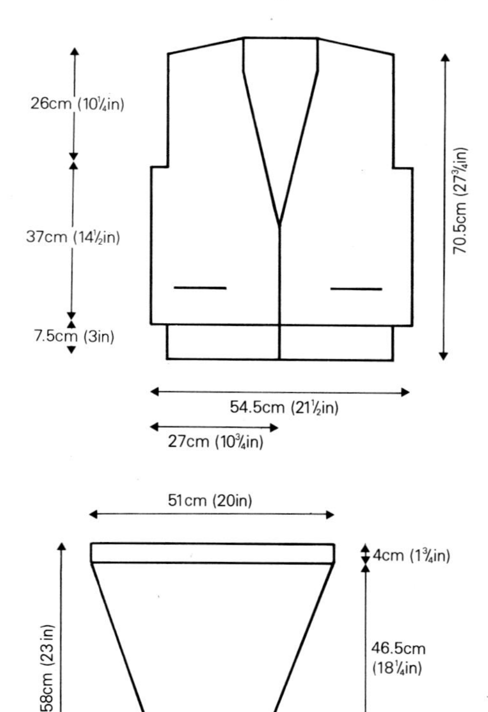

Shape shoulder
Cont in rib, cast off 11 sts at beg of next and foll alt row. Work 1 row.
Cast off rem 10 sts.

RIGHT FRONT
Work as given for left front, reversing all shapings and placing pocket lining as foll:
Next row Patt 25 sts, sl next 25 sts on to a stitch holder, now patt across 25 sts of pocket lining, patt to end.

SLEEVES
Work as given for sweater sleeves.

TO MAKE UP
Join both shoulder seams.
Set Sleeve in flat, joining last few row of sleeve to cast-off sts at underarm.
Join side and sleeve seams.
Pocket edgings
With RS of work facing, using 3¼mm (US3) needles and yarn B, sl sts from stitch holder on to left-hand needle and work 2.5cm (1in) in twisted K1, P1 rib.
Cast off evenly in rib.
Stitch down pocket linings to WS of fronts, and pocket edgings to RS.
Front band
With RS of work facing, using 3¼mm (US3) circular needle and yarn B, beg at lower edge right front, K up 21 sts along rib, 160 sts up right front to beg of twisted rib, 12 sts to shoulder seam, K (18, inc 1, 17) across back neck stitch holder, K up 12 sts down from shoulder seam to end of rib, 160 sts down left front to beg of lower rib, and 21 sts along rib. 423 sts.
Work 12 rows in twisted K1, P1 rib, working 4 buttonholes as foll:
6th row Rib 4, (cast off 2 sts, rib 22 including st used to cast off) 3 times, cast off 2 sts, rib to end.
7th row Rib to end, casting on 2 sts over those cast off in previous row.
When 12 rows in rib have been completed, cast off evenly in rib.
Sew on buttons.

CHILD'S SWEATER

BACK
Using 3¼mm (US3) needles and yarn D, cast on 80 sts.
Work 7.5cm (3in) in twisted K1, P1 rib as given for adult's sweater back.
Change to 4mm (US6) needles and work in patt from chart as given for adult's sweater back but foll colour sequence table for child's sweater. Work 54 rows in chart patt, ending with a WS row.
Shape armholes
Keeping chart patt correct, cast off 5 sts at beg of next 2 rows. 70 sts. **
Patt 44 rows straight, omitting parts of motifs at side edges between 61st and 80th rows.
Change to yarn D and work 8 rows in twisted K1, P1 rib, ending with a WS row.
Shape shoulders
Cast off 20 sts at beg of next 2 rows.
Leave rem 30 sts on a stitch holder.

FRONT
Work as given for back to **.
Patt 34 rows straight, ending with a WS row.
Divide for neck
Next row Patt 28 sts, turn, leaving rem sts on a spare needle and cont on these sts only for first side of neck.
Dec 1 st at neck edge on next 8 rows. 20 sts. Patt 1 row.
Change to yarn D and work 8 rows in twisted K1, P1 rib.
Shape shoulder
Cast off.
With RS of work facing, return to sts on spare needle, rejoin yarn to next st, cast off 14 sts, patt to end. 28 sts.
Complete second side of neck to match first side, reversing shapings and working 1 more rib row before shoulder shaping.

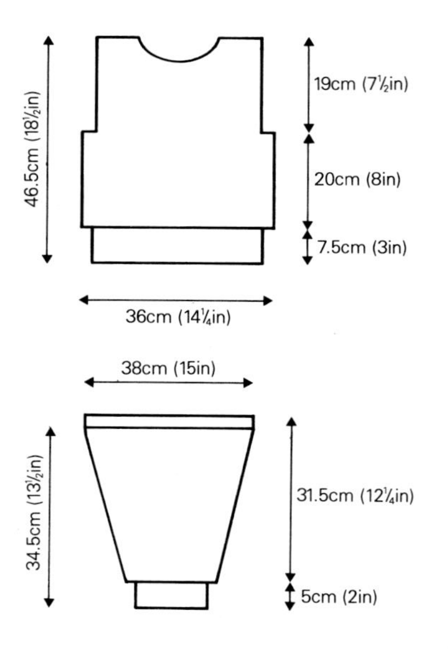

SLEEVES
Using 3¼mm (US3) needles and yarn D, cast on 30 sts. Work 5cm (2in) in twisted K1, P1 rib, ending with a RS row.
Next row Rib 2, (make 1, rib 3) 9 times, make 1, rib 1. 40 sts.
Change to 4mm (US6) needles and commence chart patt as given for back, *at the same time* inc 1 st at each end of 3rd and every foll 4th row until there are 50 sts, then of every foll 5th row until there are 58 sts, then of every foll 3rd row until there are 84 sts, working the incs into patt. Patt 2 rows. Change to yarn D and work 8 rows in twisted K1, P1 rib.
Cast off loosely and evenly in rib.

TO MAKE UP
Join right shoulder
Neckband
With RS of work facing, using 3¼mm (US3) needles and yarn D, K up 17 sts down left side of front neck, 14 sts across centre front neck, 17 sts up right side of front neck and 30 sts from stitch holder at back neck. 78 sts. Work 9 rows in twisted K1, P1 rib.
Cast off evenly in rib.
Join left shoulder and neckband seam.
Set sleeves in flat, joining last few rows of sleeve to cast-off sts at underarm.
Join side and sleeve seams.

Right *The Scotty Cardigan and the child's sweater in bright modern colours.*

CARRIE WHITE

If you board the local bus deep in the Welsh countryside near Newtown you might find it carrying not only people but parcels of yarn. These mixed bags of wool, cotton, chenille and silk will be transformed into subtly shaded flowers and patterns that city ladies all around the world will wear and treasure. Carrie White employs knitters in remote farmhouses and isolated cottages to produce the elaborate floral designs that characterize her work.

Teaching jobs brought Carrie and her husband, Jeremy, to Wales in the early 1970s. They are happy with a life where roses around the door and hens out the back are a reality. Behind the idyllic exterior is dedication, hard work, a sound business sense and a special ability to produce designs that are on a different plane to topical fashion. A Carrie White cardigan will still look fresh five years after it has left its country birthplace.

Despite this enduring quality, the fashion world demands two new collections a year, and Carrie continues to provide a changing bouquet each season. She is primarily a textile designer who designs for the medium rather than attempting to squeeze ideas into a knitted form. The limitations of the domestic knitting machines that her outworkers use do not deter her from achieving the desired result. The effect, even on close inspection, is of a hand-knitted garment.

Jeremy gave up teaching to assist Carrie in running the business. A large chart on the kitchen wall records and forecasts the state of play, and there are no set hours for work. Much planning is done at the breakfast table as orders from all over the world are processed into lists, supplies and instructions for the knitters. Finishers sew up the work and all is checked for size and quality before the shippers arrive.

In an area where jobs are scarce, they are proud to contribute to rural life by providing regular employment for 22 people. Catch the bus back to Newtown, and it is likely that those parcels by the driver are cardigans, waistcoats and sweaters destined for New York, Paris and London.

★ ★

BIJAR SWEATER

Summer

KITS A yarn kit is available for this design. *See page 160 for details.*

SIZE

To fit one size up to 101cm (40in) bust

MATERIALS

450g Handknit Double Knitting Cotton in ecru 251 (A); 100g in violet 256 (B); 50g each in peacock 259 (C), fuchsia 258 (D), sunflower 261 (E), taupe 253 (F)
100g Cotton Chenille in lavender 357 (G); 50g each in grey/green 361 (H), and cloud blue 360 (J)
50g Cabled Mercerised Cotton in spode 307 (L)
50g Salad Days Knobbly Cotton in hyacinth 566 (M)
Equivalent yarn double knitting
1 pair each 3¼mm (US3) and 4mm (US6) needles.

NOTE Use yarns L and M double.

TENSION

20 sts and 24 rows to 10cm (4in) over patt on 4mm (US6) needles.

BACK

Using 3¼mm (US3) needles and yarn A, cast on 112 sts. Work 12 rows in K2, P2 rib, dec 1 st at end of last row. 111 sts.
Change to 4mm (US6) needles and beg colour patt from chart as foll, weaving yarn A and border patt yarns into back of work, but using separate balls of yarn for motifs.
1st row (RS) K1A, 1B, 5A, 1B, 2A, * 3A, (1B, 5A) 4 times, 1B, 2A; rep from * to last 11 sts, 3A, 1B, 5A, 1B, 1A.
2nd row P to end in B.
These 2 rows establish the position of the chart. Cont in patt as set, working in st st throughout, work 1st-10th rows then rep 11th-70th rows until 72 rows in all have been worked from chart, end with a WS row.
Shape armholes
Keeping chart patt correct, cast off 10 sts at beg of next 2 rows. 91 sts.
Work 58 rows straight, ending with a WS row.
Shape shoulders and back neck
Next row Cast off 7 sts, patt 20 sts including st used to cast off, turn, leaving rem sts on a spare needle, cont on these sts only for first side of neck.
Cast off 3 sts at beg of next row, 7 sts at beg of foll row and 3 sts at beg of next row. Cast off rem 7 sts.
With RS of work facing, return to sts on spare needle, sl centre 37 sts on to a stitch holder, rejoin yarn, patt to end. 27 sts.
Next row Cast off 7 sts, patt to end. 20 sts.

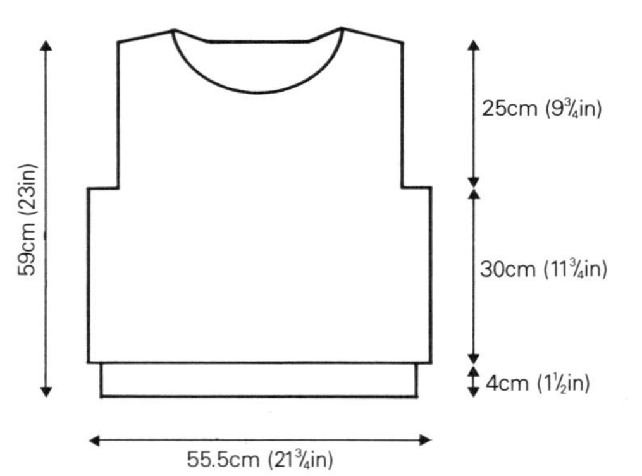

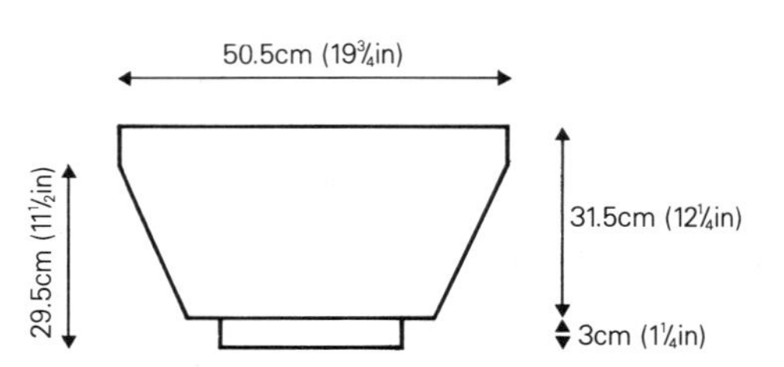

Right *Motifs from a Kurdish carpet influenced the design of Carrie White's Bijar Sweater in cool summer cottons.*

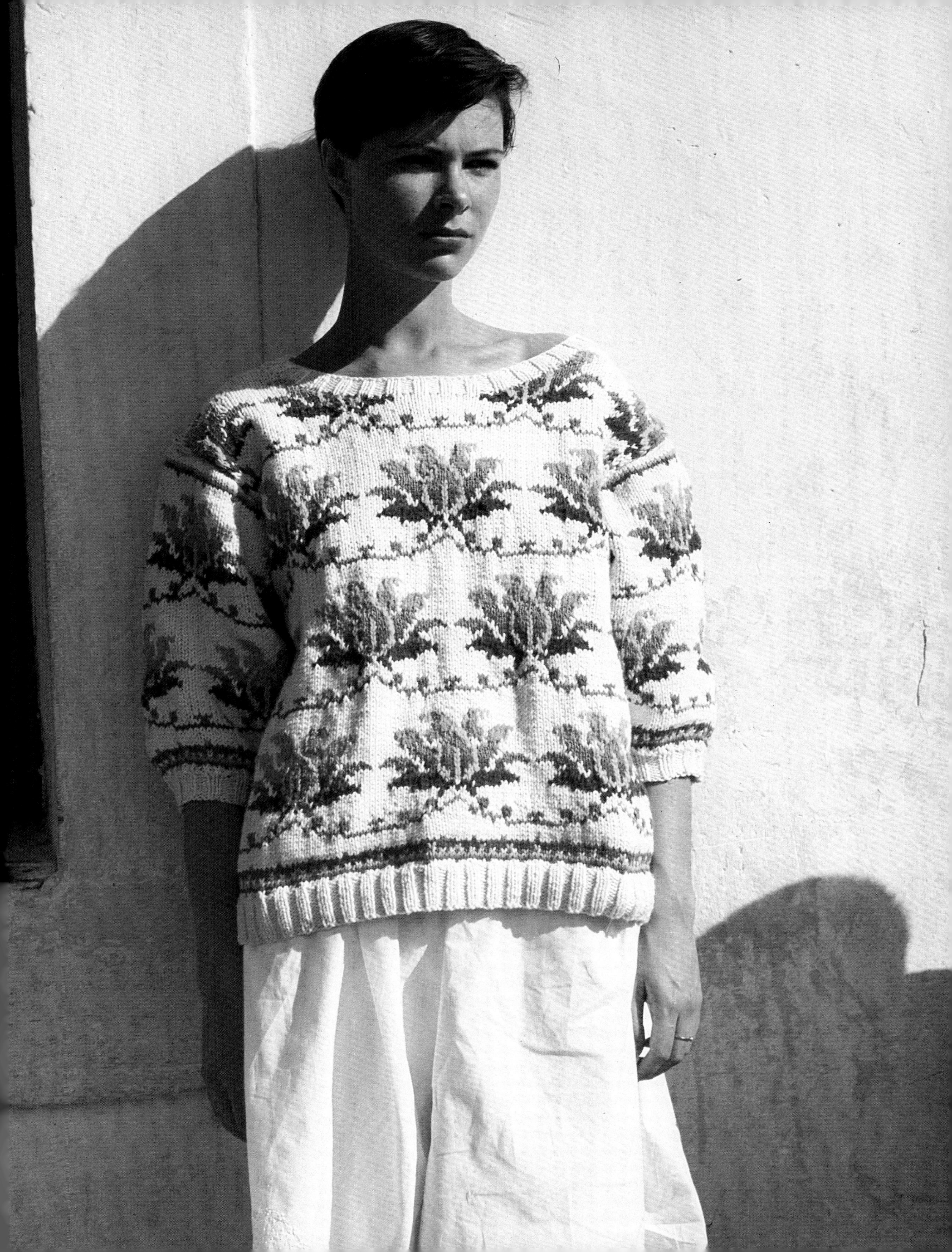

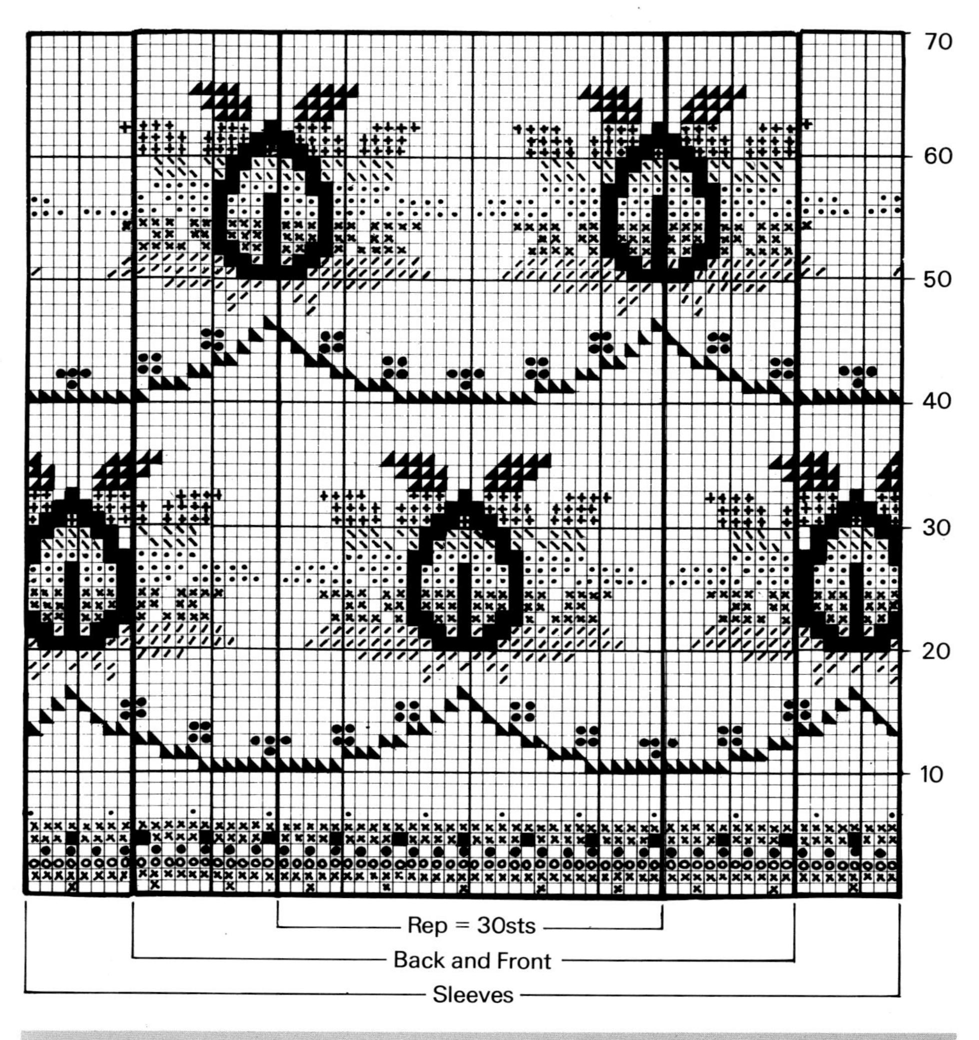

KEY

- □ = A
- ☒ = B
- ○ = C
- ● = D
- ■ = E
- ◣ = F
- ⟋ = G
- ◢ = H
- ⊞ = J
- ⟍ = L
- · = M

Complete second side of neck to match first side, reversing shapings.

FRONT

Work as given for back to **.
Now work 36 rows straight, ending with a WS row.

Divide for neck

Next row Patt 38 sts, turn, leaving rem sts on a spare needle and cont on these sts only for first side of neck.
Cast off 3 sts at beg of next and foll 2 alt rows, then 2 sts at beg of next 2 alt rows and 1 st at beg of foll 4 alt rows. 21 sts.
Now work straight until front matches back to beg of shoulder shaping, ending at armhole edge.

Shape shoulder

Cast off 7 sts at beg of next and foll alt row.
Work 1 row.
Cast off rem 7 sts.
With RS of work facing, return to sts on spare needle, sl centre 15 sts on to a stitch holder, rejoin yarn to next st, patt to end of row. 38 sts.
Complete second side of neck to match first side, reversing shapings.

SLEEVES

Using 3¼mm (US3) needles and yarn A, cast on 48 sts.
Work 9 rows in K2, P2 rib.
Next row Rib 6, (make 1, rib 2) 18 times, make 1, rib 6. 67 sts.
Change to 4mm (US6) needles and beg colour patt from chart working between sleeve markers, work 1st-70th rows, then 1st-3rd rows again, then 3 rows in A only, *at the same time* inc 1 st at each end of 2nd row and foll 7 alt rows, then at each end of every foll 4th row until there are 101 sts, working the incs into patt. Cast off.

TO MAKE UP

Join right shoulder using a backstitch seam.

Neckband

With RS of work facing, using 3¼mm (US3) needles and yarn A, K up 28 sts down left side of front neck, K 15 sts from stitch holder at front neck, K up 28 sts up right side of front neck, 6 sts down left back neck, K 37 sts from stitch holder at back neck and K up 6 sts up right back neck. 120 sts.
Work 6 rows in K2, P2 rib.
Cast off loosely and evenly in rib.
Join left shoulder and neckband seam.
Set sleeves in flat joining last few rows of sleeve to cast-off sts at underarm.
Join side and sleeve seams.

Left *Carrie White is better known as the designer of colourful machine-knits like this beautiful jacket.*

Carrie White

★★

BIJAR CARDIGAN

Winter

SIZE

To fit one size up to 106cm (42in) bust/chest

MATERIALS

900g Rowanspun in ecru 765 (A); 200g in iris 757 (E)
100g Designer Double Knitting each in yellow 13 (B), cyclamen 93 (C) and deep purple 99 (D); 50g each in blue fleck 51F (G) and beige fleck 82F (J)
100g Cotton Chenille each in grey/green 361 (F), lavender 357 (H), periwinkle 358 (M) and cloud blue 360 (L)
Equivalent yarn Aran-weight
1 pair each 3¾mm (US5) and 4½mm (US7) needles

NOTE When working yarns B, C, D, G and J, use 2 strands together.

TENSION

18 sts and 25 rows to 10cm (4in) over st st on 4½mm (US7) needles.

BACK

Using 3¾mm (US5) needles and yarn A, cast on 108 sts.
Work in K2, P2 rib as foll:
1st row (RS) K1, (P2, K2) to last 3 sts, P2, K1.
2nd row P1, (K2, P2) to last 3 sts, K2, P1.
Rep these 2 rows until work measures 7.5cm (3in) from cast-on edge, ending with a RS row.
Next row Rib 4, (make 1, rib 25) 4 times, make 1, rib 4. 113 sts.
Change to 4½mm (US7) needles and beg colour patt from chart 1 on page 40 working between back markers, weaving yarn A and border patt yarns into back of work but using small separate balls of yarn for motifs where convenient to do so. Work 94 rows marking each end of 16th and 44th rows for pockets, ending with a WS row.
Shape armholes
Keeping chart patt correct, cast off 12 sts at beg of next 2 rows. 89 sts.
Cont in chart patt until 119 rows have been worked, then work 48th-98th rows again, ending with a WS row.
Shape shoulders
Cast off 15 sts at beg of next 2 rows and 14 sts at beg of foll 2 rows.
Cast off rem 31 sts.

LEFT FRONT

Using 3¾mm (US5) needles and yarn A, cast on 73 sts.
Next row (RS) With yarn A, K1, (P2, K2) 14 times, K3E, K to end in A.
Next row P13A, P3E, with yarn A (P2, K2) 14 times, P1.
Rep these 2 rows until work measures 7.5cm (3in), ending with a WS row.
Change to 4½mm (US7) needles and beg colour patt from chart 1, working 57 sts between markers for left front, and cont to work 13 sts in yarn A and 3 sts in yarn E as set in st st for front opening facing.
Work 94 rows straight, marking side seam edge on 16th and 44th rows for pocket, ending with a WS row.
Shape armhole
Keeping chart patt and facings correct, cast off 12 sts at beg of next row. 61 sts.
Cont in chart patt until 119 rows have been worked, then work 48th-98th rows again, ending at armhole edge.
Shape shoulder
Cast off 15 sts at beg of next row and 14 sts at beg of foll alt row. 32 sts.
Shape collar
Keeping facings and chart patt correct, work straight until 119th row of chart is completed, then work 3 rows in A only.
Cast off.

RIGHT FRONT

Work as given for left front reversing facing and all shapings.

SLEEVES

Using 3¾mm (US5) needles and yarn A, cast on 46 sts.
Work in K2, P2 rib as foll:
1st row (RS) K2, (P2, K2) to end.
2nd row P2, (K2, P2) to end.
Rep these 2 rows until work measures 14cm (5½in), from cast-on edge, ending with a RS row.
Next row Rib 1, (make 1, rib 2) 22 times, make 1, rib 1. 69 sts.
Change to 4½mm (US7) needles and beg colour patt from chart 1, working between sleeve markers, *at the same time* inc 1 st at each end of 3rd and every foll 5th row until there are 107 sts, working the incs into patt.
Work 2 rows straight. (95 patt rows have been worked.)
Now beg colour patt from chart 2 on page 40, beg with a P row, inc 1 st at each end of 3rd row. 109 sts.
When chart 2 is complete, cast off loosely and evenly.

TO MAKE UP

Join both shoulders using a backstitch seam.
Join back collar seam.
Stitch collar to neck edge. Fold facing on to WS at 3-st stripe, using the middle st as the foldline. Slipstitch in place down both fronts and across back neck.
Pocket edgings
With RS of work facing, using 3¾mm (US5) needles and yarn A, K up 26 sts between pocket markers on left front.
Work 6 rows in K2, P2 rib as given for sleeve.
Cast off evenly in rib.
Work right front pocket edging to match.
Pocket linings
With RS of work facing, using 4½mm (US7) needles and yarn A, K up 22 sts between pocket markers on left back side seam.
Work 54 rows in st st, beg with a P row.
Cast off. Work right front pocket lining to match.
Set in sleeves flat, joining last few rows of sleeve to cast-off sts at underarm.
Join sleeve and side seam above and below opening.
Fold pocket lining in half. Join cast-off edge to front between pocket markers. Join pocket sides.
Catch down pocket edgings to RS back.
Fold back cuffs.

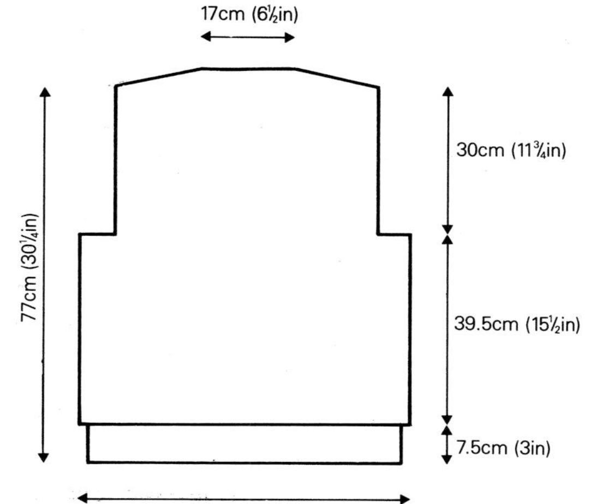

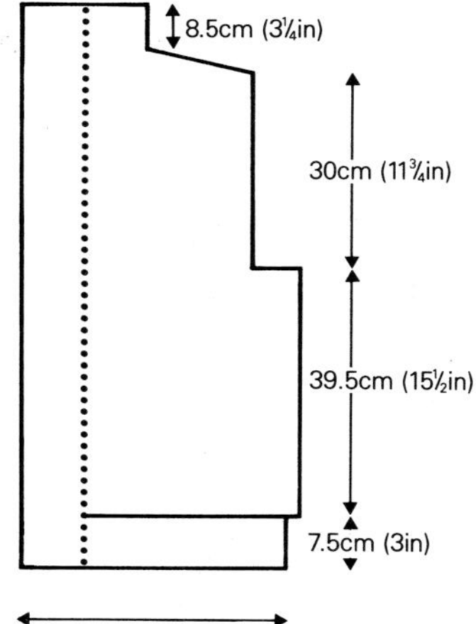

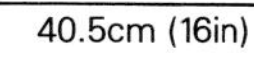

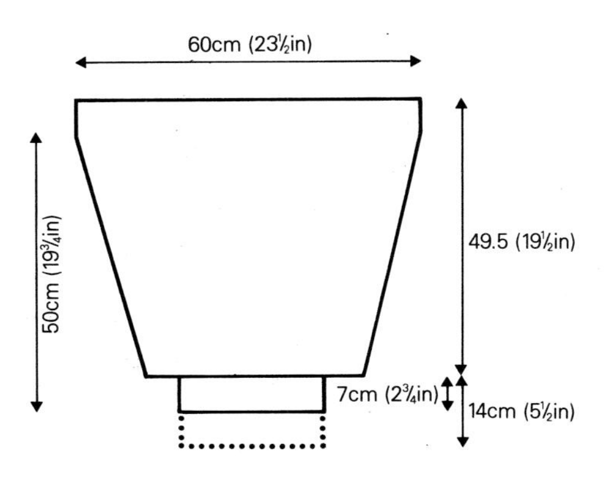

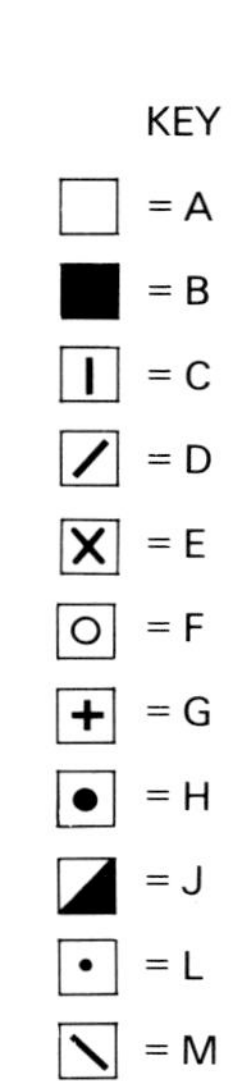

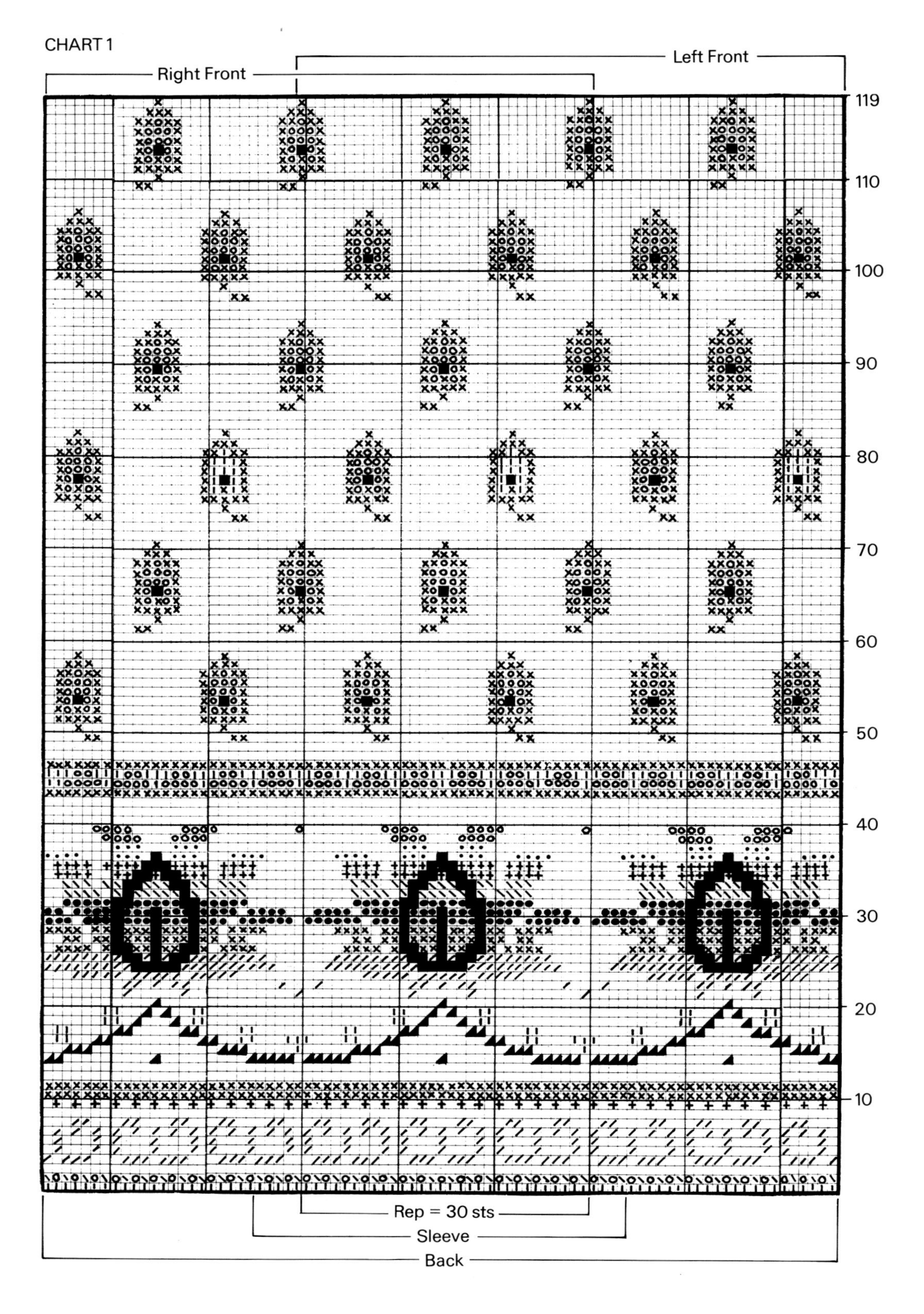

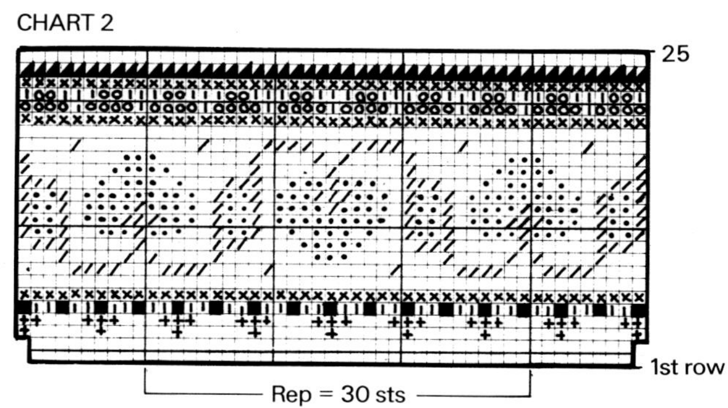

Pages 38-39 *Both the Bijar Sweater and the Bijar Cardigan (also shown opposite) mix textures as well as colours. The cardigan combines intricate borders with a simple stylized* boteh *motif repeated on a white background. The original* boteh *motifs were those swirling pear shapes on traditional Paisley and Kashmiri shawls.*

JEAN MOSS

Unwittingly you may own a Jean Moss sweater for she is the unnamed designer behind much of the Laura Ashley and Ralph Lauren knitwear labels. Jean's early ambitions included hairdressing and reception work, and she and her husband had a brief career in spaghetti Westerns. But with a growing family to provide for they bought an isolated farmhouse in Yorkshire where they planned to work as well as live. Jean had always knitted, so they used this skill to create their cottage industry. Together they knitted all day every day for two years (using domestic machines) to supply a shop in Camden Town, London.

A search for wider horizons took them to the British Export Council's fair where Ralph Lauren was enchanted by the Fair Isle patterns and the traditional cables and textures that Jean uses. This introduction marked a big change in their business, with Jean designing within the guidelines of the Lauren style, and outknitters employed to produce the orders. Their farmhouse was soon stuffed to the eaves with yarn and knitwear, and the articulated lorries needed to collect and deliver frequently embedded themselves in the mud track to their door.

Jean has continued to produce her own hand-knitted collections which she now sells only in America. Her approach is eclectic; seeing little patterns in everyday objects around her she puts them into her knitting adding her own colours as she goes along.

★ ★

BELLMANEAR SWEATER AND SLIPOVER

Winter

KITS A yarn kit is available for the sweater in this design. See page 160 for details.

SIZE

To fit one size up to 96cm (38in) bust/chest

MATERIALS

Sweater

200g Botany Wool in grey 61 (A); 75g mahogany 71 (H); 50g each in blue 55 (B), dark green 420 (C), navy 97 (D) and plum 70 (G); 25g each in dark tan 77 (E) and rose 69 (F)

Slipover

125 g in dark green 420 (A); 50g in brown 616 (H); 25g each in grey/blue 52 (B), mahogany 71 (C), grey 61 (D), brick 45 (E), ochre 14 (F) and navy 97 (G)

Equivalent yarn four-ply

1 pair each 2¼mm (US1) and 3¼mm (US3) needles

Set of four double-pointed 2¼mm (US1) needles

TENSION

30 sts and 36 rows to 10cm (4in) over patt on 3¼mm (US3) needles.

SWEATER

BACK

Using 2¼mm (US1) needles and A, cast on 106 sts. Work 6cm (2¼in) in K1, P1 rib.

Next row Rib 3, (make 1, rib 2, make 1, rib 3, make 1, rib 2) 14 times, make 1, rib 2, make 1, rib 3. 150 sts.

Change to 3¼mm (US3) needles and beg colour patt from chart on page 44, weaving contrast colours into back of work and using small separate balls of yarn for motifs where convenient to do so; work yarns B-H in st st, and yarn A as shown in chart key.

Work 208 rows straight, placing sleeve markers at each end of 106th row, end with a WS row.

Shape shoulders

Cast off 24 sts at beg of next 2 rows, and 25 sts at beg of foll 2 rows. 52 sts.

Leave these sts on a stitch holder.

FRONT

Work as given for back until front is 18 rows less than back to shoulder, end with WS row.

Divide for neck

Next row Patt 65 sts, turn, leaving rem sts on a spare needle and cont on these sts only for first side of neck.

Dec 1 st at neck edge on every row until there are 49 sts. Patt 1 row, ending at armhole edge.

Shape shoulder

Cast off 24 sts at beg of next row.

Work 1 row. Cast off rem 25 sts.

With RS of work facing return to sts on spare needle, sl centre 20 sts on to a stitch holder, rejoin yarn to next st, patt to end. 65 sts. Complete second side of neck to match first side, reversing shapings, and working 1 more row before neck shaping.

Right *Two traditional Fair Isle garments – a long-sleeved crew-neck sweater (for which a kit is available) and a classic v-neck slipover.*

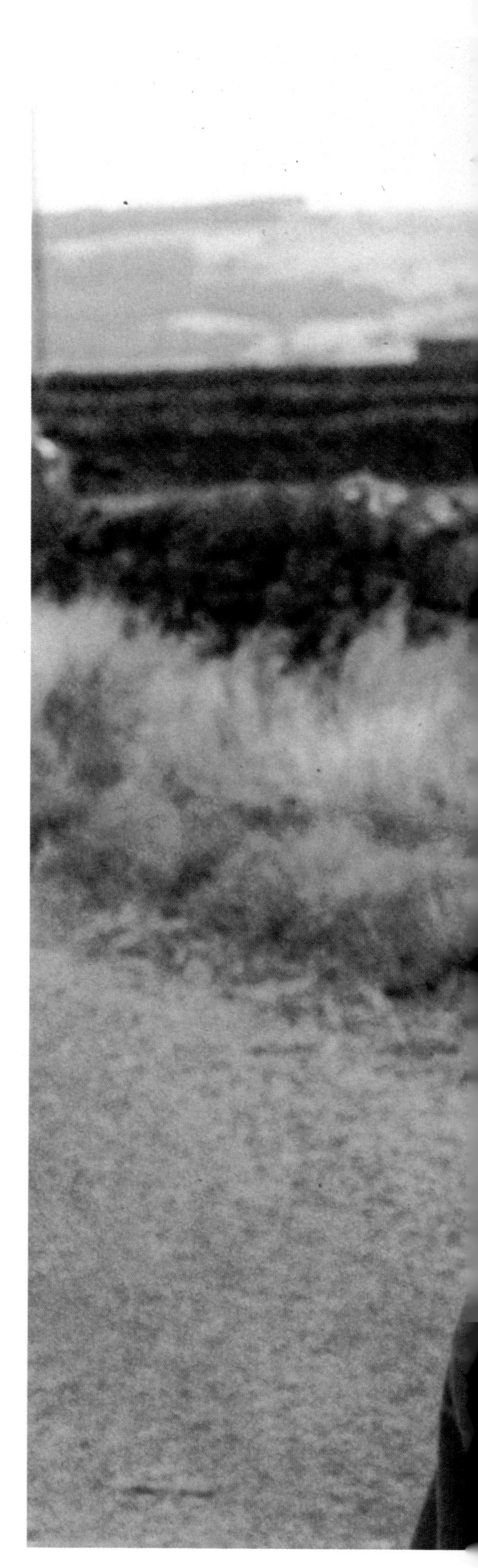

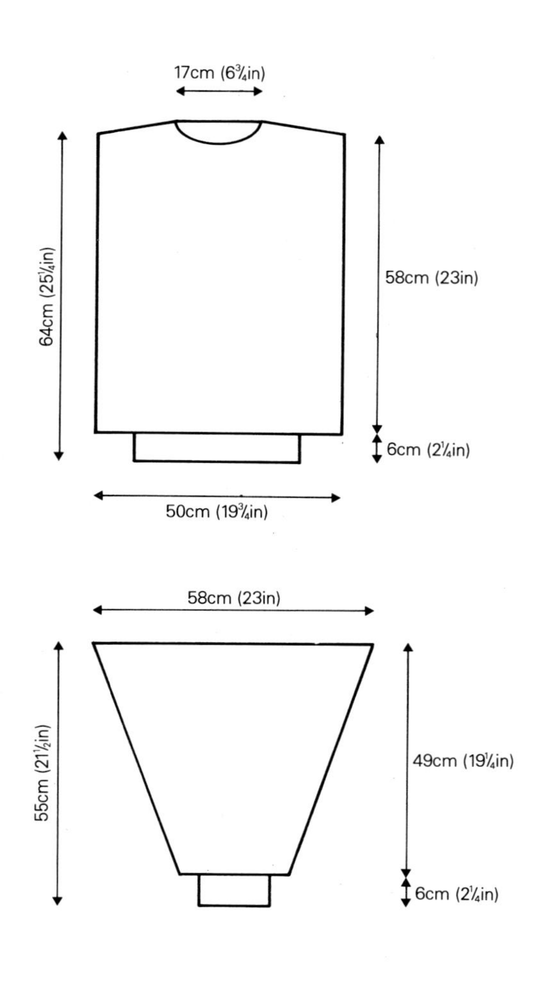

SLEEVES

Using 2¼mm (US1) needles and yarn A, cast on 50 sts.
Work 6cm (2¼in) in K1, P1 rib.
Next row Rib 4, (make 1, rib 2, make 1, rib 3) 8 times, make 1, rib 2, make 1, rib 4. 68 sts.
Change to 3¼mm (US3) needles and beg colour patt from 23rd row of chart as given for back, working between sleeve markers, *at the same time* inc 1 st at each end of every 3rd row until there are 172 sts, working the extra sts into patt.
Now work straight until 178 patt rows in all have been worked, ending with 12th patt row.
Cast off loosely and evenly.

TO MAKE UP

Join both shoulders using a backstitch seam.

Neckband

With RS of work facing, using double-pointed needles and yarn A, beg at left shoulder, K up 26 sts down left side of neck, K 20 sts from stitch holder at front neck, K up 26 sts up right side of front neck, and K across 52 sts from back neck stitch holder. 124 sts.
Work 6 rounds in K1, P1 rib.
Cast off evenly in rib.
Set in sleeves flat between sleeve markers on back and front.
Join side and sleeve seams.

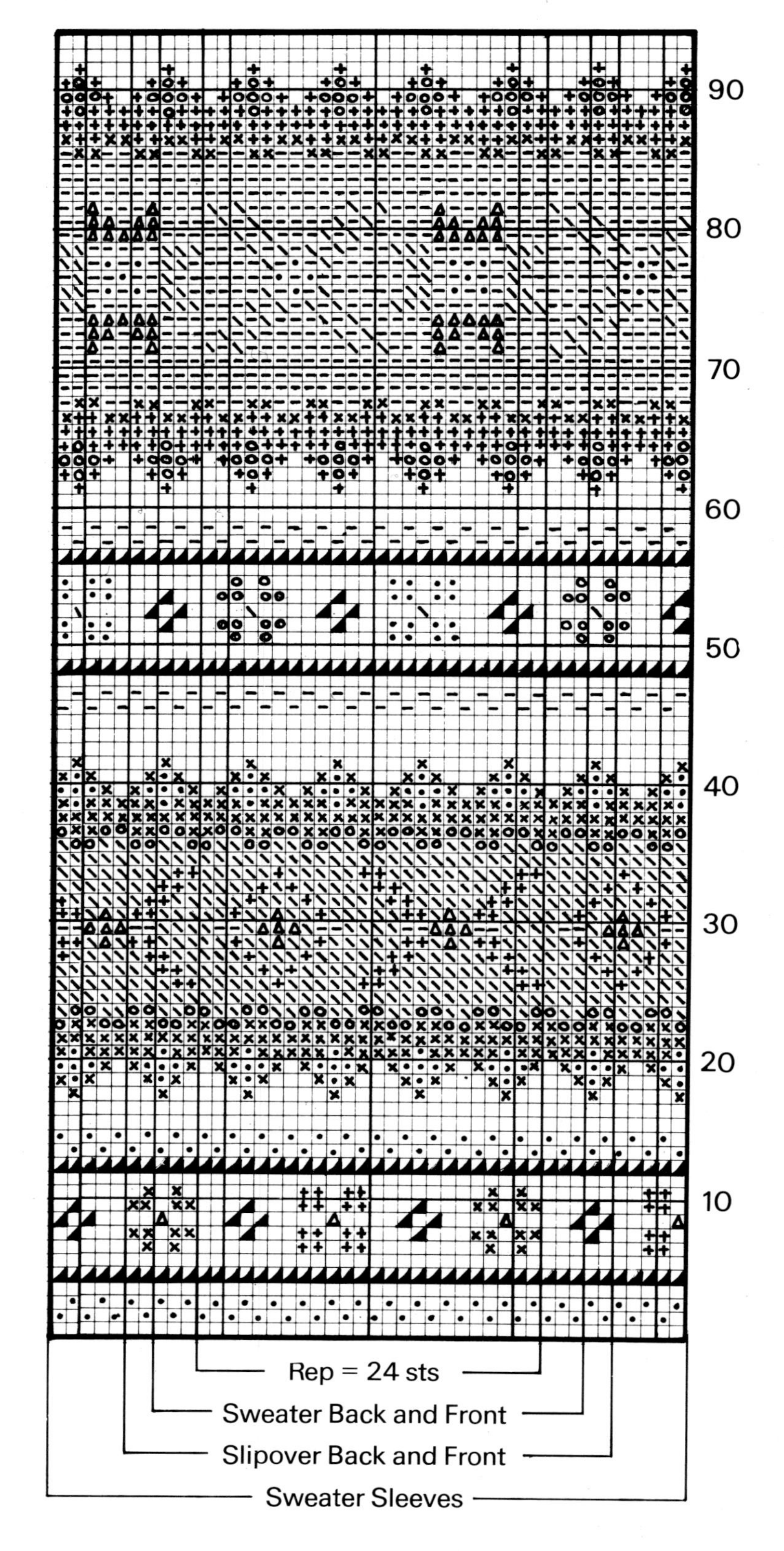

KEY

☐ = With A, K on RS, P on WS
◪ = With A, P on RS, K on WS
⊡ = B
⊞ = C
☒ = D
△ = E
⊙ = F
⧅ = G
H = ⊟

SLIPOVER

BACK

Using 2¼mm (US1) needles and yarn A, cast on 112 sts.
Work 7.5cm (3in) in K2, P2 rib.
Next row (WS) Rib 8, (make 1, rib 2, make 1, rib 3, make 1, rib 2) 14 times, rib 6. 154 sts.
Change to 3¼mm (US3) needles and beg colour patt from chart, weaving contrast colours into back of work and using small separate balls of yarn for motifs where convenient to do so; work yarns B-H in st st, and yarn A as shown in chart key.
Work straight until back measures 38cm (15in) from cast-on edge, end with WS row.
Shape armholes
Cast off 8 sts at beg of next 2 rows. 138 sts.
Dec 1 st at each end of every row until 102 sts rem, ending with a WS row. **
Now cont in patt until back measures 63.5cm (25in) from cast-on edge, ending with a WS row.
Shape shoulders
Cast off 14 sts at beg of next 4 rows.
Leave rem 46 sts on a spare needle.

Above *Jean Moss's Bellmanear Sweater and Slipover.*

FRONT

Work as given for back to **.
Divide for neck
Next row Patt 49 sts, K2 tog, turn, leaving

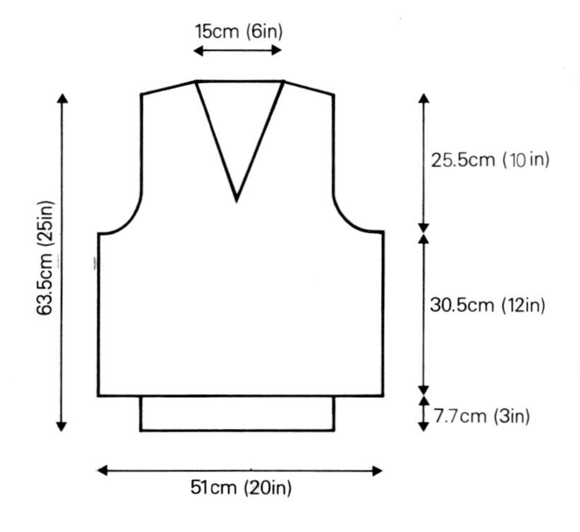

rem sts on a spare needle, patt to end and cont on these sts only for first side of neck.
Now dec 1 st at neck edge on next and every foll 3rd row until 28 sts rem.
Now work straight until front matches back to shoulder, end at armhole edge.
Shape shoulder
Cast off 14 sts at beg of next row.
Work 1 row.
Cast off rem 14 sts.
With RS of work facing, return to sts on spare needle, rejoin yarn to next st, K2 tog, patt to end. 50 sts.
Complete second side of neck to match first, reversing shapings.

TO MAKE UP

Join both shoulders using a backstitch seam.
Neckband
With RS of work facing, using double-pointed 2¼mm (US1) needles and yarn A, beg at centre V, K up 73 sts up right side of front neck, K 46 sts from stitch holder at back neck and K up 73 sts down left side of front neck. 192 sts.
Work 9 rounds in K2, P2 rib, dec 1 st at each end of every round.
Cast off evenly in rib.
Armbands
With RS of work facing, using 2¼mm (US1) needles and yarn A, K up 200 sts evenly around armhole edge.
Work 9 rows in K2, P2 rib.
Cast off evenly in rib.
Join side and armband seams.

★ ★ ★

WHARRAM SWEATER

Summer

SIZE
To fit one size up to 96cm (38in) bust

MATERIALS
250g Sea Breeze Soft Cotton in pine forest 538 (A); 100g in rain cloud 528 (D); 50g each in smoke 527 (B), polka 530 (C), ecru 522 (E), bermuda 539 (F) and wheat 523 (G)
Equivalent yarn four-ply
1 pair each 2¼mm (US1) and 3¼mm (US3) needles
Set of four double-pointed 2¼mm (US1) needles

TENSION
32 sts and 38 rows to 10cm (4in) over patt on 3¼mm (US3) needles.

BACK
Using 2¼mm (US1) needles and yarn A, cast on 110 sts.
Work 6cm (2¼in) in K2, P2 rib.
Next row Rib 8, (make 1, rib 2, make 1, rib 1, make 1, rib 2) 19 times, make 1, rib 7. 168 sts.
Change to 3¼mm (US3) needles and beg colour patt from chart, weaving contrast colours into back of work and using small separate balls of yarn for motifs where convenient to do so; beg with a K row, work yarns A, B, C, E, F and G in st st, and yarn D as shown in chart key. Working between markers for back, cont in patt until work measures 38cm (14¾in) from cast-on edge, ending with a WS row.
Shape armholes
Cast off 8 sts at beg of next 2 rows. 152 sts.
Now work straight until back measures 62cm (24¼in) from cast-on edge, ending with a WS row.
Shape shoulders
Cast off 23 sts at beg of next 4 rows. 60 sts.
Leave these sts on a stitch holder.

FRONT
Work as given for back until front measures 16 rows less than back to beg of shoulder shaping.
Divide for neck
Next row Patt 61 sts, turn, leaving rem sts on a spare needle and cont on these sts only for first side of neck.
Dec 1 st at neck edge on every row until 46 sts rem, ending at armhole edge.

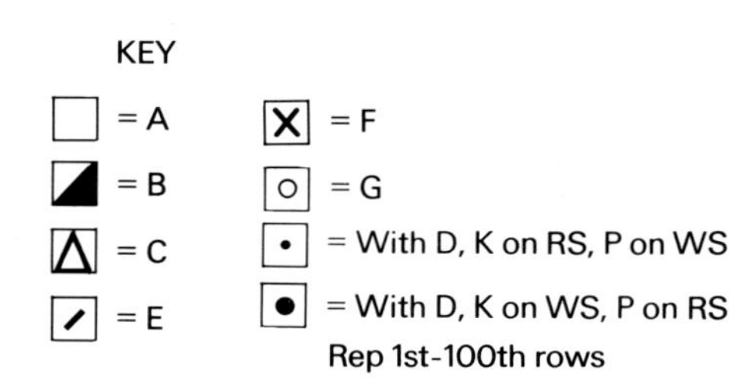

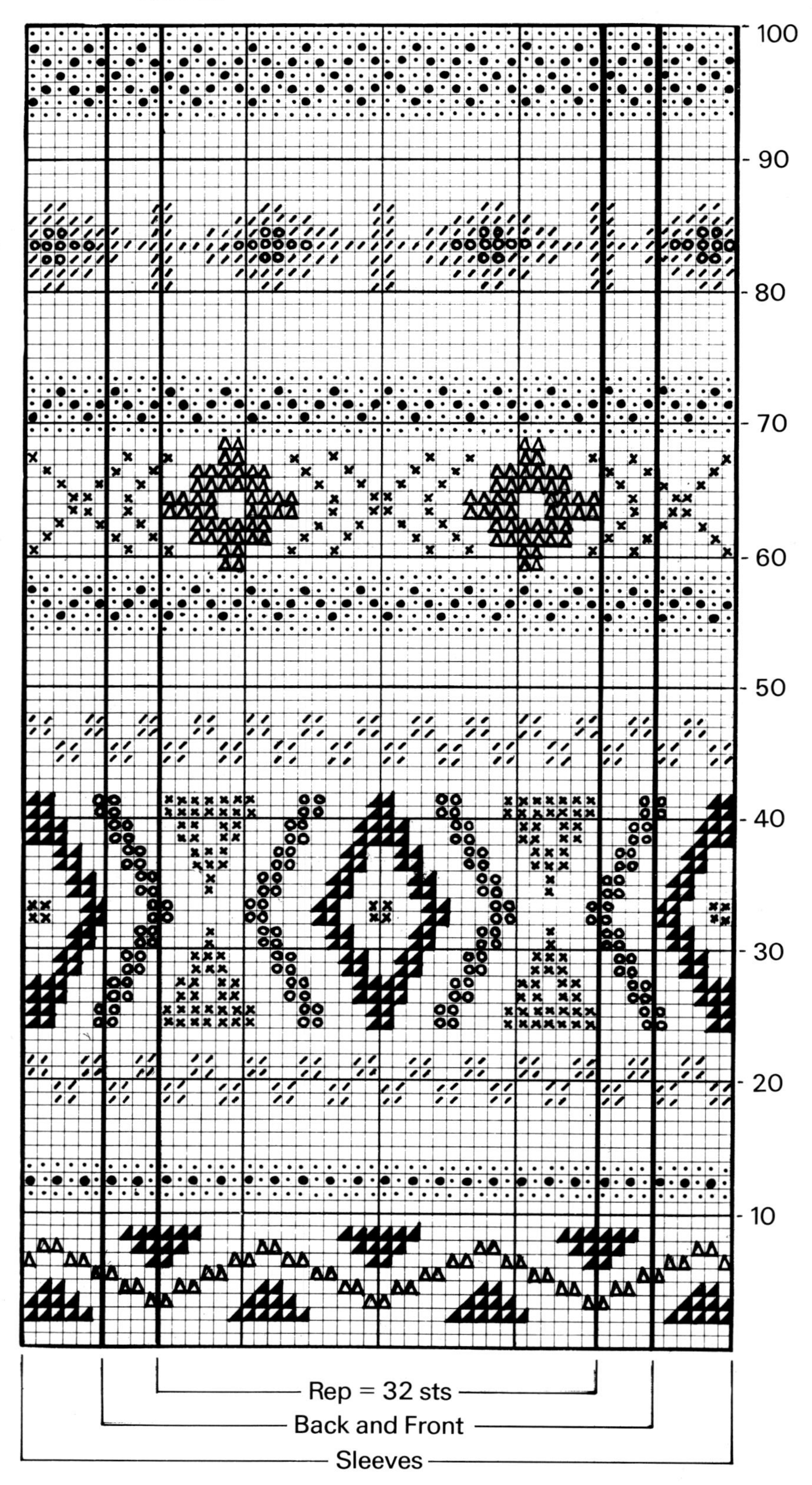

Shape shoulder
Cast off 23 sts at beg of next row.
Work 1 row.
Cast off rem 23 sts.
With RS of work facing, return to sts on spare needle, sl centre 30 sts on to a stitch holder, rejoin yarn to next st, patt to end of row.
Complete second side of neck to match first side, reversing shapings.

SLEEVES

Using 2¼mm (US1) needles and yarn A, cast on 130 sts.
Work 2cm (¾in) in K2, P2 rib.
Next row Rib 6, (make 1, rib 7) 17 times, make 1, rib 5. 148 sts.
Measure 18.5cm (7¼in) down from beg of armhole shaping on back and mark chart patt row.
Change to 3¼mm (US3) needles and beg colour patt from chart, working between sleeve markers, and beg on same row as marked patt row on back. Cont in patt until work measures 20.5cm (8in) from cast-on edge and sleeve patt matches back to beg of armhole shaping. With yarn A only, work 2.5cm (1in) in st st. Cast off loosely and evenly.

TO MAKE UP

Join both shoulders using a backstitch seam.
Neckband
With RS of work facing, using double-pointed 2¼mm (US1) needles and yarn A, K up 21 sts down left side front neck, 30 sts from stitch holder at centre front, 21 sts up right side front neck and 60 sts from stitch holder at back neck. 132 sts.
Work 2cm (¾in) in K2, P2 rib in rounds.
Cast off evenly in rib.
Set in sleeve flat, matching last few rows of sleeve to cast-off sts at underarm.
Join side and sleeve seams.

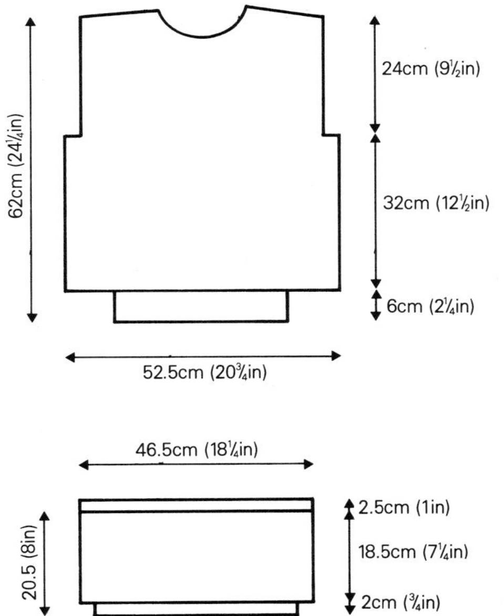

Right *Jean Moss's Wharram Sweater. The soft shape, unusual colouring and geometric design are all typical of her work.*

EDINA RONAY

Kilims, bead and needlepoint cushions, embroidery, mother of pearl inlaid furniture and Victorian tiles surround you in Edina Ronay's decorative drawing room. There is a hint of un-Englishness, and although Edina has lived in Britain since she was two, the Hungarian verve and colour sense remain a driving force within her. From England she has absorbed an understanding of classic styles and, perhaps from her admiraton of Schiaparelli, a dimension of sophistication. The resulting mixture is elegant and irresistible.

Edina was a model and an actress before she gave in to the pull that had always attracted her to fashion. She collected antique clothes, altered them to suit the current trend, and sold them through the shop in the Kings Road that she shared with Lena Stengard. Some Fair Isle knits from the 30s and 40s occasionally passed through their hands, and their lively beauty caught her attention. When they discovered a box of Fair Isle knitting patterns from the same era it presented an opportunity to make a collection to complement the antique outfits.

Showing these sweaters at a fashion trade fair in 1978 was so successful that a new business was born in those few important days. The old clothes were left behind, and the Fair Isles she now designs have shed their rustic roots to become the delicate patterning for clothes knitted in silks and luxury fibres that co-ordinate with her beautifully cut classic separates. Since then Edina Ronay has become a major fashion company but, in her own words, 'knitwear will always remain the jewel in the collection'.

★ ★

FAIR ISLE SWEATER

Summer

SIZES

To fit 86[91, 97]cm (34[36, 38]in) bust

MATERIALS

250[300, 350]g Sea Breeze Soft Cotton in wheat 523 (A); 100g in pine forest 538 (C); 100[100, 150]g in ecru 522 (D); 50g each in antique pink 533 (B) and smoke 527 (E)

Equivalent yarn four-ply

1 pair 2¼mm (US1), 2¾mm (US2) and 3¼mm (US3) needles

TENSION

32 sts and 32 rows to 10cm (4in) over Fair Isle patt on 3¼mm (US3) needles.

BACK

Using 2¾mm (US2) needles and yarn A, cast on 153[161, 169] sts.

Work 5cm (2in) K1, P1 rib.

Change to 3¼mm (US3) needles and commence Fair Isle patt from chart as foll:

1st row (RS) K to end in A.

2nd row P0[4A,(3A, 1B, 4A)], *4A, 1B, 4A; rep from * to last 0[4, 8] sts, P0[4A,(4A, 1B, 3A)].

These 2 rows set the position of chart. **

Cont in patt, work in st st until back measures 52cm (20½in) from cast-on edge, ending with a WS row.

Shape armholes

Keeping patt correct, cast off 4 sts at beg of next 2 rows, 145[153, 161] sts.

Cast off 2 sts at beg of next 6 rows. 133[141, 149] sts.

Now dec 1 st at each end of next and every foll alt row until 105[111, 117] sts rem.

Work straight until back measures 71cm (28in) from cast-on edge, ending with a WS row.

Shape shoulders

Cast off 29[31, 33] sts at beg of next 2 rows.

Leave rem 47[49, 51] sts on a spare needle.

POCKET LININGS (make 2)

Using 3¼mm (US3) needles and yarn A, cast on 40 sts.

Work 50 rows in st st, beg with a K row.

Leave these sts on a spare needle.

FRONT

Work as given for back to **.

Cont in patt, work 58 rows, thus ending with a WS row.

Place pocket linings

Next row Patt 19[20, 21] sts, sl next 40 sts on to a stitch holder, now K across 40 sts of first pocket lining, patt 35[41, 47] sts, sl next 40 sts on to a stitch holder, now K across 40 sts of second pocket lining, patt to end of row.

Cont in patt until front measures 2 rows less than back to beg of armhole shaping, ending with a WS row.

Divide for neck

Next row Patt 76[80, 84] sts, turn, leaving rem sts on a spare needle, patt to end. Cont on these sts only for first side of neck.

Shape armhole and front neck

Next row Cast off 4 sts, patt to last 2 sts, K2 tog.

Work 1 row.

Now cast off 2 sts at beg of next and 2 foll alt rows, then dec 1 st at armhole edge on

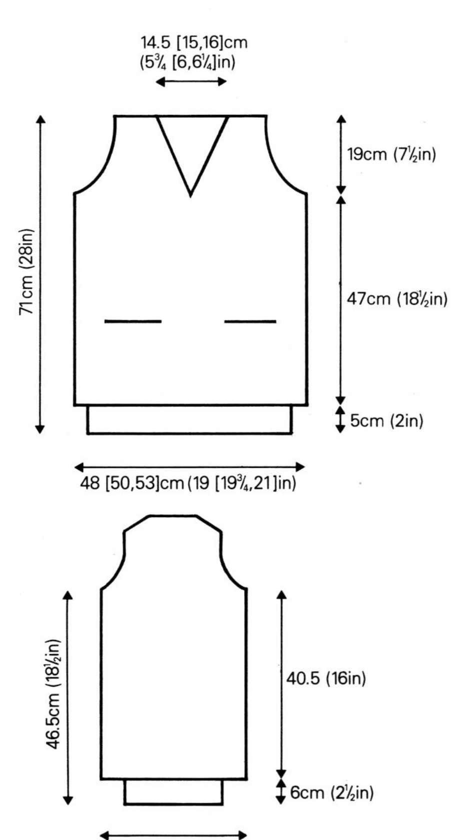

Right *A gorgeous slinky Fair Isle sweater in the palest of pastel colours.*

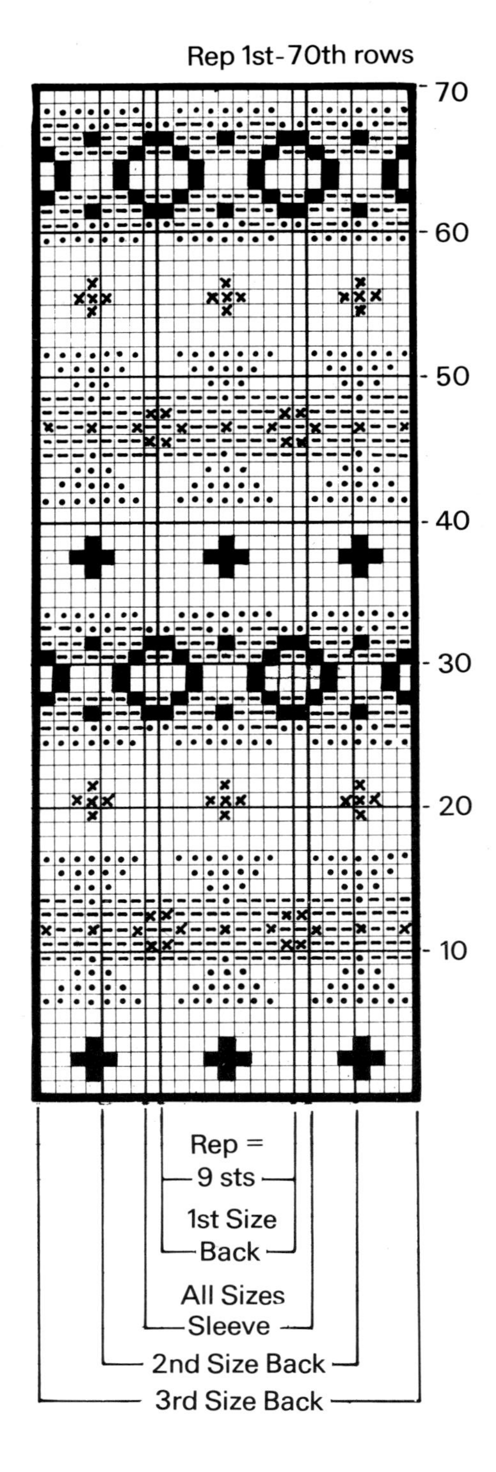

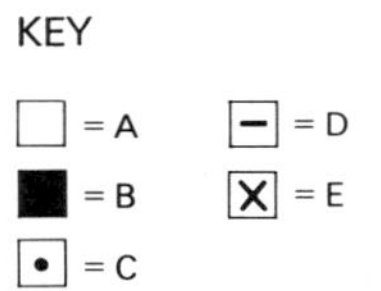

foll 14[15, 16] alt rows, *at the same time* dec 1 st at neck edge on next and every foll alt row until 33[35, 37] sts rem.
Work 2 rows straight, then cont to dec 1 st at neck edge only on next and every foll 3rd row until 29[31, 33] sts rem.
Now work straight until front matches back to shoulder.
Cast off.
With RS of work facing, return to sts on spare needle, sl centre st on to a safety pin, rejoin yarn to next st and patt to end of row.
76[80, 84] sts. Work 2 rows.
Complete armhole shaping and second side of neck to match first side, reversing shapings.

SLEEVES

Using 2¼mm (US1) needles and yarn A, cast on 62 sts.
Work 6cm (2½in) in K1, P1 rib.
Next row Rib 3, (make 1, rib 1, make 1, rib 2) 19 times, make 1, rib 2. 101 sts.
Measure 40.5cm (16in) down from beg of

Edina Ronay and her partner Lena Stengard first became known for their marvellously sympathetic adaptations of the knitwear designs of the thirties and forties. They took traditional Fair Isles and those ladylike sweaters with lots of lace and bobbles, neat collars and puffed sleeves, and created timeless garments with a thoroughly modern feel, of which these (above and opposite) *are just two examples.*

armhole shaping on back and mark chart patt row.
Change to 3¼mm (US3) needles and commence chart patt, beg on same row as marked patt row on back. Rep patt sts 11 times across each row, working first and last sts as indicated.
Cont in patt until work measures 46.5cm (18 in) from cast-on edge, and sleeve patt matches back to beg of armhole shaping.

Shape sleeve top

Keeping patt correct, cast off 4 sts at beg of next 2 rows, then 2 sts at beg of foll 6 rows. Now dec 1 st at beg of next 16 rows. 65 sts.
Work 16 rows straight.
Dec 1 st at each end of next 6 rows.
Cast off 2 sts at beg of next 4 rows and 3 sts at beg of foll 4 rows. 33 sts.
Next row (K2 tog) 8 times, K1, (K2 tog) 8 times. 17 sts.
Cast off evenly.

TO MAKE UP

Join right shoulder using a backstitch seam.

Neckband

With RS of work facing, using 2¼mm (US1) needles and yarn A, K up 72 sts down left side of front neck, K1 from safety pin at centre front, K up 72 sts up right side of front neck, and K 47[49, 51] sts from stitch holder at back neck. 192[194, 196] sts.
Work 7 rows in K1, P1 rib, dec 1 st at either side of centre st on every row as foll:
1st row (WS) Rib to within 2 sts of centre st, P2 tog, P1, P2 tog tbl, rib to end.
2nd row Rib to within 2 sts of centre st, K2 tog tbl, K1, K2 tog, rib to end.
Rep these 2 rows twice more, then 1st row once.
Change to 2¾mm (US2) needles and cast off loosely in rib, dec on cast-off row as before.
Join left shoulder and neckband seam.

Pocket edgings

With RS of work facing, using 2¾mm (US2) needles and yarn A, sl sts from stitch holder on to left-hand needle and work 7 rows K1, P1 rib.
Sew pocket linings in position on WS of front and catch down pocket tops neatly on RS.
Join side seams.
Join underarm seams.
Set in sleeves taking care to match pattern and easing the fullness evenly across shoulders.

★

CABLE AND CHECK SWEATER

Winter

SIZE

To fit one size up to 101cm (40in) bust/chest

MATERIALS

900g Lightweight Double Knitting in cream 2

Equivalent yarn double knitting

1 pair each 3mm (US2) and 3¼mm (US3) needles

Cable needle

TENSION

30 sts and 37 rows to 10cm (4in) over patt on 3¼mm (US3) needles.

SPECIAL ABBREVIATION

C8b (cable 8 back) – sl next 4 sts on to a cable needle and hold at back of work, K4, then K4 from cable needle.

BACK

Using 3mm (US2) needles, cast on 150 sts. Work 29 rows in garter st (K every row).

Next row K7, (make 1, K8) 17 times, make 1, K7. 168 sts.

Change to 3¼mm (US3) needles and beg cable and check patt as foll:

1st row (RS) K8, (P8, K8) 10 times.

2nd row P8, (K8, P8) 10 times.

3rd-10th rows Rep 1st-2nd rows 4 times.

11th row P8, (K8, C8b, K8, P8) 5 times.

12th row (K8, P24) 5 times, K8.

13th row P8, (K24, P8) 5 times.

14th row As 12th row.

15th-20th rows Rep 13th-14th rows 3 times.

21st row K8, (P8, C8b, P8, K8) 5 times.

22nd row As 2nd row.

23rd-30th rows Rep 1st-2nd rows 4 times.

Rep 11th-30th rows to form patt. **

Cont in patt until work measures 76cm (30in) from cast-on edge, ending with a WS row.

Shape shoulders

Cast off 54 sts at beg of next 2 rows.

Cast off rem 60 sts.

POCKET LININGS (make 2)

Using 3mm (US2) needles, cast on 48 sts. Work 85 rows in garter st.

Leave these sts on a stitch holder.

FRONT

Work as given for back to **.

Cont in patt until work measures 25.5cm (10in) from cast-on edge, ending with a WS row.

Place pocket linings

Next row Patt 16 sts, sl next 48 sts on to a stitch holder, patt across 48 sts of first pocket lining, patt 40 sts, sl next 48 sts on to a stitch holder, patt across 48 sts of second pocket lining, patt to end of row.

Now cont in patt until front measures 76 rows less than back to shoulder, ending with a WS row.

Divide for neck

Next row Patt 84 sts, turn, leaving rem sts on a spare needle and cont on these sts only for first side of neck.

* Keeping patt correct, dec 1 st at neck edge on next and foll alt row. Work 2 rows. ** 82 sts. Rep from * to ** until 54 sts rem. Cast off.

With RS of work facing, return to sts on spare needle, rejoin yarn to next st, patt to end of row.

Complete second side of neck to match first, working from * to end.

SLEEVES

Using 3mm (US2) needles, cast on 66 sts. Work 25 rows in garter st.

Next row K2, (make 1, K7) 9 times, make 1, K1. 76 sts.

Change to 3¼mm (US3) needles and cont in patt as foll:

1st row (RS) P2, (K8, P8) 4 times, K8, P2.

2nd row K2, (P8, K8) 4 times, P8, K2.

3rd-10th rows Rep 1st-2nd rows 4 times.

11th row P2, (K8, P8, C8b, P8) twice, K8, P2.

These 11 rows set the position of the cable and check patt.

Cont in patt as set, *at the same time* inc 1 st at each end of next and every foll 3rd row until there are 168 sts, working incs into patt.

Now work straight until sleeve measures 48.5cm (19in) from cast-on edge, ending with a WS row.

Cast off very loosely.

POCKET EDGINGS

With RS of work facing, using 3mm (US2) needles, sl 48 sts from stitch holder at pocket top on to left-hand needle.

Work 10 rows in garter st. Cast off.

COLLAR

Using 3mm (US2) needles, cast on 60 sts. Work 44 rows in garter st. Leave these sts on a spare needle and work a second piece to match.

Next row K across both sets of sts to join both halves of collar. 120 sts.

Now work 12 rows in garter st across both sets of sts.

Cast off 30 sts at beg of next 2 rows. 60 sts.

Now dec 1 st at each end of next and every foll 3rd row until 52 sts rem.

Work 1 row.

*** Dec 1 st at each end of next and foll alt row. Work 2 rows. ****

Rep from *** to **** until 32 sts rem.

Dec 1 st at each end of next and every foll 3rd row until 2 sts rem.

Next row K2 tog.

Fasten off.

TO MAKE UP

Join both shoulders using a backstitch seam.

Join back collar seam. Place back collar seam at centre back neck and stitch collar to neck edge.

Place markers 28cm (11in) down from shoulder seams on back and front.

Set in sleeves between markers using a backstitch seam.

Join side and sleeve seams.

Sew pocket linings in position on WS of fronts. Catch down pocket tops on RS of fronts.

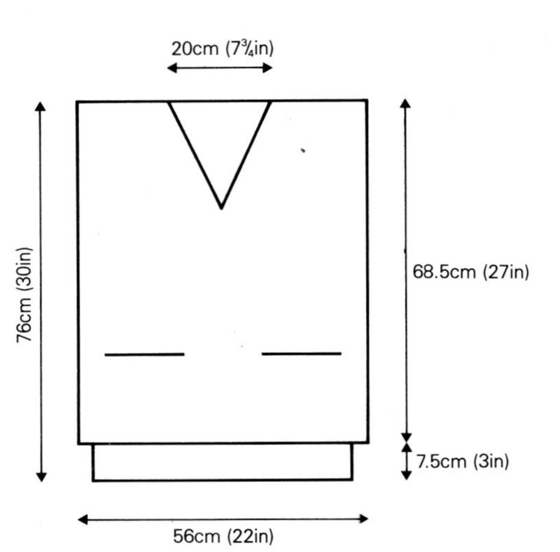

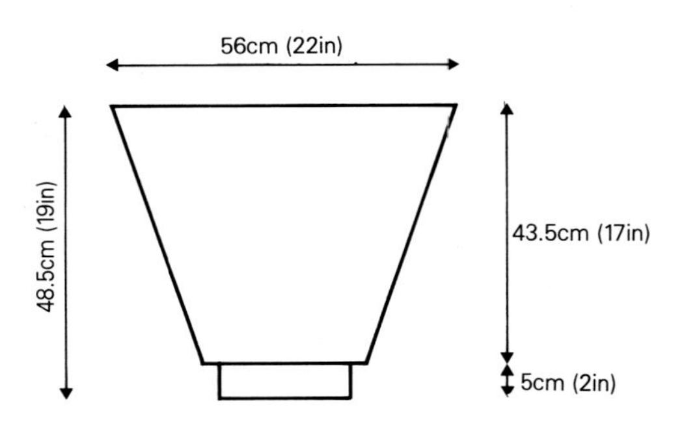

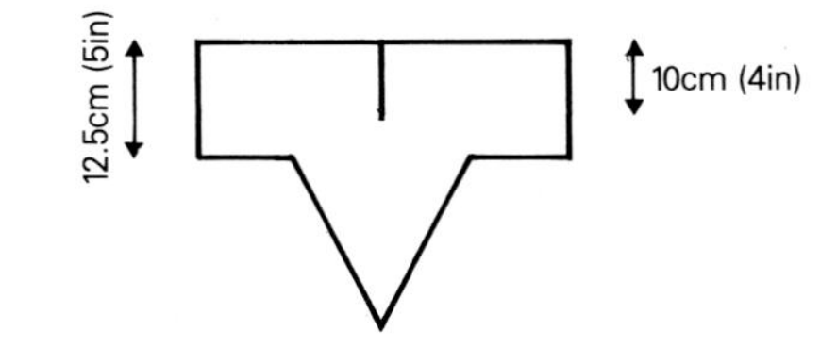

Right *Edina Ronay's version of a traditional creamy Aran sweater – long and loose and very easy to knit in a mixture of basketweave pattern and simple cables. The garter-stitch collar is made separately and sewn on.*

LENA STENGARD

As a model she travelled the world and met fashion buyers, photographers, magazine editors, and designers. When Lena Stengard went into producing fashion knitwear she not only had the right contacts everywhere, but the confidence of manner and looks that enabled her to walk straight into the New York buyers' offices, and sell.

She had always loved clothes, and found she had a business buying and selling secondhand clothes when her passion for collecting them outstripped her purse. This path led her to Edina Ronay, and together they progressed from a market stall to a shop in the Kings Road, and then into the international fashion business. She remembers the fun and the crazy excitement of her first London showings when they couldn't write fast enough to take the orders. When the partnership dissolved she took two years off, but in 1984 started again in no small way. She showed some designs to the Laura Ashley organization who wanted nearly 3000 sweaters in black and white. It proved to be a tough order to fulfil, 'knitters hate using black, and all the white ones came back grubby and had to be washed'. Unable to face another such order she sought a new client and rang Ralph Lauren to ask if he might be interested in using her skills. He was, and she found it sheer joy to work with him. In 1986 when the business was going well, the yen for a country house and life with her children got the better of her and she closed up the spectacular riverside studio in Chelsea. She and her husband bought an enormous house in Gloucestershire and had another baby. Her energy is forceful, so it cannot be long before she is back in business, and whatever it is she decides to do it will doubtless be in the grand manner and the European style that inevitably is hers.

★ ★ ★

FLORAL SWEATER

Summer

SIZES

To fit 86[96]cm (34[38]in) bust/chest

MATERIALS

250[300]g Sea Breeze Soft Cotton in turkish plum 529 (A); 100[150]g) in signal red 532 (C); 150g in fiord 531 (D); 100g in polka 530 (E); 50[100]g in baize 540 (B); 50g in sienna 535 (F)

Equivalent yarn four-ply

1 pair 2¾mm (US2) and 3¼mm (US3) needles

TENSION

32 sts and 36 rows to 10cm (4in) over patt on 3¼mm (US3) needles.

BACK

Using 2¾mm (US2) needles and yarn A, cast on 122[142] sts.

Work 7.5cm (3in) in K1, P1 rib, ending with a RS row.

Next row Rib 5, (make 1, rib 2, make 1, rib 3) 23[27] times, rib 2. 168[196] sts.

Change to 3¼mm (US3) needles and beg colour patt from chart, working in st st throughout between markers for back, using separate balls of yarns for flowers and stems, twisting yarns between colours to avoid holes, and weaving background yarns into back of work (flower centres may be Swiss-darned on completion); cont in patt until work measures 63.5[66]cm (25[26]in) from cast-on edge, ending with a WS row.

Shape shoulders

Cast off 49[60] sts at beg of next 2 rows.

Leave rem 70[76] sts on a spare needle.

FRONT

Work as given for back until front measures 24 rows less than back to shoulder.

Divide for neck

Next row Patt 66[78] sts, turn, leaving rem sts on a spare needle and cont on these sts only for first side of neck.

Dec 1 st at neck edge on every row until 49[60] sts rem.

Work 6[5] rows straight, ending at armhole edge.

Cast off.

With RS of work facing, return to sts on spare needle, sl next 36[40] sts on to a stitch holder, patt to end.

Complete second side of neck to match first side, reversing shapings and working 1 more row before shoulder shaping.

SLEEVES

Using 2¾mm (US2) needles and yarn A, cast on 60[64] sts.

Work 7.5cm (3in) in K1, P1 rib, ending with a RS row.

Next row Rib 4[6], (make 1, rib 1, make 1, rib 2) 18 times, rib to end. 96[100] sts.

Change to 3¼mm (US3) needles and work in colour patt from chart between sleeve markers, *at the same time* inc 1 st at each end of 5th and every foll 3rd row until there are 184[192] sts, working the incs into patt.

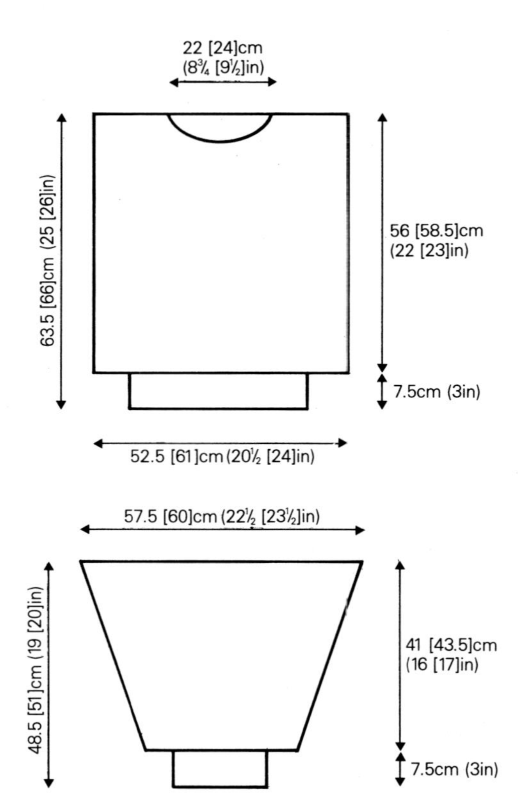

Right *Lena Stengard's Floral Sweater – a classic crew-neck in light, summery cotton yarns.*

Now work straight until sleeve measures 48.5[51]cm (19[20]in) from cast-on edge. Cast off loosely and evenly.

TO MAKE UP

Join right shoulder.

Neckband

With RS of work facing, using 2¾mm (US2) needles and yarn A, K up 24 sts down left side of neck, K 36[40] sts from stitch holder at front neck, K up 24 sts up right side of neck, and K 70[76] sts from stitch holder at back neck. 154[164] sts.
Work 2.5cm (1in) in K1, P1 rib.
Cast off evenly in rib.
Join left shoulder and neckband seam.
Place markers 28.5[30]cm (11¼[11¾]in) down from shoulder seams on back and front. Set in sleeves between markers using a backstitch seam. Join side and sleeve seams.

Detailed pictorial motifs have been a recurring theme in Lena Stengard's work. The sweater shown below combines simplicity and complexity and is typical of her approach.

KEY

- □ = A
- ◪ = B
- ● = C
- ○ = D
- · = E
- ☒ = F

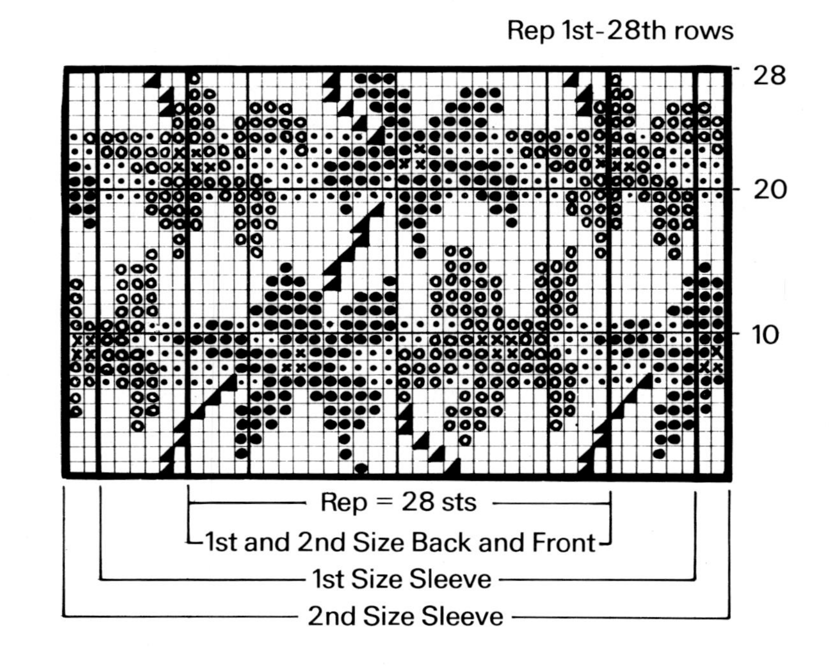

Lena Stengard

★ ★ ★

ROSE FAIR ISLE CARDIGAN

Winter

SIZE

To fit one size up to 96cm (38in) bust

MATERIALS

350g Lightweight Double Knitting in mink 616 (A); 150g in sea blue 53 (B); 100g each in blue/grey 88 (C), purple 93 (E), maroon 601 (G) and brown/pink 70 (H); 50g each in plum 602 (D) and deep rose 412 (J)
100g Grainy Silk in blackcurrant 812 (F)
Equivalent yarn double knitting
1 pair each 3mm (US2) and 3¾mm (US5) needles
10 buttons

TENSION

26 sts and 29 rows to 10cm (4in) over patt on 3¾mm (US5) needles.

BACK

Using 3mm (US2) needles and yarn A, cast on 120 sts.
Work 5cm (2in) in K1, P1 rib.
Next row (WS) Rib 7, (make 1, rib 7) 15 times, make 1, rib 8. 136 sts.
Change to 3¾mm (US5) needles and beg colour patt from chart, working in st st throughout beg with a K row and between markers for back; weave yarn A into back of work but use small separate balls of yarn for other colour areas, twisting yarns tog on WS at colour joins to avoid holes.
Cont in patt until back measures 44cm (17¼in) from cast-on edge, ending with a WS row.
Shape armholes
Keeping patt correct, cast off 5 sts at beg of next 2 rows, 3 sts at beg of foll 2 rows and 2 sts at beg of next 4 rows. 112 sts.
Now dec 1 st at beg of next 6 rows. 106 sts.
Work straight until back measures 66cm (26in) from cast-on edge, ending with a WS row.
Shape shoulders
Cast off 10 sts at beg of next 6 rows.
Leave rem 46 sts on a stitch holder.

POCKET LININGS (make 2)

Using 3¾mm (US5) needles and yarn A, cast on 32 sts.
Work 15cm (6in) in st st, ending with a WS row. Leave these sts on a stitch holder.

LEFT FRONT

Using 3mm (US2) needles and yarn A, cast on 60 sts.
Work 5cm (2in) in K1, P1 rib.
Next row (WS) Rib 2, (make 1, rib 8) 7 times, make 1, rib 2. 68 sts.
Change to 3¾mm (US5) needles and beg colour patt from chart, working between left front markers, cont in patt until work measures 21.5cm (8½in) from cast-on edge ending with a WS row.
Place pocket lining
Next row Patt 16 sts, sl next 32 sts on to a stitch holder, patt across 32 sts of pocket lining, patt 20 sts.

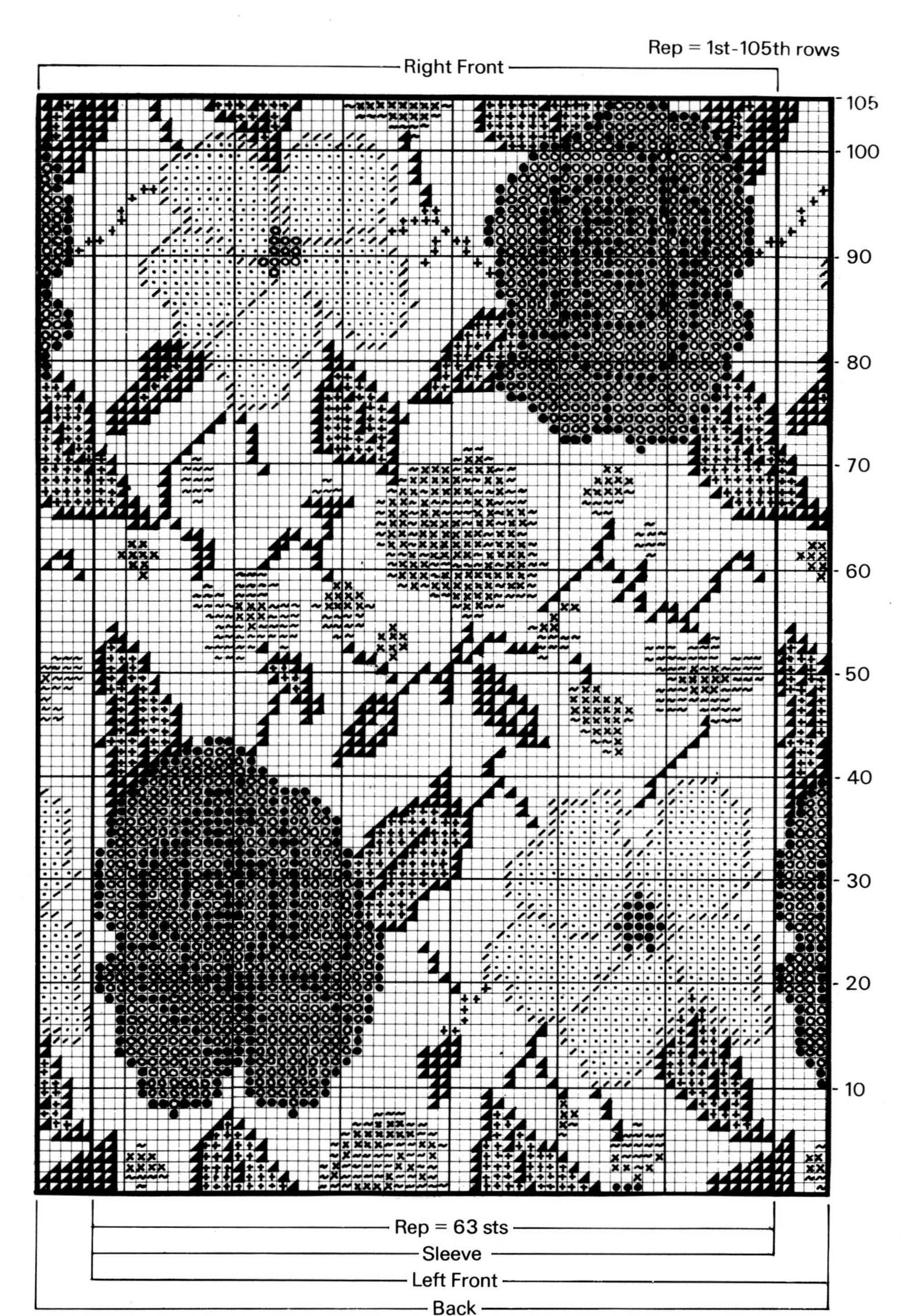

KEY

□ = A
◪ = B
⊞ = C
⧄ = D
⊡ = E
⊙ = F
● = G
~ = H
⊠ = J

Cont in patt until left front matches back to beg of armhole shaping, ending with a WS row.
Shape armhole
Cast off 5 sts at beg of next row, 3 sts at beg of foll alt row and 2 sts at beg of next 2 alt rows, then dec 1 st at beg of foll 3 alt rows. 53 sts.
Now work straight until front measures 19 rows less than back to shoulder, ending with a RS row.

Shape neck
Cast off 8 sts at beg of next row, 3 sts at beg of foll 2 alt rows and 2 sts at beg of next 3 alt rows, then dec 1 st at beg of foll 3 alt rows. 30 sts.
Work 2 rows, ending at armhole edge.
Shape shoulder
Cast off 10 sts at beg of next and foll alt row. 10 sts.
Work 1 row.
Cast off.

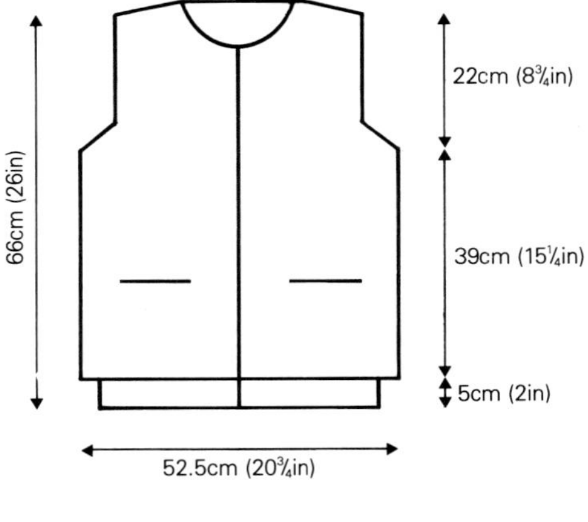

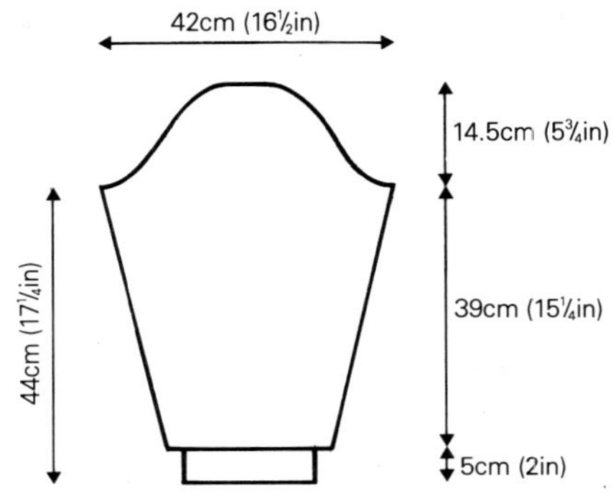

RIGHT FRONT
Work as given for left front, working between right front markers on chart and reversing pocket position and shapings.

SLEEVES
Using 3mm (US2) needles and yarn A, cast on 52 sts.
Work 5cm (2in) in K1, P1 rib.
Next row (WS) Rib 1, (make 1, rib 5) 10 times, make 1, rib 1. 63 sts.
Change to 3¾mm (US5) needles and work in chart patt between sleeve markers, *at the same time* inc 1 st at each end of 3rd and every foll 4th row until there are 79 sts, then of every foll 5th row until there are 109 sts, working the incs into patt.
Now work straight until sleeve measures 44cm (17¼in) from cast-on edge, ending with a WS row.
Shape top
Cast off 5 sts at beg of next 2 rows, 3 sts at beg of foll 2 rows and 2 sts at beg of next 18 rows. 57 sts.

Left *The Rose Fair Isle Cardigan – finely drawn floral motifs in a close blend of pinks and browns; definitely for dedicated knitters only. In contrast* (right), *an example of Lena's way with bolder patterns and colours.*

Now dec 1 st at beg of next 8 rows, then cast off 2 sts at beg of foll 10 rows and 5 sts at beg of next 2 rows.
Cast off rem 19 sts.

TO MAKE UP
Join both shoulders using backstitch seams. Join side and sleeve seams. Set in sleeves.
Pocket tops
With RS of work facing, using 3mm (US2) needles and yarn A, sl 32 sts from stitch holder at pocket top on to left-hand needle.
Work 4 rows in K1, P1 rib.
Buttonhole row Rib 15, yo, K2 tog, rib to end.
Work 3 more rows in rib. Cast off in rib.
Sew pocket lining in position on WS of fronts.
Catch down pocket tops to RS.
Neckband
With RS of work facing, using 3mm (US2) needles and yarn A, K up 36 sts up right front neck, K 46 sts across back neck stitch holder, K up 36 sts down left front neck.
118 sts. Work 2cm (¾in) in K1, P1 rib.
Cast off in rib.
Button band
Using 3mm (US2) needles and yarn A, cast on 11 sts.
Work in K1, P1 rib as foll:
1st row K2, (P1, K1) to last st, K1.
2nd row (K1, P1) to last st, K1.
Rep these 2 rows until band when slightly stretched fits up left front edge.
Cast off in rib.
Sew buttonband to left front opening edge.
Mark the positions of 8 buttons, the first to come 2cm (¾in) from lower edge, the last 2cm (¾in) from top edge, and the rest spaced evenly between.
Buttonhole band
Work as for button band, making buttonholes opposite button markers as foll:
Buttonhole row (RS) Rib 5, yo, K2 tog, rib to end.
Sew buttonhole band to right front opening edge.
Sew on buttons.

JANE WHEELER

It is possible that Jane Wheeler inherited her familiarity with wool from her ancestors, Flemish weavers who settled in the flat Norfolk countryside where she still lives. Knitted wool is a comforting fabric in this windswept land where spring comes late as if it knew not to hurry, for the slow road to Norfolk leads nowhere else.

There is nothing slow about Jane however. By her own admission she is prolific, and looking around her cottage stuffed with wool, sweaters, paintings and a piano and violin that are obviously used, it is evident that the creative urge is overriding. She paints as much as she knits. Larger than life musicians dominate the canvasses and you can almost hear the notes pouring forth from their instruments. The same evocative movement is present in her knitting. She responds to shape for the fashion element, but where decoration and texture are concerned she lets her imagination run, pushing the technique as far as she can to achieve her aims in knitted form.

At college she explored Persian miniatures, illuminated manuscripts, Japanese prints and Elizabethan embroidery, and became an expert on Victorian shawls, so it is not surprising that she discovered knitting could be more exciting than the dishcloths she was taught to make at school. Patterns, colours and ideas from trips abroad often find their way into her collections, but the end results remain English and countrified.

With the help of 150 knitters and a part-time organizer, she produces a considerable number of sweaters that have been finding markets around the world since 1973. Meanwhile she has never let knitting take over her life. There has always been a horse to ride, a musical instrument to be mastered, or canvas and oil that demand her attention, but with these activities come more ideas and the lure of the yarn is never far away.

★ ★

TOPKAPI FLOWER JACKET

Summer

SIZE
To fit one size up to 101cm (40in) bust/chest

MATERIALS
650g Handknit Double Knitting Cotton in ecru 251 (A); 150g in peacock 259 (B) and 100g in navy 277 (C)
150g Sea Breeze Soft Cotton in frolic 534 (D) and polka 530 (E)
Equivalent yarn double knitting
1 pair each 3¼mm (US3), 4mm (US6) and 4½mm (US7) needles
3¼mm (US3) circular needle
4 buttons

NOTE When working with yarns D and E, use 2 strands together.

TENSION
20 sts and 28 rows to 10cm (4in) over st st on 4mm (US6) needles.
23 sts and 23 rows to 10cm (4in) over sleeve patt on 4½mm (US7) needles.

BACK
Using 3¼mm (US3) needles and yarn A, cast on 120 sts.
Work 5cm (2in) in K3, P2 rib.
Change to 4mm (US6) needles and work 10 rows in st st, beg with a K row.
Now beg colour patt from chart 1 on page 62, working in st st throughout, beg with a K row, and using small separate balls of yarn for each motif, twisting yarns together at colour joins to avoid holes.
Work 160 rows straight.
With A only, work 8 rows in st st.
Shape shoulders
Cast off 50 sts at beg of next 2 rows.
Leave rem 20 sts on a stitch holder.

POCKET LININGS (make 2)
Using 4mm (US6) needles and A, cast on 28 sts.
Work 18cm (7in) in st st, beg with a K row.
Leave these sts on a stitch holder.

LEFT FRONT
Using 3¼mm (US3) needles and yarn A, cast on 60 sts.
Work 5cm (2in) in K3, P2 rib.
Change to 4mm (US6) needles and work 10 rows in st st, beg with a K row.
Now beg colour patt from chart 1 on page 62, working between left front markers, work 46 rows straight, ending with a WS row.
Place pocket lining
Next row Patt 16 sts, sl next 28 sts on to a stitch holder, patt across 28 sts of first pocket lining, patt to end of row.
Work 96 rows straight, ending with a RS row.
Shape neck
Next row Patt 7 sts and place these sts on a safety pin, patt to end of row. 53 sts.
Work 1 row. Now dec 1 st at neck edge on next and foll 2 alt rows. 50 sts.
Work straight until front matches back to beg of shoulder shaping, ending with a WS row.
Cast off

RIGHT FRONT
Work as given for left front, reversing shapings.

SLEEVES
Using 3¼mm (US3) needles and yarn A, cast on 53 sts.
Work 5cm (2in) in K3, P2 rib, inc 1 st at end of last row. 54 sts.
Change to 4½mm (US7) needles and work in colour patt from chart 2 on page 62, work in st st weaving contrast colours into back of work.
Work 88 rows, *at the same time* inc 1 st at each end of 3rd and every foll alt row until there are 130 sts, working the extra sts into patt.
Cast off loosely and evenly.

Right *The motif for the Topkapi Flower Jacket is of Turkish origin.*

TO MAKE UP

Pocket edgings

With RS of work facing, using 3¼mm (US3) needles and yarn A, sl sts from stitch holder at pocket top on to left-hand needle. Work 2.5cm (1in) in K3, P2 rib.
Cast off evenly in rib.
Sew pocket edgings to RS of fronts and pocket linings to WS.

Button band

With RS of work facing, using 3¼mm (US3) circular needle and yarn A, K up 123 sts evenly along left front edge (work in rows).
Work 2.5cm (1in) in K3, P2 rib.
Cast off evenly in rib.

Buttonhole band

Work as given for button band making 3 buttonholes on 3rd row of rib as foll:
Buttonhole row (WS) Rib 37, (yo, P2 tog, rib 37) twice, yo, P2 tog, rib 6.
Join both shoulders using a backstitch seam.

Neckband

With RS of work facing, using 3¼mm (US3) needles and yarn A, K up 5 sts across top of buttonhole band, 7 sts from safety pin at neck edge, 23 sts up right front neck, 19 sts (dec 1 st at centre back) across stitch holder at back neck, 22 sts down left front neck, 7 sts from safety pin and 5 sts across top of button band. 88 sts.
Work 2.5cm (1in) in K3, P2 rib, making a buttonhole on 2nd row as foll:
Buttonhole row (RS) Rib 3, yo, P2 tog, rib to end.
Cast off evenly in rib.
Place markers 28cm (11in) down from shoulder seams on back and fronts.
Set in sleeves between markers using a backstitch seam.
Join side and sleeve seams.
Sew on buttons.

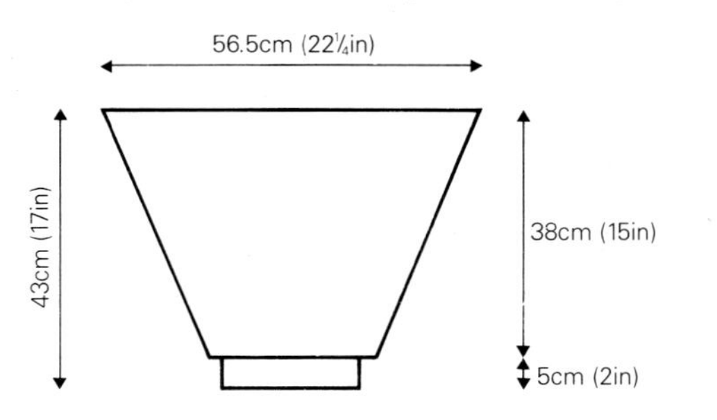

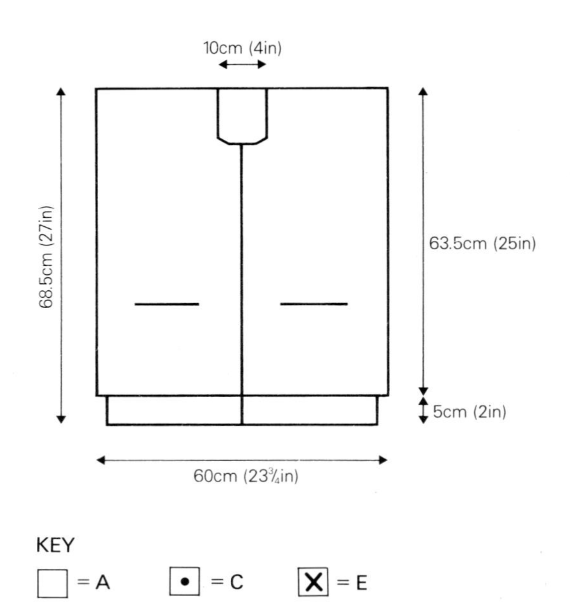

CHART 2 Rep 1st-42nd rows

42
40
30
20
10

Rep = 22 sts
Sleeves

KEY

□ = A
[I] = B
[•] = C
[/] = D
[X] = E

CHART 1 Rep 1st-80th rows

80
70
60
50
40
30
20
10

Right Front
Left Front
Back

★★

TOPKAPI LILY COAT

Winter

SIZE
To fit one size up to 101cm (40in) bust

MATERIALS
1,325g Lightweight Double Knitting in black 62 (A); 200g in pale grey 64 (E); 175g in blue grey 88 (B); 125g in grey 61 (D)
200g Rowanspun Tweed in grey 764 (C)
Equivalent yarn Aran-weight
1 pair each 5mm (US8) and 4mm (US6) needles
6 buttons

NOTE When using yarns A, B, D and E, use 2 strands together.

TENSION
18 sts and 24 rows to 10cm (4in) over st st on 5mm (US8) needles.

BACK
Using 5mm (US8) needles and A, cast on 120 sts.
Change to 4mm (US6) needles and work in moss st as foll:
1st row (RS) (K1, P1) to end.
2nd row (P1, K1) to end.
Rep these 2 rows twice more.
Change to 5mm (US8) needles and work in colour patt from chart 1 on page 64, working in st st throughout beg with a K row, and using small separate balls of yarn for each motif, twisting yarns together at colour joins to avoid holes.
Cont in patt until back measures 117cm (46in) from cast-on edge, ending with a WS row.
Shape shoulders
Cast off 47 sts at beg of next 2 rows. 26 sts.
Leave these sts on a stitch holder.

POCKET LININGS (make 2)
Using 5mm (US8) needles and yarn A, cast on 23 sts.
Work 15cm (6in) in st st, beg with a K row.
Leave these sts on a stitch holder.

LEFT FRONT
Using 5mm (US8) needles and yarn A, cast on 67 sts.
Change to 4mm (US6) needles and work in moss st as foll:
1st row (RS) (K1, P1) to last st, K1.
Rep this row 5 times more.
Change to 5mm (US8) needles and beg colour patt from chart 1, working between left front markers as foll:
1st row (RS) K49A, 3B, 1A, 2B, 5A, sl next 7 sts on to a safety pin for front band.
This row establishes the position of chart patt and front band.
Cont as set until left front measures 76cm (30in) from cast-on edge, ending with a WS row.
Place pocket lining
Next row Patt 18 sts, sl next 23 sts on to a stitch holder, patt across 23 sts of first pocket lining, patt to end of row. Now work straight until front measures 109cm (43in) from beg, ending with a RS row.
Shape neck
Next row Patt 8 sts, sl these sts on to a safety pin, patt to end of row.
Work 1 row.
Cast off 2 sts at neck edge on next row, and dec 1 st at neck edge on foll 3 alt rows. 47 sts.
Work straight until left front matches back to beg of shoulder shaping, ending with a WS row.
Cast off.

RIGHT FRONT
Work as given for left front, but working between right front markers on chart 1, reversing front band, and all shapings, and placing pocket lining as foll:
Next row Patt 19 sts, sl next 23 sts on to a stitch holder, patt across 23 sts of second pocket lining, patt to end.

FRONT BANDS (alike)
Using 3¾mm (US5) needles and yarn A, sl 7 sts left for front band on to left-hand needle.
Work in moss st as given for left front until band when slightly stretched fits up front opening edge to beg of neck shaping.
Leave these sts on a stitch holder.

SLEEVES
Join both shoulders using a backstitch seam.
Place markers 30.5cm (12in) below shoulder seams on back and fronts.
With RS of work facing, using 5mm (US8) needles and yarn A, K up 108 sts evenly between markers.
Next row P to end.
Now work in colour patt from chart 1, turning chart upside down and working between sleeve markers as foll:

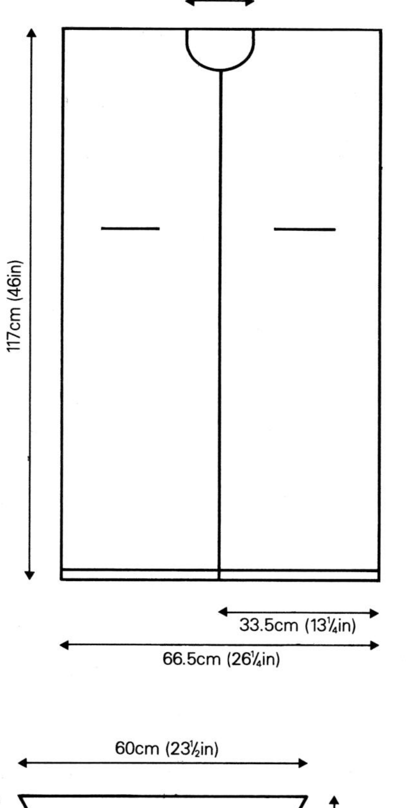

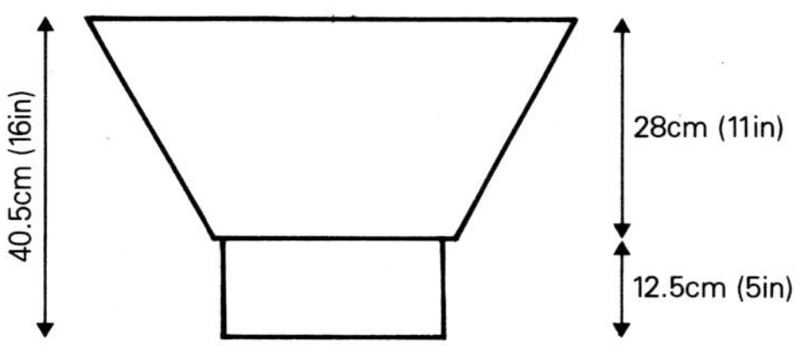

1st row K24A, patt 1st row of chart, K24A. This row establishes the position of chart patt.
Cont in patt, *at the same time* dec 1 st at each end of next and every foll 3rd row until 94 sts rem, then every foll alt row until 54 sts rem.
Now work straight until sleeve measures 28cm (11in), ending with a WS row, dec 1 st in middle of last row. 53 sts.
Change to 4mm (US6) needles and yarn D. Work 6 rows in moss st as given for left front.
Now work 20 rows in colour patt from chart 2, using small separate balls of yarn for each motif.
Change to yarn D and then work 6 rows in moss st.
Cast off evenly in moss st.

TO MAKE UP

Collar

With RS of work facing, using 4mm (US6) needles and yarn A, work in moss st across 7 sts of right front band, K across 8 sts at beg of neck shaping, K up 18 sts up right side of neck, (K12, K2 tog, K12) across stitch holder at back neck, K up 18 sts down left front neck, K across 8 sts at beg of neck shaping, and work in moss st across 7 sts of left front band. 91 sts.
Work 16 rows in moss st making a buttonhole on 7th and 8th rows as foll:
1st buttonhole row (WS) Work in moss st to last 9 sts, cast off 2 sts, moss st to end.
2nd buttonhole row Work in moss st to end, casting on 2 sts over those cast off in previous row.
Cast off evenly in moss st.
Join side and sleeve seams.

Pocket edgings

With RS of work facing, using 5mm (US8) needles and yarn A, sl 23 sts from stitch holder at pocket top on to left-hand needle. Work 6 rows in moss st as given for left front. Cast off evenly in moss st.
Sew pocket linings in position on WS of fronts. Catch down pocket edgings to RS.

Front bands

Slipstitch left front band in position down left front, stretching it slightly to fit. Mark the position of 5 buttonholes on right front band, the first 7.5cm (3in) down from beg of neck shaping and the rem 4 at 10cm (4in) intervals.
Slipstitch right front band in place, leaving 2cm (¾in) gaps opposite button markers for buttonholes. Sew on buttons.

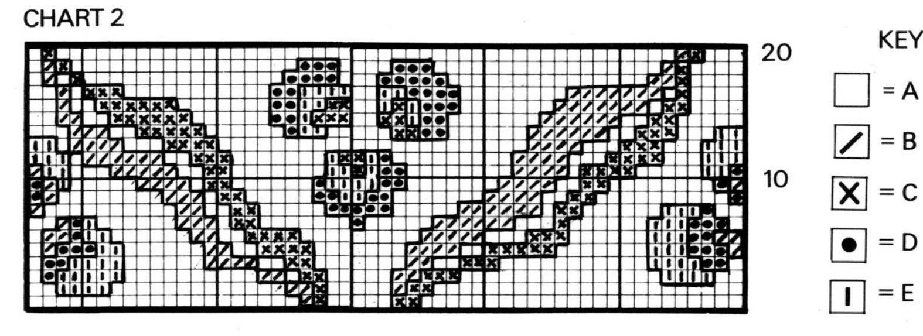

Right *The Topkapi motif lends itself to many interpretations. Here its simple swirls decorate a long sinuous winter coat. Another of Jane Wheeler's jackets, pictured on pages 66-67, has much the same quietly exotic feeling.*

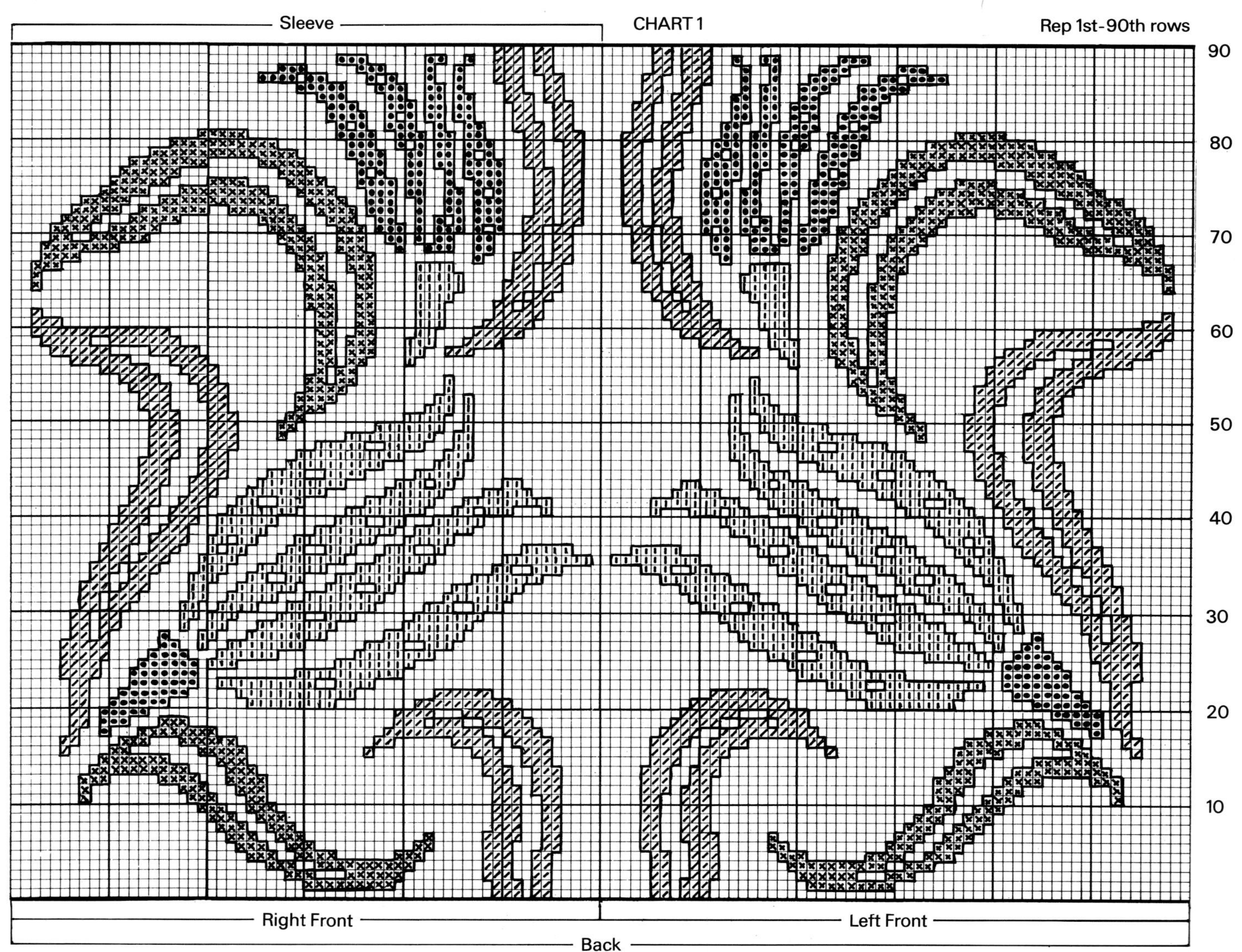

JAMIE AND JESSI SEATON

Fields are all you can see from Jamie and Jessi Seaton's studio, and for miles around that is all there is. From this remote spot they design and organize the production of hundreds of sweaters, mainly hand-knitted, for international fashion stores.
Somehow they can detect what colours, textures, shapes and motifs will sell in the smartest shops in New York and California, but their work is highly individual while merging successfully with fashion. The occasional historical theme finds its way into the designs, which is not surprising when you discover that they both set out to be archaeologists. Nine years ago they abandoned the dig and started knitting for a living.
In those early days Jamie used a machine to produce the garments that Jessi designed. She also dyed the wool, for the plentiful supplies of shades and textures that we now take for granted were not available then. Later Jamie became interested in designing and now undertakes most of this work, producing magnificent coloured charts for their knitters to use.

★ ★

CASPIAN FLOWERS

Winter

KITS A yarn kit is available for this design. *See page 160 for details.*

SIZE

To fit 91[96, 101]cm (36[38, 40]in) bust/chest

MATERIALS

400 [425, 450]g Botany Wool in black 62 (A); 50g in grey/green 100 (B); 25g each in sea green 91 (C), red 44 (D), light blue 51 (E), ginger 26 (G), rose 69 (H), plum 70 (J), royal 56 (L), taupe 102 (M), iris 501 (N), silver 120 (Q), apricot 103 (R) and aubergine 94 (S)
25g Light Tweed in atlantic 223 (T)
25g Fine Fleck Yarn each in midnight 54 (F) and light blue 51 (U)
Equivalent yarn four-ply
1 pair each 2¼mm (US1) and 2¾mm (US2) needles
1 2¼mm (US1) circular needle 80cm (30in) long

TENSION

32 sts and 42 rows to 10cm (4in) over patt on 2¾mm (US2) needles.

SHAWL-NECK SWEATER

BACK

Using 2¼mm (US1) needles and yarn A, cast on 135[143, 149] sts.
Work in twisted rib as foll:
1st row (K1 tbl, P1) to last st, K1 tbl.
2nd row (P1, K1 tbl) to last st, P1.
These 2 rows form twisted rib.
Cont in rib until work measures 10cm (4in).
Next row (WS) Rib 4[8, 11], (make 1, rib 6) 21 times, make 1, rib to end. 157[165, 171] sts.
Change to 2¾mm (US2) needles and work 4[6, 8] rows in st st, beg with a K row. Now cont in st st, beg colour patt from chart, using small separate balls of yarn for each colour area, twisting yarns tog on WS at colour joins to avoid holes, as foll:
1st row (RS) K10[14, 17]A, (1C, 33A, 1B, 33A) twice, 1C, 10[14, 17]A.
This row establishes the position of chart patt. Cont in patt, work 90[92, 94] rows, ending with a WS row.
Shape armholes
Keeping patt correct, cast off 4 sts at beg of next 2 rows, then dec 1 st at each end of next and foll 13[15, 17] alt rows. 121[125, 127] sts. **
Now work straight until 210[214, 220] rows in all have been worked in chart patt, ending with WS row. ***
Shape shoulders
Cast off 9 sts at beg of next 4 rows, then 8[9, 9] sts at beg of foll 2 rows. 69[71, 73] sts. Work 1 row. Cast off.

FRONT

Work as given for back until 137[139, 143] rows in all have been worked in chart patt, ending with a RS row.
Divide for neck
Next row Patt 49[50, 51] sts, turn, leaving rem sts on a spare needle and cont on these sts only for first side of neck.
Work 2 rows straight.
Dec 1 st at neck edge on next and foll 3rd row until 26[27, 27] sts rem. Now work straight until front matches back to shoulder, ending at armhole edge.
Shape shoulder
Cast off 9 sts at beg of next and foll alt row.
Work 1 row. Cast off rem 8[9, 9] sts.
With WS of work facing, return to sts on spare needle, rejoin yarn to next st, cast off centre 23[25, 25] sts, patt to end. Complete second side of neck to match first reversing shapings.

SLEEVES

Using 2¼mm (US1) needles and yarn A, cast on 65[67, 69] sts. Work 10cm (4in) in twisted K1, P1 rib as given for back.
Next row (WS) Rib 3[4, 6], (make 1, rib 2) 29 times, make 1, rib to end. 95[97, 99] sts.
Change to 2¾mm (US2) needles and work 2[4, 6] rows in st st, beg with a K row.
Cont in st st, work in colour patt from chart, beg at 65th row as foll:
65th row K13[14, 15]A, 1C, 33A, 1B, 33A, 1C, 13[14, 15]A.
This row establishes the position of chart patt. Cont in patt as set, *at the same time* inc 1 each end of every foll 3rd row until there are 189[193, 199] sts, working incs into patt (but do not beg a new motif if less than half of it can be worked). Now work straight until 154[156, 158] rows have been worked in chart patt, end with WS row.
Shape top
Cast off 4 sts at beg of next 2 rows, then 3 sts at beg of foll 16[16, 18] rows and 10 sts at beg of foll 8 rows. 53[57, 57] sts.
Work 1 row. Cast off.

COLLAR

Using 2¼mm (US1) circular needle and yarn A, cast on 96[102, 106] sts. Work in rows.
Work 44 rows in K1, P1 rib, *at the same time* cast on 3 sts at beg of next 16 rows and 1 st at each end of foll 28 rows. 200[206, 210] sts.
Now inc 1 st at each end of next 11 alt rows. 222[228, 232] sts.
Work 2 rows. Cast off loosely in rib.

TO MAKE UP

Join both shoulders using backstitch seams. Join cast-on edge of collar to neck edge, and row ends to cast-off sts at centre front, lapping right side of collar over left side. Join side and sleeve seams.
Set in sleeves.

CREW-NECK SWEATER (not shown)

BACK

Work as given for shawl-neck sweater to ***, ending with a WS row.
Shape shoulders
Cast off 10[11, 11] sts at beg of next 4 rows and 11[10, 10] sts at beg of foll 2 rows.
Leave rem 59[61, 63] sts on a stitch holder.

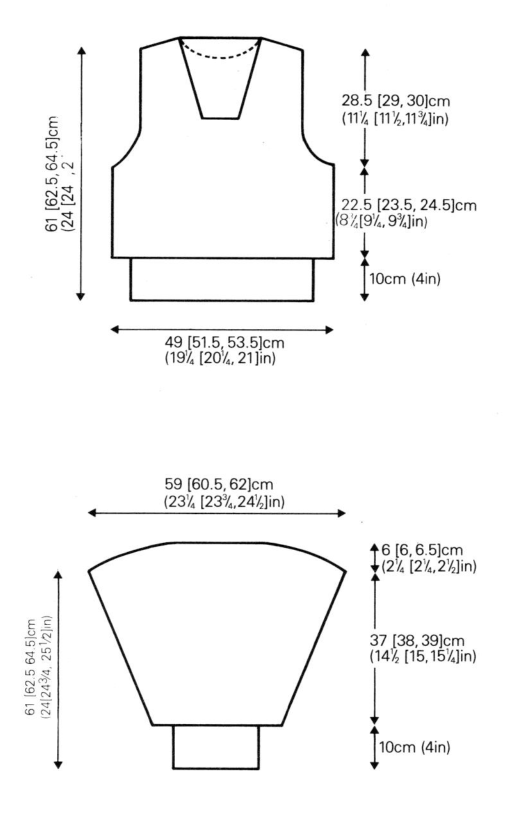

FRONT

Work as given for back until front measures 26[28, 30] rows less than back to shoulder.

Divide for neck

Next row Patt 54[55, 55] sts, turn, leaving rem sts on a spare needle and cont on these sts only for first side of neck.

Cast off 3 sts at neck edge on next and foll 5 alt rows, then dec 1 st at same edge on next 5 rows. 31[32, 32] sts.

Now work straight until front matches back to shoulder, ending at armhole edge.

Shape shoulder

Cast off 10[11, 11] sts at beg of next and foll alt row. 11[10, 10] sts.

Work 1 row.

Cast off.

With RS of work facing, return to sts on spare needle, sl centre 13[15, 17] sts on to a stitch holder, rejoin yarn to next st, patt to end.

Work 1 row.

Complete second side of neck to match first side, reversing shapings.

SLEEVES

Work as given for shawl-neck sweater.

TO MAKE UP

Join right shoulder using a backstitch seam.

Neckband

With RS of work facing, using 2¼mm (US1) needles and yarn A, K up 36[38, 39] sts down left front neck, K 13[15, 17] from stitch holder at centre front, K up 36[38, 39] sts up right front neck and K 59[61, 63] sts from stitch holder at back neck. 144[152, 158] sts.

Work 12 rows in K1, P1 rib.

Cast off evenly in rib.

Join left shoulder and neckband seam.

Join side and sleeve seams.

Set in sleeves.

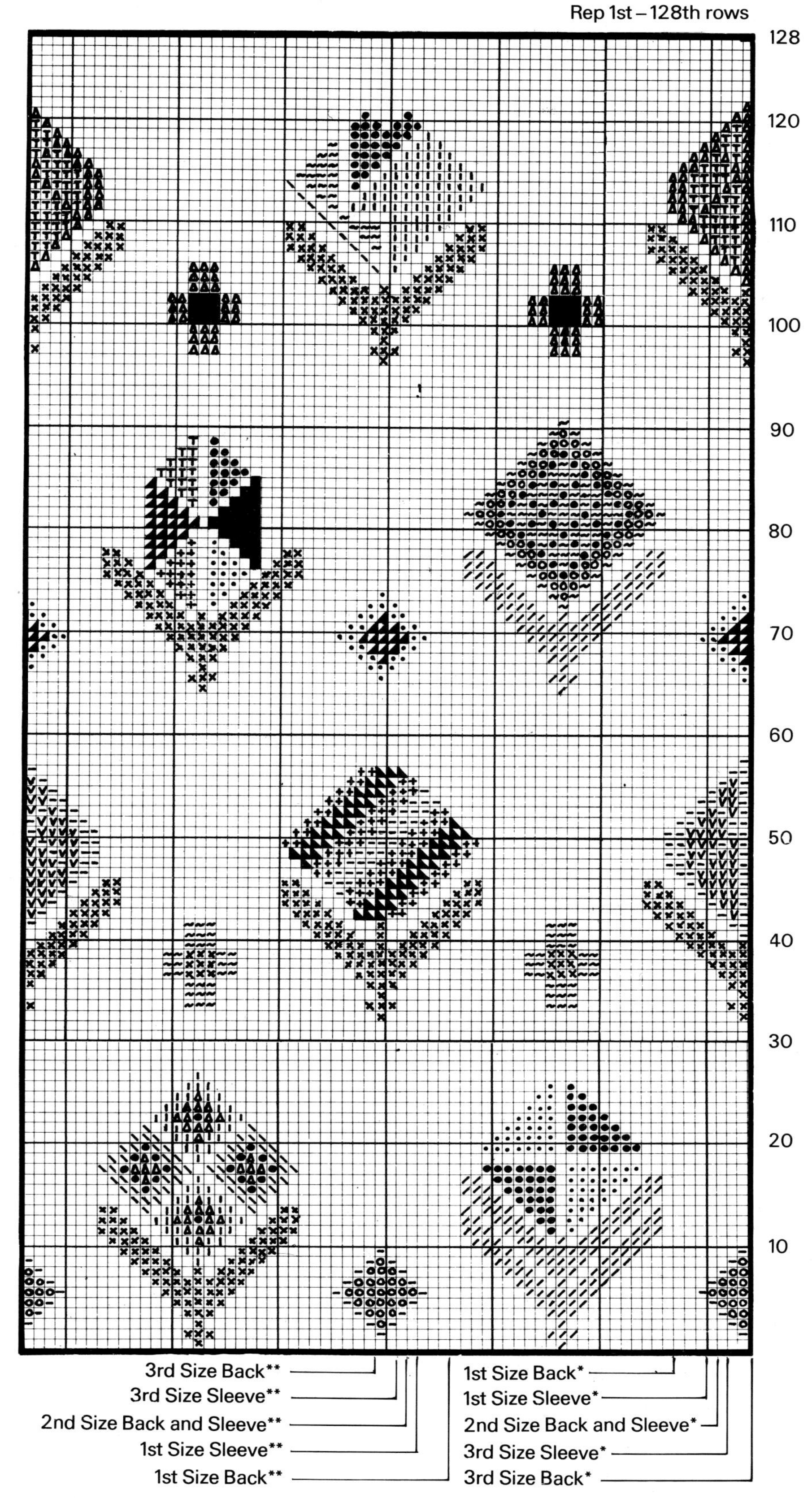

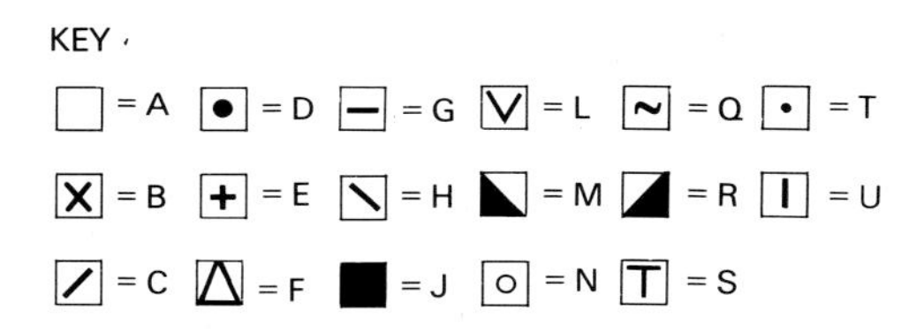

Overleaf *The Caspian Flower Sweater on the left was inspired by the beautiful prayer rugs of the Caucasus. The pattern is given for the shawl-neck version and for a crew-neck (not shown). The sweater on the right is another example of the Seatons' brilliant use of bright jewel colours on a black background.*

★ ★

RAJASTHAN SWEATER

Summer

SIZES
To fit 91[101]cm (36[40]in) bust

MATERIALS
350[400]g Sea Breeze Soft Cotton in bleached 521 (A); 50g each in fiord 531 (D), baize 540 (H), bermuda 539 (M) and polka 530 (Q)
50g [100]g Mercerised Cotton each in furnace 314 (B) and deep blue 309 (C); 50g each in livid 321 (E), blush 322 (F), rich purple 310 (G), spode 307 (J), blue scan 306 (L) and pale mauve 311 (N)
Equivalent yarn four-ply
1 pair each 2¼mm (US1) and 2¾mm (US2) needles

TENSION
33 sts and 40 rows to 10cm (4in) over patt on 2¾mm (US2) needles

SPECIAL ABBREVIATION
Make bobble – (K1, P1, K1, P1, K1) into st, (turn, P5, turn, K5) twice, turn, P5, turn, pass 2nd, 3rd, 4th and 5th sts over 1st st and off needle, then sl st on to right-hand needle.

BACK
Using 2¼mm (US1) needles and yarn A, cast on 141[151] sts.
Work in twisted rib as foll:
1st row (K1 tbl, P1) to last st, K1 tbl.
2nd row (P1, K1 tbl) to last st, P1.
Rep these 2 rows 20 times more, then work 1st row again.
Next row (WS) Rib 4[9], (make 1, rib 7) 19 times, make 1, rib to end. 161[171] sts.
Change to 2¾mm (US2) needles and work 2 rows in st st, beg with a K row.
Now cont in st st unless otherwise indicated, beg colour patt from chart, working between back markers using small separate balls of yarn for each colour area, twisting yarns tog on WS at colour joins to avoid holes, work 84[88] rows, ending with a WS row.
Shape armholes
Keeping patt correct, cast off 5 sts at beg of next 2 rows. 151[161] sts.
Work 104[110] rows straight, ending with a WS row.
Divide for neck
Next row Patt 68[71] sts, turn, leaving rem sts on a spare needle and cont on these sts only for first side of neck.
Cast off 6 sts at neck edge of next and 3 foll alt rows, then 5 sts at same edge on foll alt row, ending at armhole edge. 39[42] sts.
Shape shoulder
Cast off 10[11] sts at beg of next row, 5 sts at beg of foll row, 10[11] sts at beg of next row and 5 sts at beg of foll row. Cast off rem 9[10] sts.
With RS of work facing, return to sts on spare needle, rejoin yarn to next st, cast off centre 15[19] sts, patt to end.
Complete second side of neck to match first side, reversing shapings.

FRONT
Work as given for back.

SLEEVES
Using 2¼mm (US1) needles and yarn A, cast on 65[69] sts.
Work 43 rows in twisted rib as given for back.
Next row Rib 4[6] sts, (make 1, rib 2) 29 times, make 1, rib to end. 95[99] sts.
Change to 2¾mm (US2) needles and work 6 rows in st st, beg with a K row, inc 1 st at each end of 3rd and 6th rows. 99[103] sts.
Now work in colour patt from chart between sleeve markers, *at the same time* inc 1 st at each end of every foll 3rd row until there are 191[201] sts, working the incs into patt.
Work straight until 140[150] rows in all have been worked in chart patt.
Cast off loosely and evenly.

TO MAKE UP
Neckbands
With RS of work facing, using 2¼mm (US1) needles and yarn A, K up 40 sts down left front neck, 15[19] sts from centre front and 40 sts up right front neck. 95[99] sts.
Work 8 rows in K1, P1 rib.
Cast off loosely and evenly in rib.
Work neckband across back neck to match.
Join both shoulder seams, overlapping neckband edges front over back.
Set in sleeves, joining last few rows of sleeve to cast-off sts at underarm.
Join side and sleeve seams.

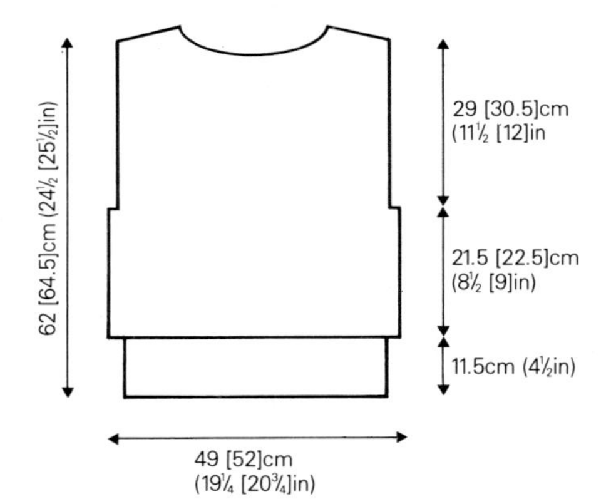

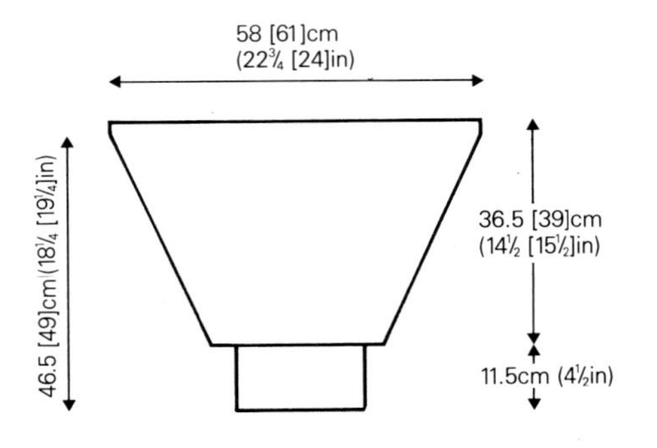

Above *The Rajasthan Sweater – a kaleidoscope of sharp geometrics and vibrant colours on a cool ground.*

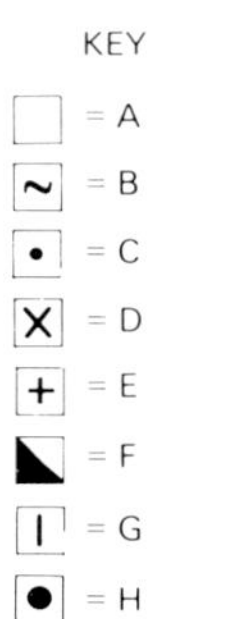

= J
= L
= M
= N
= Q
= make bobble in H (or other yarn as indicated)

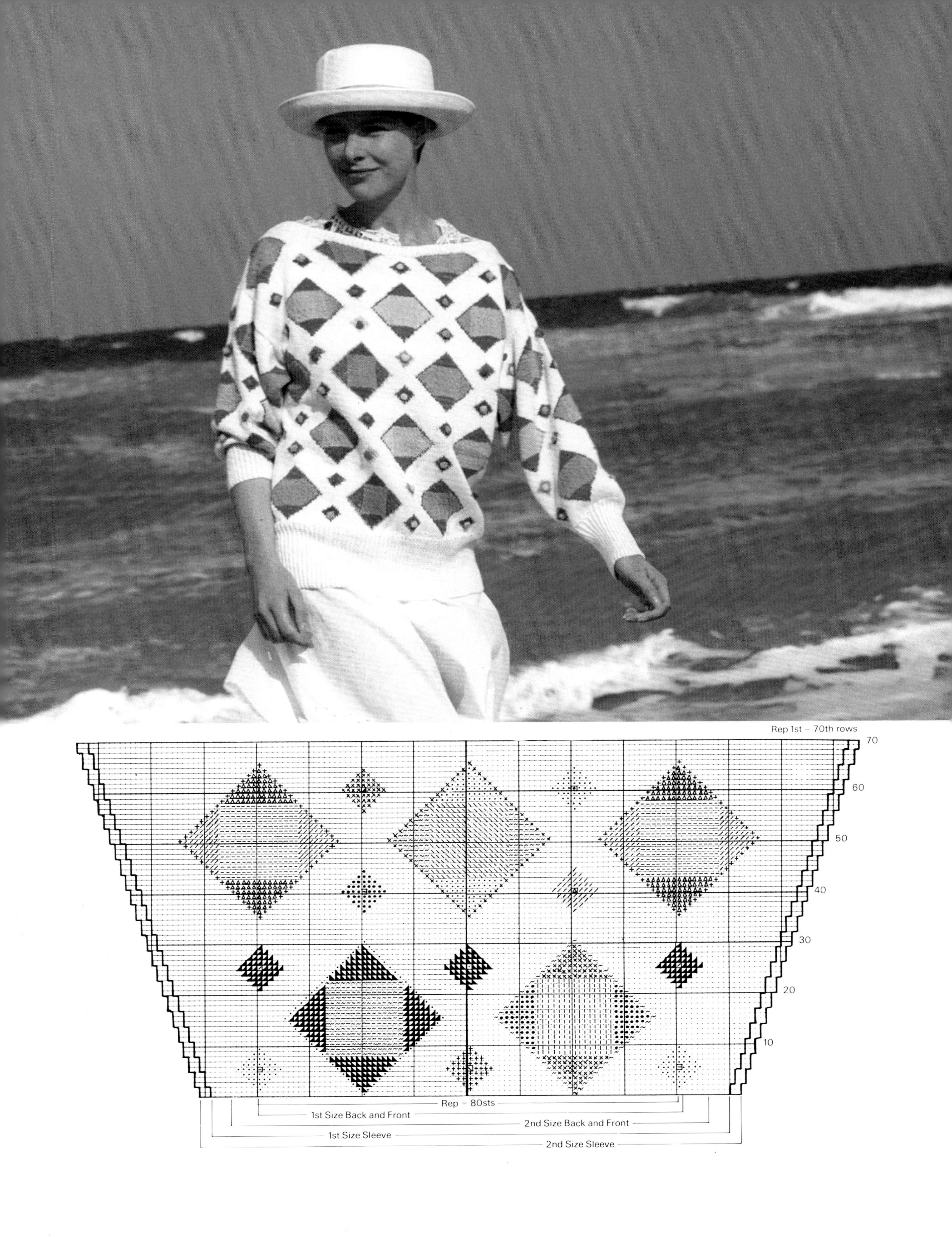
Rep 1st – 70th rows
70
60
50
40
30
20
10
Rep = 80sts
1st Size Back and Front
2nd Size Back and Front
1st Size Sleeve
2nd Size Sleeve

SUSAN DUCKWORTH

Susan Duckworth is a painter. Originally she set out to design for televison, and entered the BBC as a make-up artist. The long waits alternating with frenetic activity provided a wonderful opportunity to knit, and she used it to the full, not just to make sweaters but to explore the possibilities that yarns and needles might present. Finding it impossible to move from make-up to set design, she began to use the job to earn a living while she started a new career in knitting.

By setting up a London studio in the early 1970s and employing knitters to produce sweaters she was breaking new ground. Vision is a remarkable quality, strong in Sue as it must also be in Joseph who was one of her first customers, selling her work from his hairdressing salon, before the Joseph fashion empire existed. Since then her work has been constantly in demand from all over the world, and new ideas continue to spring from her needles.

Children's bikes litter the path to what looks like the garden shed from the outside, but turns out to be her studio. Inside the shed the walls are lined with hanks of wool, stock waiting to be shipped to Australia and the United States, and press cuttings featuring Sue's work. On the desk a computer keeps track of what the 250 knitters are working on, deals with the accounts and is generally indispensable.

The juxtapositon of high tech and hand-made is intriguing. These painters who successfully took to knitting have also turned out to be excellent businesswomen. Without this unusual combination, the rigours of finance, stock and quality control, export and marketing might suffocate the creative flair and stifle the business potential.

The opportunity for Susan Duckworth to be a much bigger concern has been present all the way along, but she keeps it the size that suits her, giving it the attention to detail that shines through her work, and balancing all with a happy family life. But it doesn't stop there. She moves, almost unconsciously, a little ahead of the tide, leaving you wondering just what will bear the Susan Duckworth label next year.

★ ★ ★

VENETIAN TILE CARDIGAN

Winter

KITS a yarn kit is available for the oatmeal colourway in the shorter length of this design. *See page 160 for details.*

SIZE

To fit up to 101cm (40in) bust/chest
Length 58.5[66]cm (23[26])in

MATERIALS

Oatmeal colourway

600[650]g Lightweight Double Knitting in oatmeal 614 (A); 75g in deep rose 411 (D), 50g each in grey blue 88 (E), mauve 611 (J) and plum 94 (N); 25g each in lavender 127 (B), soft pink 109 (F), tan 86 (G), mist 58 (H) and beige 82 (M)
50g Light Tweed in autumn 205 (L); 25g in rosemix 215 (C)
Equivalent yarn double knitting
1 pair each 3mm (US2) and 3¼mm (US3) needles
3.00mm (USD) crochet hook
8[9] buttons

TENSION

27½ sts and 38 rows to 10cm (4in) over patt on 3¼mm (US3) needles.

SPECIAL NOTE

Work blackberry st in yarns as on chart:
1st row (RS) K to end.
2nd row *(K1, P1, K1) into next st, P3 tog; rep from * to last st, (K1, P1, K1) into next st.
3rd row P to end.
4th row *P3 tog, (K1, P1, K1) into next st; rep from * to last 3 sts, P3 tog.
5th row P to end.
6th-9th rows As 2nd-5th rows.
10th-12th rows As 2nd-4th rows.
13th row K to end.
These 13 rows form blackberry st panel in centre of each 'tile'.

BACK

Using 3mm (US2) needles and yarn A, cast on 164 sts.
Work in K4, P4 rib as foll:
1st row (RS) (K4, P4) to last 4 sts, K4.
2nd row (P4, K4) to last 4 sts, P4.
These 2 rows form rib patt.
Cont in rib until work measures 5cm (2in), ending with a WS row.
Change to 3¼mm (US3) needles and work in colour and stitch patt from chart in yarn A unless otherwise indicated, working between back markers, use small separate balls of yarn for each colour area, twisting yarns tog on WS at colour joins to avoid holes. Work 1st-93rd rows, then 14th-24th[52nd] rows again, ending with a WS row.

Shape armholes

Keeping patt correct, cast off 8 sts at beg of next 2 rows. 148 sts.
Now cont in patt until 93rd row has been worked, then rep 14th-44th[52nd] rows once.
The 5th-12th chart rows form basketweave patt rep, work 0[20] rows in basketweave patt, ending with a WS row.

Shape shoulders

Keeping basketweave patt correct, cast off 17 sts at beg of next 6 rows.
Cast off rem 46 sts.

LEFT FRONT

Using 3mm (US2) needles and yarn A, cast on 82 sts.
Work 5cm (2in) in K4, P4 rib as foll:
1st row (RS) (K4, P4) to last 2 sts, K2.
2nd row P2, (K4, P4) to end. Rep these 2 rows.
Change to 3¼mm (US3) needles and beg colour and stitch patt from chart, working between left front markers, work 1st-93rd rows, then rep 14th-24th[52nd] rows again, ending with a WS row.

Shape armhole

Keeping patt correct, cast off 8 sts at beg of

next row. 74 sts.
Now cont in patt until 93rd patt row has been worked, then rep 14th-23rd[51st] rows again, ending at front opening edge.

Shape neck
Keeping patt correct, cast off 10 sts at beg of next row, then dec 1 st at neck edge on next 13 rows. 51 sts.
Work 7 rows straight, ending at armhole edge.

Shape shoulder
Cast off 17 sts at beg of next and foll alt row. 17 sts.
Work 1 row.
Cast off.

RIGHT FRONT

Work as given for left front, working between right front markers on chart, working one more row before armhole shaping and reversing all shaping and working K4, P4 rib as foll:
1st row RS K2, (P4, K4) to end.
2nd row (P4, K4) to last 2 sts, P2. Rep these 2 rows.

SLEEVES

Using 3mm (US2) needles and yarn A, cast on 58 sts.
Work 10cm (4in) in K1, P1 rib.
Next row (WS) K into front and back of every st. 116 sts.
Change to 3¼mm (US3) needles and work in patt from chart as foll:
1st row (P4, K4) twice, patt 84 sts between sleeve markers, (K4, P4) twice. This row sets the position of chart. Cont in patt as set, *at the same time* inc 1 st at each end of 5th and every foll 4th row until there are 144 sts, working the incs into basketweave patt.
Now work straight until 172 rows have been completed in chart patt.
Cast off loosely and evenly.

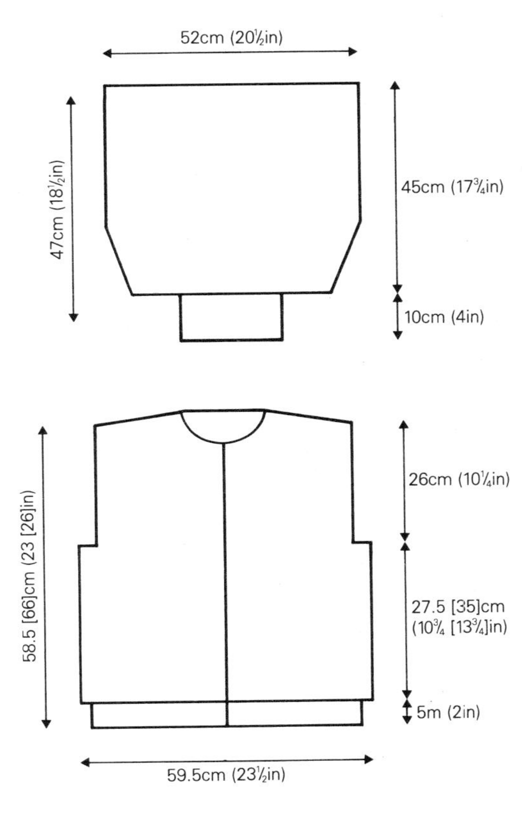

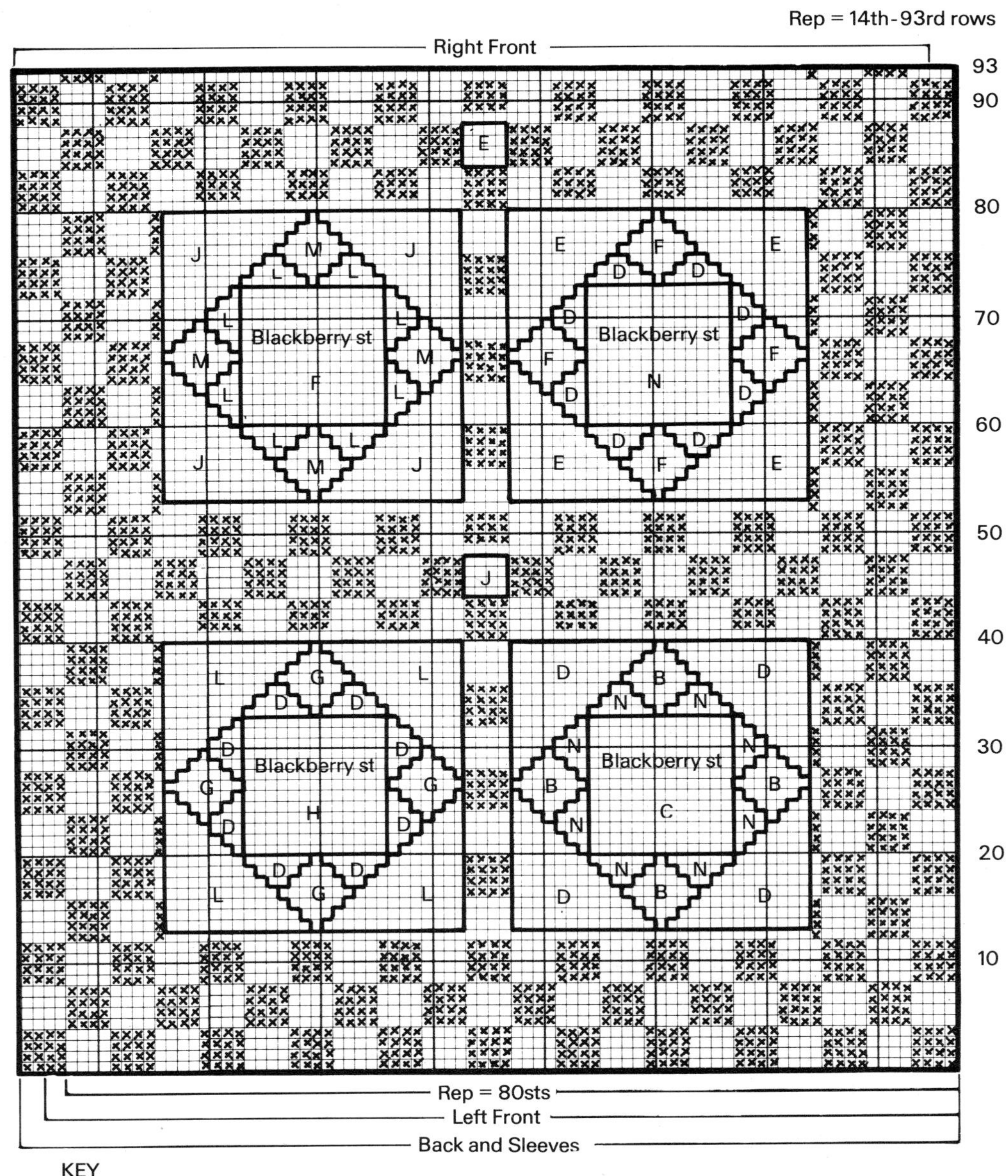

KEY
☐ = K on RS rows, P on WS rows in yarn A unless otherwise indicated
☒ = P on RS rows, K on WS rows in yarn A

BUTTON BAND

Using 3mm (US2) needles and yarn A, cast on 13 sts.
Work in K1, P1 rib until band when slightly stretched fits up left front to beg of neck shaping. Cast off in rib.
Mark the position of 8[9] buttons, the first to come 1.5cm (½in) from cast-on edge, the 2nd 1.5cm (½in) from cast-off edge and the rest spaced evenly between.

BUTTONHOLE BAND

Work as for button band, making buttonholes opposite button markers as foll:
1st buttonhole row Rib 5, cast off 3 sts, rib to end.
2nd buttonhole row Rib to end, casting on 3 sts over those cast off in previous row.

COLLAR

Using 3¼mm (US3) needles and yarn A, cast on 21 sts.
Work 42.5cm (16¾in) in blackberry st, rep 2nd-5th rows. Cast off.

TO MAKE UP

Join both shoulders using backstitch seams.
Join on buttonband and buttonhole band.
Sew collar to neck edge, beg halfway along right front band and ending halfway across left front band.

Picot edging
Using 3.00mm (USD) crochet hook and yarn A, work collar edging as foll:
1st row Work in double crochet to end.
2nd row *1 double crochet in each of next 3 double crochet, 3 chain, slipstitch into first chain; rep from * to end.
Set in sleeves, joining last few rows of sleeve to cast-off sts at underarm.
Join side and sleeve seams.
Sew on buttons.
Fold back cuffs.

Overleaf *The Venetian Tile Cardigan in two colourways. The pattern and the kit are for the oatmeal version on the left.*

★ ★ ★

BUTTERFLY FLORAL SWEATER

Summer

SIZE

To fit one size up to 96cm (38in) bust

MATERIALS

450g Mercerised Cotton in peach 313 (A); 50g each in blush 322 (B), straw 305 (C), spode 307 (D), natural 301 (E), mauve 311 (F), char 318 (G), hydro 323 (H), claret 315 (J), french blue 308 (L), jettison 317 (M), canary 320 (N) and blue scan 306 (R)

50g Sea Breeze Soft Cotton in smoke 527 (Q)

50g Salad Days Knobbly Cotton in hyacinth 566 (S)

Equivalent yarn four-ply

1 pair each 2¾mm (US2) and 3¼mm (US3) needles

TENSION

30 sts and 36 rows to 10cm (4in) over patt on 3¼mm (US3) needles.

BACK

Using 2¾mm (US2) needles and yarn A, cast on 168 sts.

Work in twisted rib as foll:

1st row (K1 tbl, P1 tbl) to end.

Rep this row until work measures 5cm (2in) from cast-on edge.

Change to 3¼mm (US3) needles and beg colour patt from chart, weaving yarn A into back of work and using small separate balls of yarn for each motif, twisting yarns between colours to avoid holes, as foll:

1st row (RS) K21A, (patt 1st row of chart) twice, K21A.

This row establishes the position of the chart.

Cont as set, working in st st throughout until back measures 42cm (16½in) from cast-on edge, ending with a WS row.

Shape armholes.

Cast off 8 sts at beg of next 2 rows. 152 sts.

Now work straight, working in st st throughout, until back measures 65cm (25¾in) from cast-on edge, ending with a WS row.

Shape shoulders

Cast off 15 sts at beg of next 4 rows and 14 sts at beg of next 2 rows (when last possible complete motifs have been worked, cont in A only).

Cast off rem 64 sts.

FRONT

Work as given for back until front measures 61cm (24in) from cast-on edge, ending with a WS row.

Divide for neck

Next row Patt 54 sts, turn, leaving rem sts on a spare needle and cont on these sts only for first side of neck.

Dec 1 st at neck edge on next 10 rows. 44 sts.

Now work straight until front matches back to shoulder, ending at armhole edge.

Shape shoulder

Cast off 15 sts at beg of next and foll alt row. 14 sts.

Work 1 row.

Cast off.

With RS of work facing, return to sts on spare needle, rejoin yarn to next st, cast off 44 sts, patt to end.

Complete second side of neck to match first, reversing shapings.

SLEEVES

Using 2¾mm (US2) needles and yarn A, cast on 63 sts.

Work 10cm (4in) in twisted K1, P1 rib.

Next row Rib 2, (make 1, rib 2) to last 3 sts, make 1, rib 3. 93 sts.

Change to 3¼mm (US3) needles and beg colour patt from chart as foll:

Next row (RS) K15A, patt 1st row of chart, K15A.

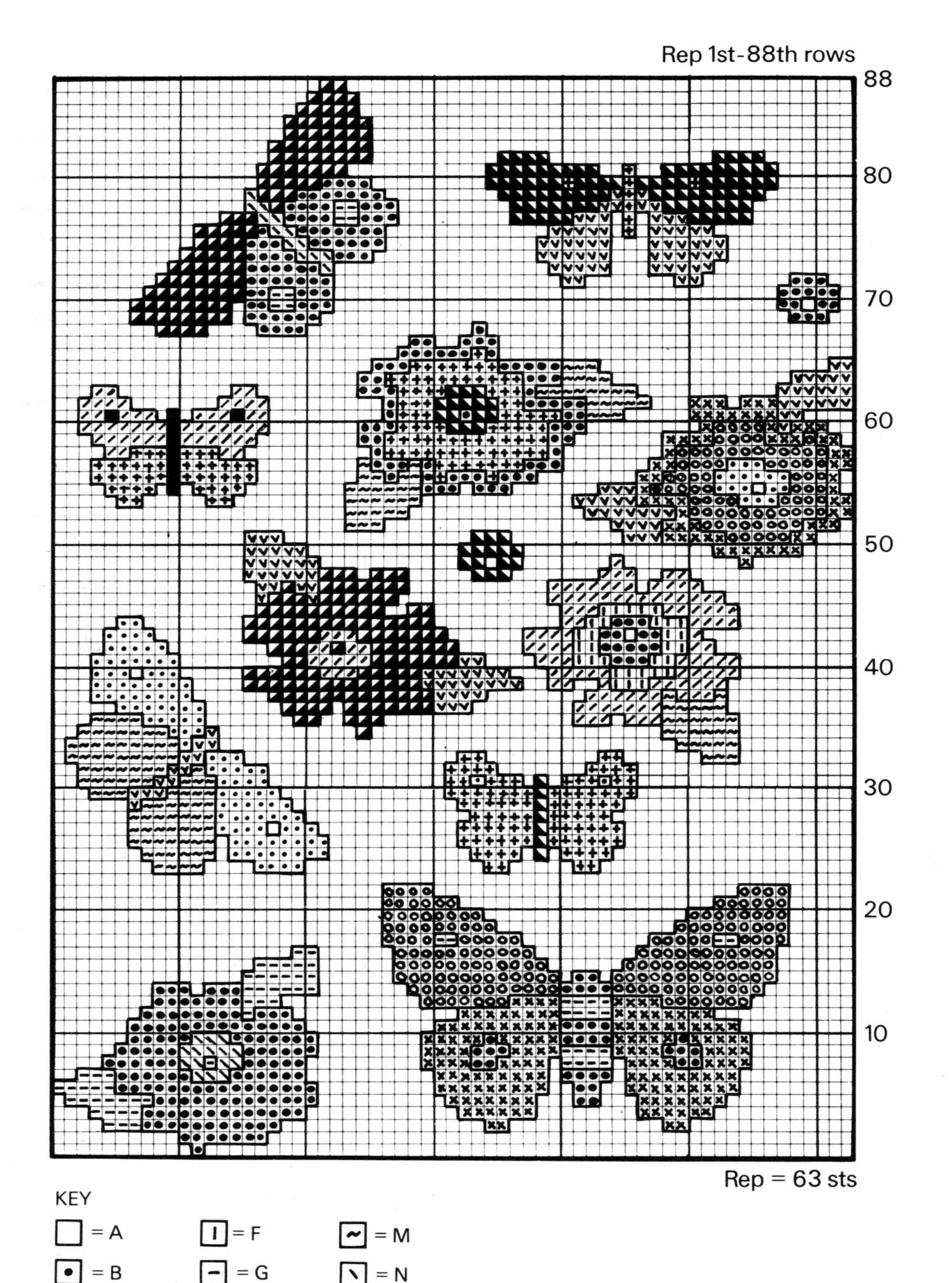

This row establishes the position of the chart.
Cont in patt, *at the same time* inc 1 st at each end of 2nd and every foll 3rd row until there are 139 sts, working the incs in st st in A. Now work straight until sleeve measures 49cm (19¼in) from cast-on edge, ending with a WS row.
Cast off loosely and evenly.

TO MAKE UP

Join right shoulder using a backstitch seam.

Neckband

With RS of work facing, using 2¾mm (US2) needles and yarn A, K up 17 sts down left side of neck, 44 sts across front neck, 17 sts up right side of neck and 66 sts across centre back. 144 sts.
Work 6 rows in K1, P1 rib.
Cast off loosely and evenly in rib.
Join left shoulder and neckband seam.
Set in sleeves joining last few rows of sleeve to cast-off sts at underarm.
Join side and sleeve seams.

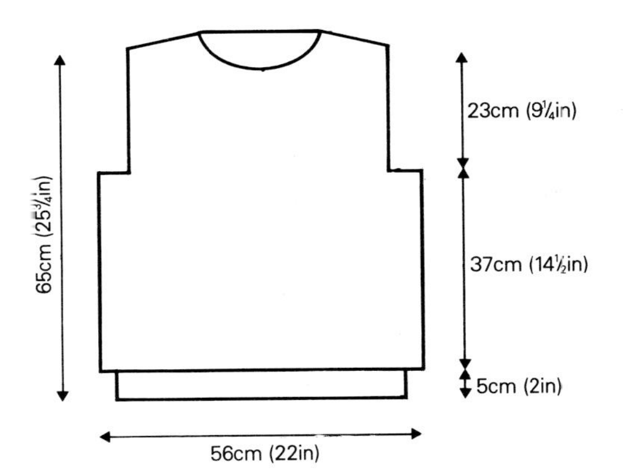

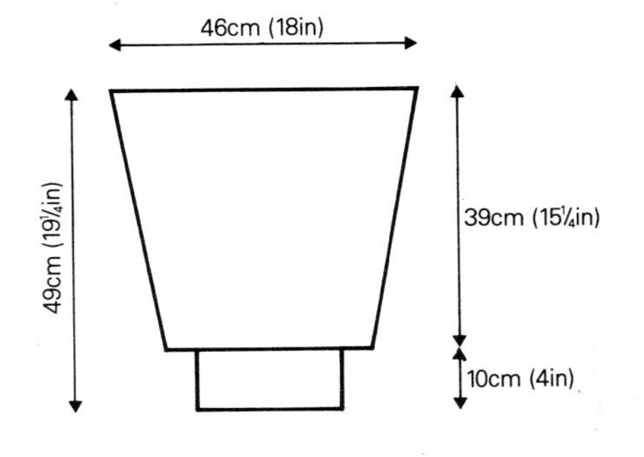

Right *Susan Duckworth's Butterfly Floral Sweater – a marvellous example of her ability to handle intricate motifs and a huge range of glowing colours with a delicate touch. In fine mercerised cotton, it will not be the easiest of garments to knit, but the results will be spectacular.*

THE MODERNS THE MODERNS THE MODERNS THE MODERNS

MARTIN KIDMAN

What would you expect the brains behind the Joseph Tricot label to be like? Joseph, one of the most successful fashion producer/retailers of the 1980s, must surely be choosy. A young man straight from college was something of a surprise, but John Lennon specs framed a pair of eyes that belied unusual powers of concentration and a calmness not acquired in the rag trade.

The Martin Kidman story could not have happened ten years ago, for fashion knitwear is still relatively young, and what now presents itself as a knitwear tradition was in the mid-70s only just emerging from the post-war love affair with nylon. Twin-set manufacturers did not use designers; art colleges had not even considered running knitting courses; and no little girl or boy had grown up dreaming of ribs and purls.

For Martin, however, knitting was one of the many options in the fashion course at college, and it was from his college show that the Joseph talent spotters snapped him up – including the garments he had knitted for his graduation. This became part of the Spring 85 Joseph Tricot collection, and Martin had started his career before he even knew it.

His engaging designs are the second surprise, reminiscent of comforting things like being cosy indoors when outside the cold wind bites, but they also encompass a fashion flair and a touch of exotica that no-one else can copy. Among snowflakes and running deer a cuddly cherub proffers a golden garland.

His slightly reclusive nature is paradoxical in the extrovert world of fashion. A chatty budgerigar and a parrot in a suburban Edwardian parlour, complete with chintz covers and Indian carpet, provide the setting. The family photos on the wall observe the scene; the budgie comments; and Martin works in tidy order, enjoying the glitz and fun but unseduced by the drum rolls and little gold chairs that herald the opening of another season's show.

★ ★

HORSES & FLOWERS SWEATERS

Summer and Winter

KITS A yarn kit is available for the adult sweater. See page 160 for details.

SIZE

Adult's Sweater

To fit one size up to 101cm (40in) bust/chest

Child's Sweater

To fit one size up to 71cm (28in) chest

MATERIALS

Adult's sweater

700g Sea Breeze Soft Cotton in signal red 532 (A); 100g in baize 540 (B)

100g Salad Days Knobbly Cotton in electric blue 570 (C)

100g Handknit Double Knitting Cotton in yellow 271 (G); 50g in amethyst 278 (D), mango 262 (E) and fuchsia 258 (F)

Equivalent yarn double knitting

1 pair each 4mm (US6) and 4½mm (US7) needles

Child's Sweater

175g Botany Wool in red 44 (A); 50g each in royal 56 (C) and yellow 12 (G); 25g each in green 90 (B), mauve 611 (D), orange 25 (E) and pink 95 (F)

Equivalent yarn four-ply

1 pair each 2¾mm (US2) and 3¼mm (US3) needles

2.50mm (USC) crochet hook

5 buttons (child's sweater)

NOTE When working yarns A and B for adult's sweater, use 3 strands together. When working yarn C for adult's sweater, use 2 strands together.

TENSION

Adult's Sweater

20 sts and 25 rows to 10cm (4in) over motif patt on 4½mm (US7) needles.

Child's Sweater

28 sts and 36 rows to 10cm (4in) over motif patt on 3¼mm (US3) needles.

ADULT'S SWEATER

BACK

Using 4mm (US6) needles and yarn A, cast on 120 sts.

Work 5cm (2in) in K2, P2 rib.

Change to 4½mm (US7) needles and colour patt from chart 1 on page 84. Work in st st, beg with a K row, weaving contrast colours into back of work for border patt, but working motifs with small separate balls of yarn, twisting yarns tog between colours on WS to avoid holes.

Work 140 rows from chart ending with a WS row.

Shape shoulders

Using yarn A, cast off 42 sts at beg of next 2 rows.

Leave rem 36 sts on a stitch holder.

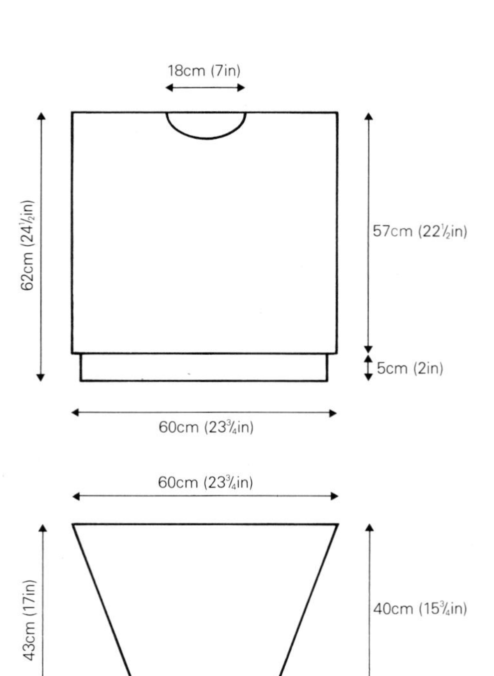

Right *The adult version of the Horses & Flowers Sweater is worked in vivid primary cottons.*

CHART 1

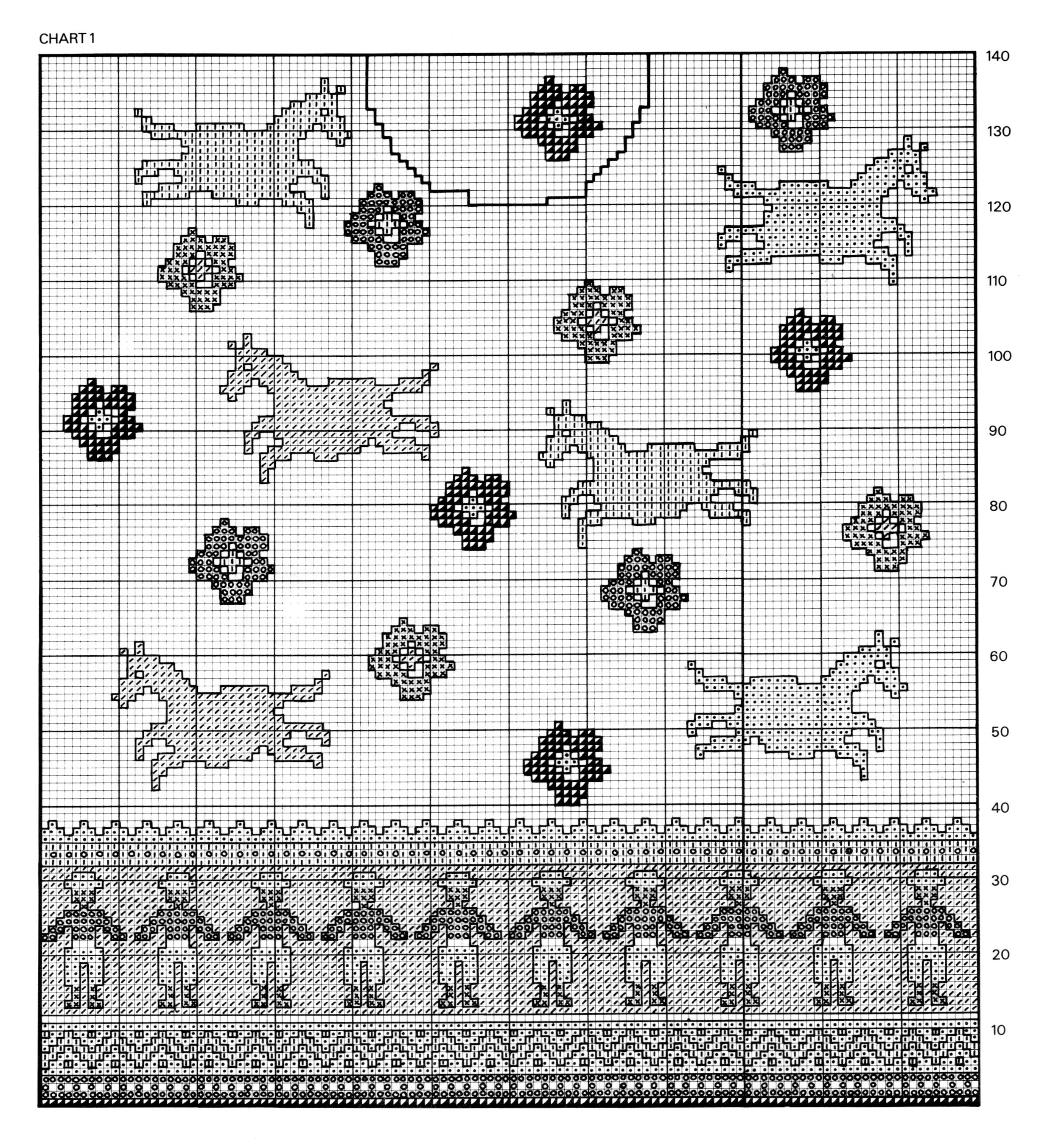

FRONT

Work as given for back until 120 rows of chart have been completed, thus ending with a WS row.

Shape neck

Next row Patt 55 sts, turn, leaving rem sts on a spare needle and cont on these sts only for first side of neck.

Next row Cast off 5 sts, patt to end. 50 sts.

Work 1 row. Dec 1 st at neck edge on next 5 rows. 45 sts.

Work 1 row. Now dec 1 st at neck edge on next row and foll 2 alt rows. 42 sts. Now work straight until 140 rows of chart have been completed.

Cast off.

With RS of work facing, return to sts on spare needle, sl centre 10 sts on to a stitch holder, rejoin yarn to rem sts and complete second side of neck to match first side, reversing shapings.

SLEEVES

Using 4mm (US6) needles and yarn A, cast on 60 sts.

Work 3cm (1¼in) in K2, P2 rib.

Change to 4½mm (US7) needles and beg colour patt from chart 2. Work in st st beg with a K row, *at the same time* inc 1 st at each end of 4th and every foll 3rd row until there are 120 sts.

Now work straight until 96 rows of chart have been completed.

Cast off loosely and evenly.

TO MAKE UP

Join right shoulder using a backstitch seam.

Neckband

With RS of work facing, using 4mm (US6) needles and yarn A, K up 23 sts down left front neck, K 10 sts from stitch holder at centre front, K up 23 sts up right front neck and K 36 sts from stitch holder at centre back. 92 sts. Work 7 rows in K2, P2 rib.

Cast off evenly in rib.

Join left shoulder and neckband seam.

Place markers 30cm (12in) below shoulder seam on back and front.

Set in sleeves between markers using a backstitch seam.

Join side and sleeve seams.

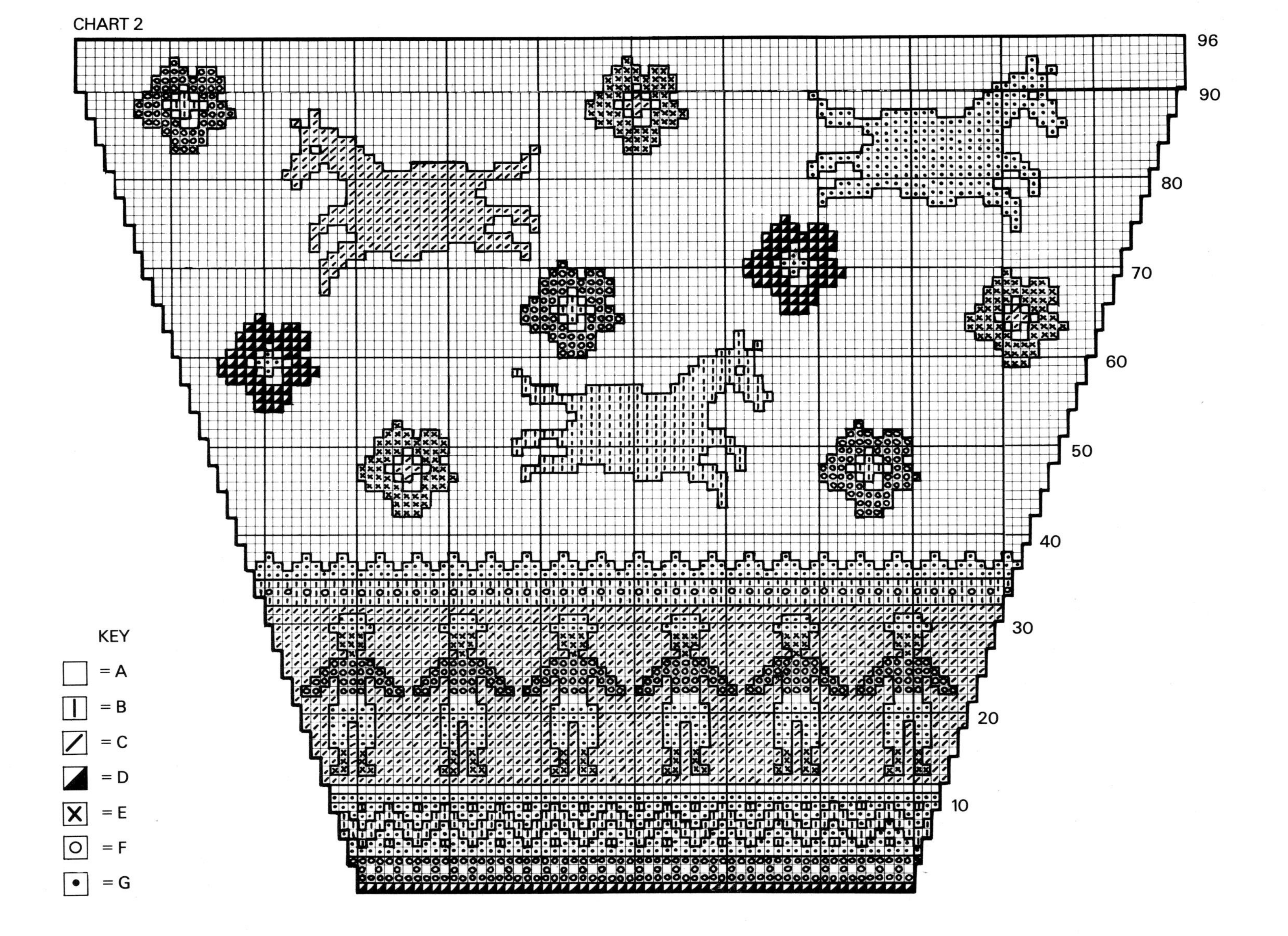

CHILD'S SWEATER

BACK

Using 2¾mm (US2) needles and yarn A, cast on 120 sts.
Work 5cm (2in) in K2, P2 rib.
Change to 3¼mm (US3) needles and beg colour patt from chart 1 as given for adult's sweater. **
Work as given for back of adult's sweater to end.

FRONT

Work as given for back to **.
Work as given for front of adult's sweater to end.

SLEEVES

Using 2¾mm (US2) needles, and yarn A cast on 60 sts.
Work 5cm (2in) in K2, P2 rib.
Change to 3¼mm (US3) needles and beg colour patt from chart 2 as given for adult's sleeve.
Work as given for adult's sleeve to end.

TO MAKE UP

Join left shoulder using a backstitch seam.

Neckband

Using 2¾mm (US2) needles, work as given for adult's sweater.
Mark 7cm (2¾in) in from armhole edge on left shoulder seam and join this section.

Make button loops

Using 2.50 (USC) crochet hook and yarn A, beg at neckband edge and work 24 double crochet evenly along left back shoulder, then work 19 double crochet across left front shoulder, interrupted by 5 3-chain loops evenly spaced for button loops.
Place markers 21cm (8¼in) down from shoulder seams on back and front. Set in sleeves between markers. Join side and sleeve seams. Sew on buttons.

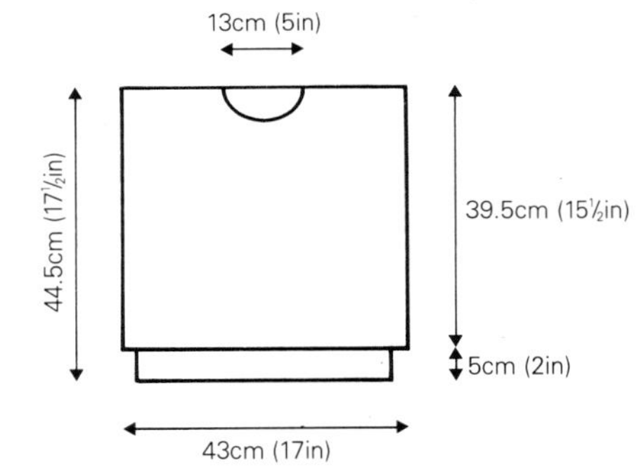

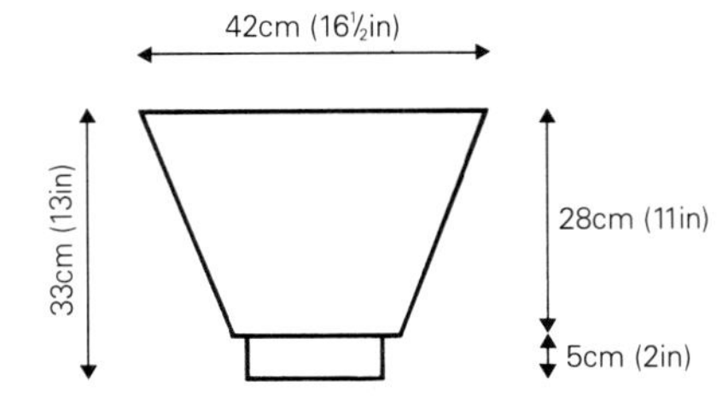

Left *The child's Horse & Flowers Sweater in soft Botany wool.*

Right *Another Martin Kidman exercise in sharp geometrics.*

★ ★

HUNT SWEATER

Winter

KITS A yarn kit is available for this design. See page 160 for details.

SIZE

To fit one size up to 111cm (44in) bust/chest

MATERIALS

950g Designer Double Knitting in charcoal 625 (A); 50g in mist 118 (L)
150g Lightweight Double Knitting in jade 100 (Q); 100g each in wine 85 (C) and beige 82 (D); 50g each in olive brown 87 (E), pale blue 48 (F), dark gold 9 (H), natural 613 (N) and rust 27 (R); 25g each in pale pink 79 (B), rose 412 (G), loden 89 (J), cream 1 (M) and soft gold 10 (S)
Equivalent yarn double knitting
1 pair each 4mm (US6) and 4½mm (US7) needles

NOTE All yarns are used double throughout.

TENSION

18 sts and 24 rows to 10cm (4in) over patt on 4½mm (US7) needles.

BACK

Using 4mm (US6) needles and yarn A double, cast on 124 sts.
Work 10 rows in K2, P2 rib.
Change to 4½mm (US7) needles and beg colour patt from chart 1, work in st st beg with a K row, weaving contrast colours into back of work, but working motifs with small separate balls of yarn, twisting yarns between colours on WS to avoid holes (if preferred, colours Q and S can be Swiss-darned after the main patt is completed).
Work 160 rows from chart, thus ending with a WS row.
Shape shoulders
Cast off 46 sts at beg of next 2 rows.
Leave rem 32 sts on a stitch holder.

FRONT

Work as given for back until 142 rows of chart have been completed.
Divide for neck
Next row Patt 57 sts, turn, leaving rem sts on a spare needle and cont on these sts only for first side of neck.
Dec 1 st at neck edge on next 9 rows. 48 sts.
Work 1 row. Now dec 1 st at neck edge on next and foll alt row. 46 sts.
Work 4 rows straight.
Cast off.
With RS of work facing, return to sts on spare needle, sl centre 10 sts on to a stitch holder, rejoin yarn to next st, and complete second side of neck to match first reversing shapings, working 1 more row before shoulder shaping.

SLEEVES

Using 4mm (US6) needles and yarn A double, cast on 54 sts.

Above *Animal motifs are a favourite Martin Kidman device and in the Hunt Sweater* (right), *the pattern for which is given here, he brings a fresh eye to a traditional theme.*

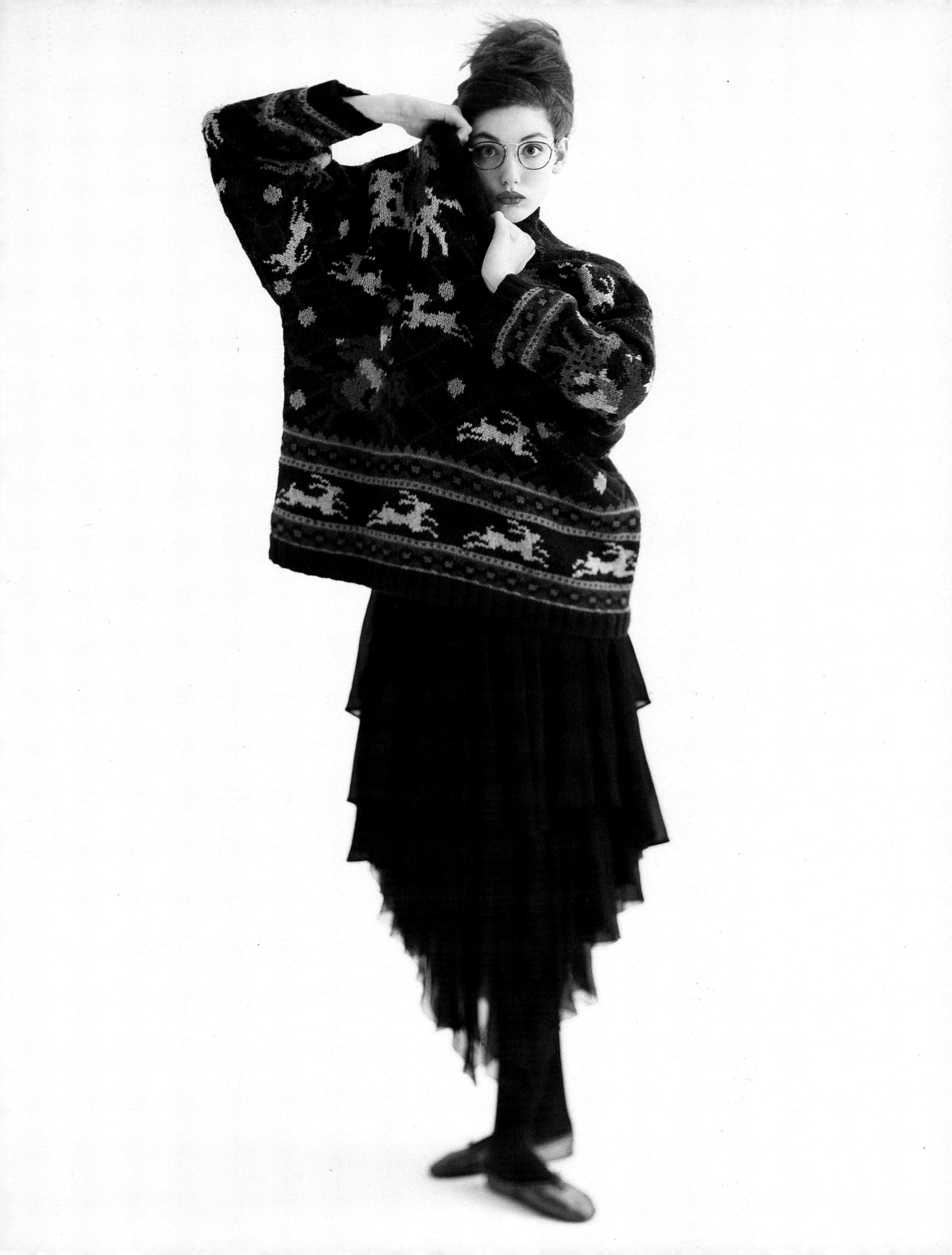

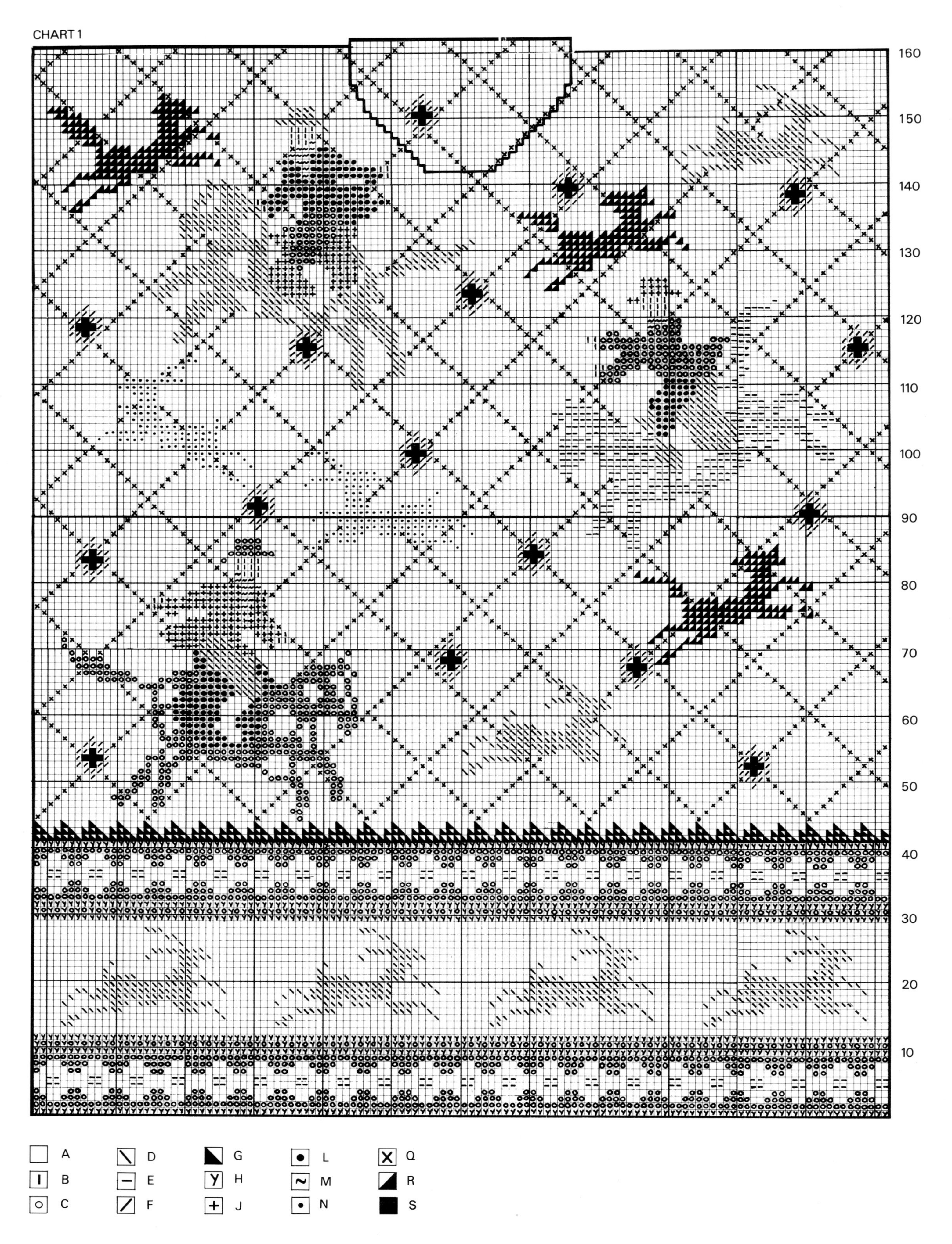
CHART 1
160
150
140
130
120
110
100
90
80
70
60
50
40
30
20
10
A
B
C
D
E
F
G
H
J
L
M
N
Q
R
S

Work 10 rows in K2, P2 rib.
Change to 4½mm (US7) needles and beg colour patt from chart 2, work in st st beg with a K row, *at the same time* inc 1 st each end of 3rd and every foll alt row until there are 90 sts, then at each end of every foll 4th row until there are 112 sts.
Work 6 rows straight.
Cast off loosely and evenly.

TO MAKE UP

Join right shoulder using a backstitch seam.

Neckband

With RS of work facing, using 4mm (US6) needles and yarn A double, K up 23 sts down left front neck. K 10 sts from stitch holder at front neck, K up 23 sts up right front neck and K 32 sts from stitch holder at back neck. 88 sts.
Work 14 rows in K2, P2 rib.
Cast off in rib.
Join left shoulder and neckband seam.
Fold neckband in half on to WS and slipstitch loosely in place.
Place markers 31cm (12¼in) below shoulder seams on back and front.
Set in sleeves between markers.
Join side and sleeve seams.

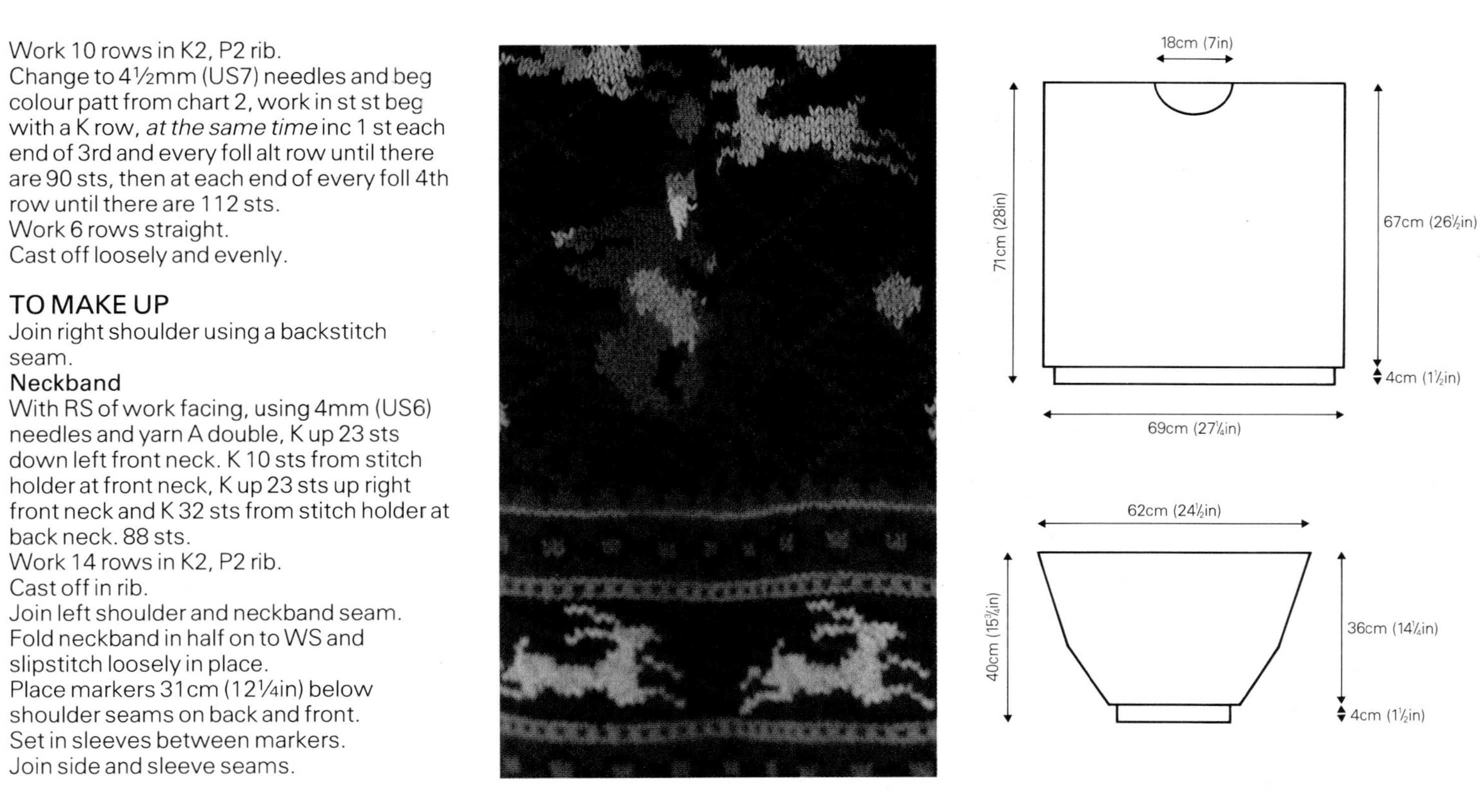

CHART 2

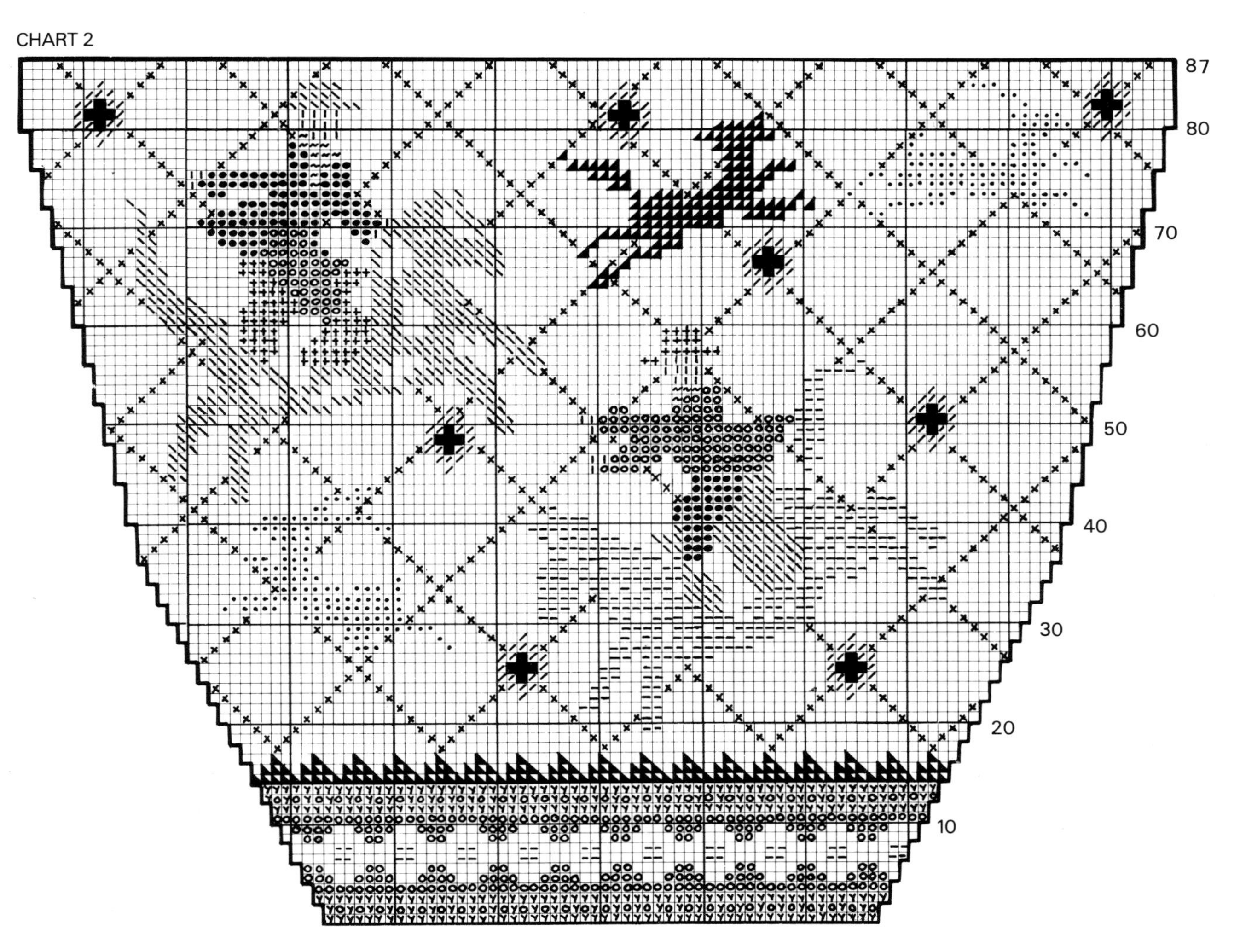

ANNABEL FOX

Energy exudes from a small, neat person who has very clear ideas about where she is going. In the few years since Annabel Fox graduated she has made a strong impact on knitwear design, displaying a versatility that enables her to change from large patterns, bold colours and loose shapes one year, to single muted shades for her collecton of body-clinging cables and ribs the next. There is no loss of integrity along the way that might be true of a follower rather than the fashion leader that Annabel has proved herself to be.

As well as building the Annabel Fox knitwear business, she is a design consultant for a major jeanswear company. After the limitations of mass production and of fabrics created by someone else, she enjoys the greater control that knitting offers over pattern, weight and texture, as well as the shape of garments.

Annabel knitted her first sweater at college during a fashion and textiles course. While still a student she started up a business in an old warehouse in London's dockland producing handknits to commission. In the early days she knitted them all herself hardly putting down her needles for months on end until her family started to knit to help out. Her sister is still involved with the business and now assists with quality control and the organization of the 250 outknitters that Annabel employs.

There is a lot to be done to keep all this going, and Annabel manages all aspects of the business herself; but she also cooks for relaxation, gardens, collects lace, and is helping her husband to restore their terrace house in Brighton. When they talk of having a farm and a family it is no idle dream, for it is clear that Annabel will simply add it to the list, achieve it soon and keep on developing her knitwear business too.

★ ★

TUTTI FRUTTI

Summer

SIZES

Adult's sweater
To fit 86[91, 96]cm (34[36, 38]in) bust
Child's sweater
To fit 61[66, 71]cm (24[26, 28]in) chest

MATERIALS

Adult's sweater
600[650, 700]g Handknit Double Knitting Cotton in ecru 251 (A); 100 g each in yellow 271 (B) and hastings green 281 (F); 50g each in pink 272 (C), flame 254 (D) and navy 277 (E)
Child's sweater
300[300, 350]g Handknit Double Knitting Cotton in flesh 268 (A); 50g each in yellow 271 (B), pink 272 (C), flame 254 (D), navy 277 (E) and hastings green 281 (F)
Equivalent yarn double knitting
1 pair each 3¼mm (US3) and 4mm (US6) needles

TENSION

20 sts and 28 rows to 10cm (4in) over st st on 4mm (US6) needles.

ADULT'S SWEATER

BACK

Using 3¼mm (US3) needles and yarn A, cast on 100[102, 104] sts.
Work 7cm (2¾in) in K1, P1 rib.
Next row Rib 3[1, 6], (make 1, rib 5[4, 3]) 19[25, 31] times, make 1, rib to end. 120[128, 136] sts.
Change to 4mm (US6) needles and beg colour patt from chart 1 on page 94, at 9th[5th, 1st] row working in st st throughout beg with a K row; use small separate balls of yarn for each colour area twisting yarns tog on WS at colour joins to avoid holes, work 76[80, 84] rows straight.
Shape armholes
Keeping patt correct, cast off 4 sts at beg of next 2 rows. 112[120, 128] sts. **
Now work 74 rows straight, ending with a WS row.
Shape shoulders
Cast off 13[17, 21] sts at beg of next 2 rows, and 24 sts at beg of foll 2 rows.
Leave rem 38 sts on a stitch holder.

FRONT

Work as given for back to **.
Work 58 rows straight, end with a WS row.
Divide for neck
Next row Patt 46[50, 54] sts, turn, leaving rem sts on a spare needle and cont on these sts only for first side of neck.
Cast off 3 sts at beg of next row and 2 sts at beg of foll alt row.
Now dec 1 st at neck edge on next 4 alt rows. 37[41, 45] sts. Work 4 rows straight, ending at armhole edge.
Shape shoulder
Cast off 13[17, 21] sts at beg of next row. 24 sts.

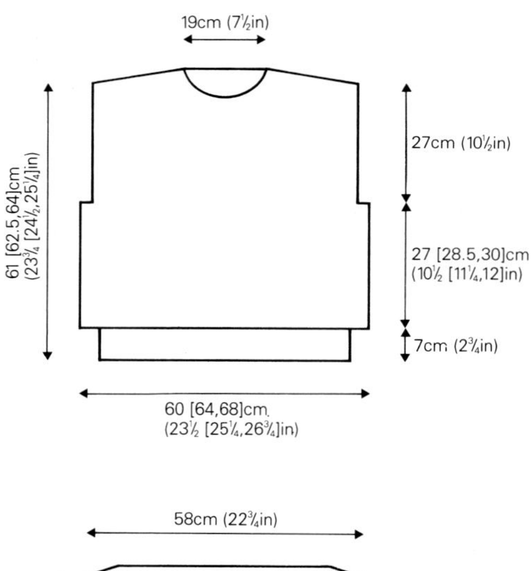

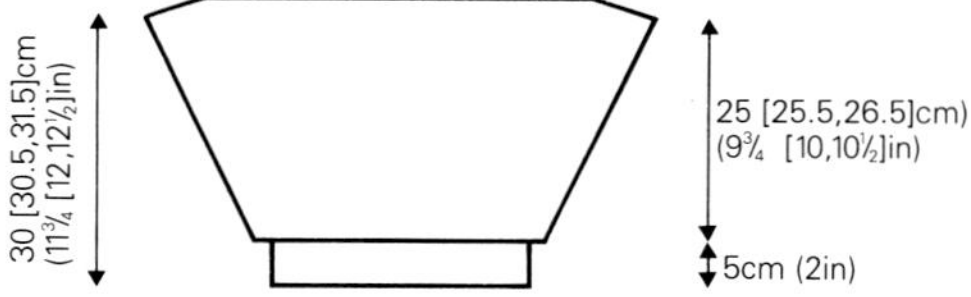

Right *Tutti Frutti is a typically direct and disarmingly simple design from Annabel Fox. Just one type of yarn is used – a soft thick cotton in luscious marshmallow colours.*

CHART 1
160
150
140
130
120
110
100
90
80
70
60
50
40
30
20
10
1st Size Back & Front
2nd Size Back & Front
3rd Size Back & Front

Work 1 row.
Cast off.
With RS of work facing, return to sts on spare needle, sl centre 20 sts on to a stitch holder, rejoin yarn to next st, patt to end. 46[50, 54] sts. Work 1 row.
Complete second side of neck to match first side, reversing shapings.

SLEEVES

Using 3¼mm (US3) needles and yarn A, cast on 68 sts.
Work 5cm (2in) in K1, P1 rib.
Change to 4mm (US6) needles and beg colour patt from chart 2, work in st st, beg with a K row, *at the same time* inc 1 st at each end of 3rd and every foll alt row until there are 96 sts, then every foll 3rd row until there are 116 sts.
Work 11[13, 15] rows straight, ending with a WS row.

Shape top

Cast off 6 sts at beg of next 2 rows, 5 sts at beg of foll 2 rows and 3 sts at beg of next 2 rows.
Cast off rem 88 sts.

TO MAKE UP

Join right shoulder using a backstitch seam.

Neckband

With RS of work facing, using 3¼mm (US3) needles and yarn A, K up 21 sts down left side of neck, K 20 sts from stitch holder at centre front, K up 21 sts up right side of neck and K 38 sts from stitch holder at back neck. 100 sts. Work 3cm (1¼in) K1, P1 rib.
Cast off loosely and evenly in rib.
Join left shoulder and neckband seam. Set in sleeves. Join side and sleeve seams.

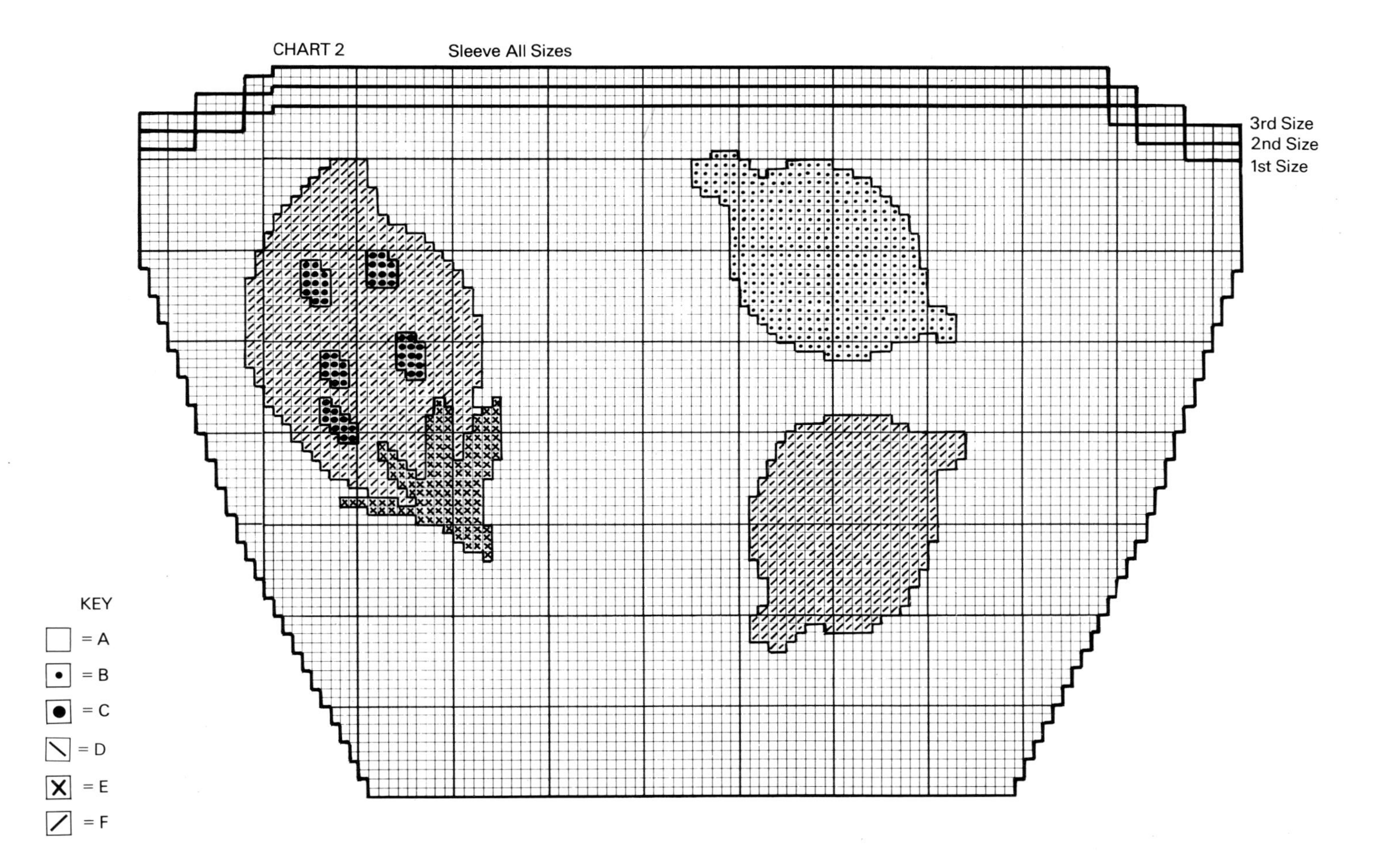

CHILD'S SWEATER

BACK

Using 3¼mm (US3) needles and yarn A, cast on 62[68, 74] sts.
Work 4cm (1½in) in K1, P1 rib.
Next row Rib 1[4, 7], (make 1, rib 12) 5 times, make 1, rib to end. 68[74, 80] sts.

Change to 4mm (US6) needles and beg colour patt from chart 3 at 11th[7th, 1st] row.
Working in st st throughout, beg with a K row, use small separate balls of yarn for each colour area and twist yarns tog on WS at colour joins to avoid holes.
Work 54[58, 64] rows straight.

Shape armholes
Keeping patt correct, cast off 2 sts at beg of next 4 rows. 60[66, 72] sts. **
Work 44 rows straight.
Divide for neck
Next row Patt 16[19, 22] sts, turn, leaving

Right *The child's Tutti Frutti.*

CHART 3

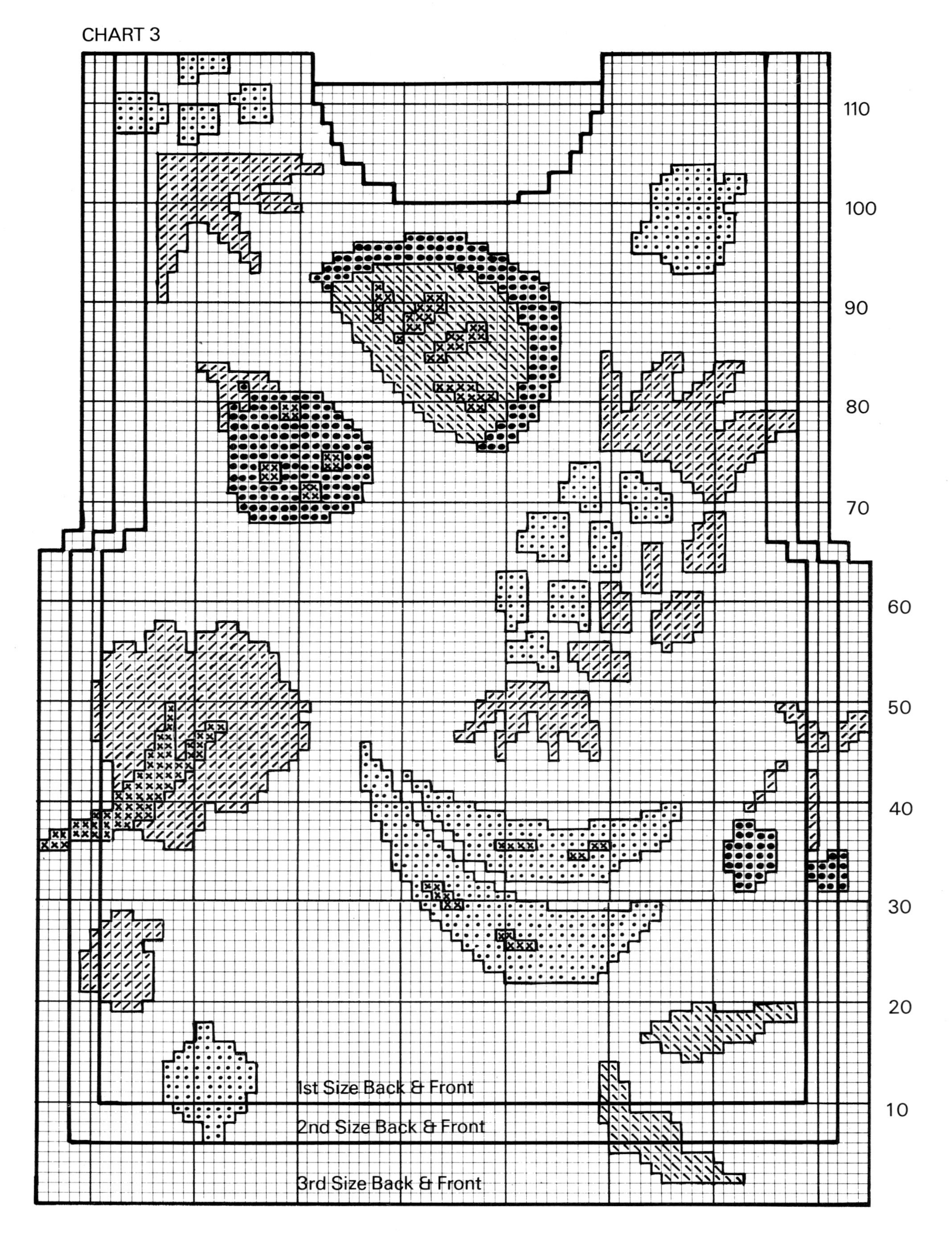

KEY

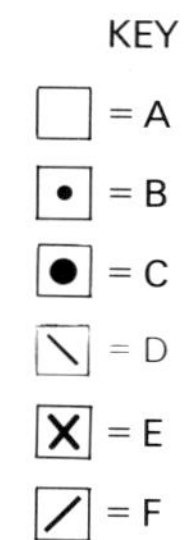

rem sts on a spare needle and cont on these sts only for first side of neck.
Work 2 rows straight. Cast off.
With RS of work facing return to sts on spare needle, sl centre 28 sts on to a stitch holder, rejoin yarn to next st, patt to end. 16[19, 22] sts.
Complete second side of neck to match first side.

FRONT

Work as given for back to **.
Work 32 rows straight.

Divide for neck

Next row Patt 24[27, 30] sts, turn, leaving rem sts on a spare needle and cont on these sts only for first side of neck.
Cast off 3 sts at beg of next row, 2 sts at beg of foll alt row, then dec 1 st at neck edge on next 3 alt rows. 16[19, 22] sts.
Work 5 rows straight. Cast off.
With RS of work facing, return to sts on spare needle, sl centre 12 sts on to a stitch holder, rejoin yarn to next st, patt to end. 24[27, 30] sts.
Work 1 row.
Complete second side of neck to match first side, reversing shapings and working 1 less row before casting off.

SLEEVES

Using 3¼mm (US3) needles and yarn A, cast on 32 sts.
Work 4cm (1½in) in K1, P1 rib.
Next row Rib 2, (make 1, rib 2, make 1, rib 3) 6 times. 44 sts.
Change to 4mm (US6) needles and beg colour patt from chart 4, working in st st beg with a K row, *at the same time* inc 1 st at each end of 4th and every foll 3rd row until there are 76 sts. Work 21[23, 25] rows straight, ending with a WS row.

Shape top

Cast off 3 sts at beg of next 4 rows and 4 sts at beg of foll 8 rows. Cast off rem 32 sts.

TO MAKE UP

Join right shoulder using a backstitch seam.

Neckband

With RS of work facing, using 3¼mm (US3) needles and yarn A, K up 18 sts down left side front neck, K 12 sts from stitch holder at centre front, K up 18 sts up right side front neck, and 28 sts across back neck. 76 sts. Work 3cm (1¼in) in K1, P1 rib.
Cast off loosely and evenly in rib.
Join left shoulder and neckband seam.
Set in sleeves. Join side and sleeve seam.

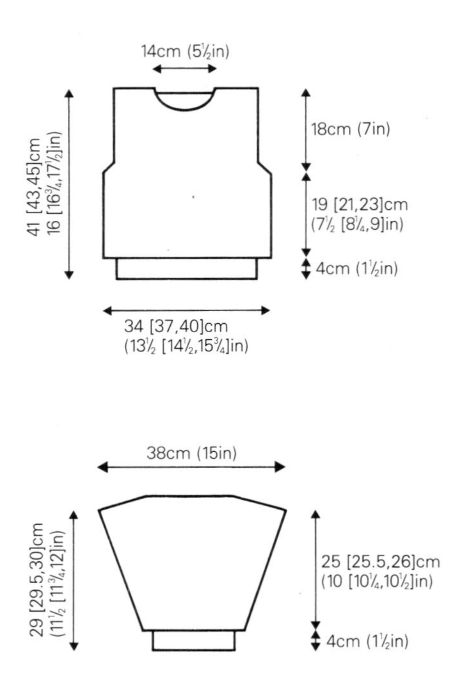

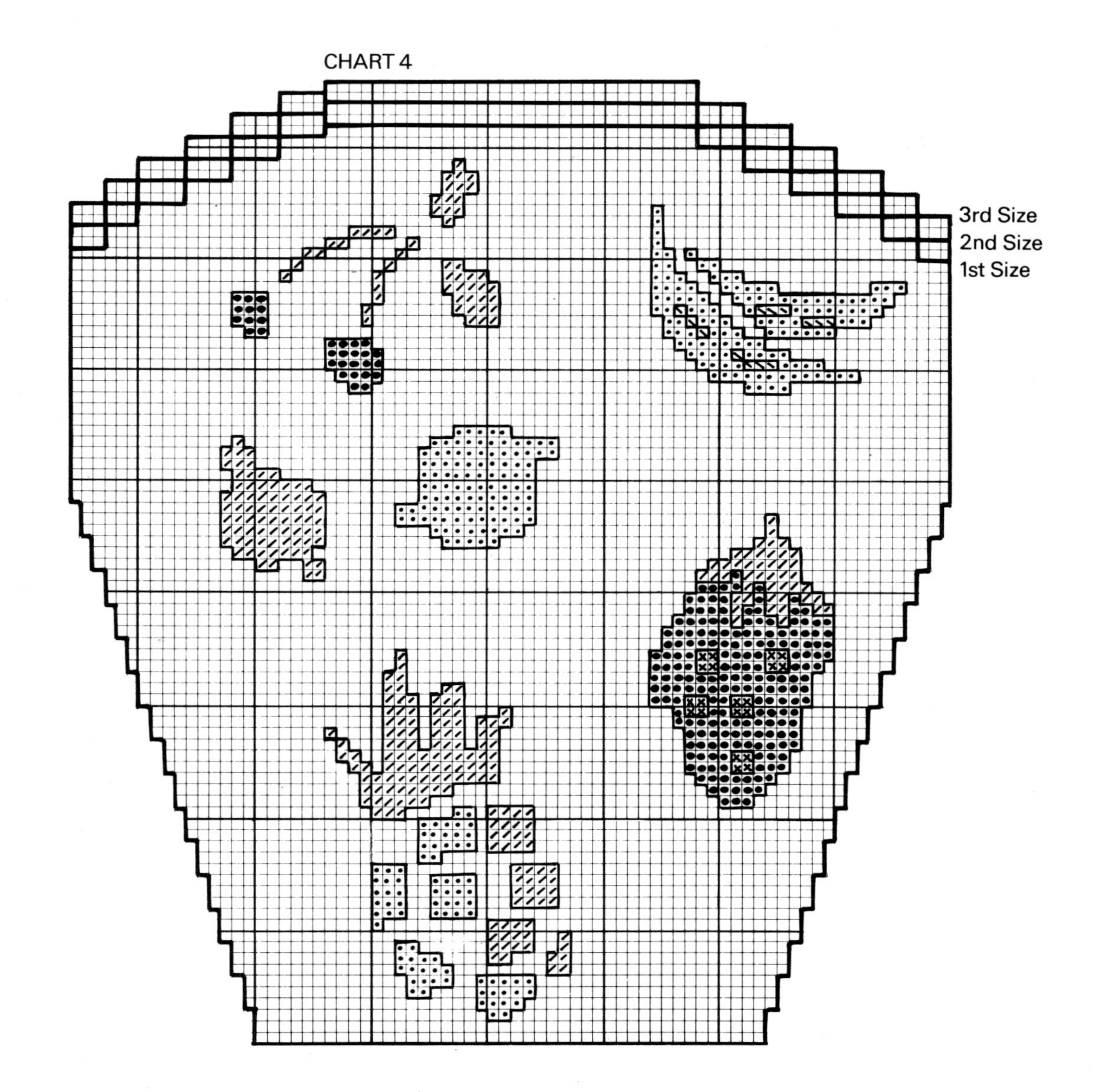

KEY
- = A
- = B
- = C
- = D
- = E
- = F

★★

SIOUX SWEATER

Winter

SIZES

To fit up to 86-91[96-101]cm (34-36[38-40]in) bust

MATERIALS

400g Classic Tweed in black 452 (A); 50[100]g in ecru 451 (B)
100g Designer Double Knitting each in beige fleck 82F (C) and green 90 (E); 50[100]g in turquoise 125 (D)
100g Fine Cotton Chenille each in saville 387 (F) and cardinal 379 (G); 50g in purple 384 (H)
Equivalent yarn double knitting
1 pair each 3¼mm (US3) and 4mm (US6) needles

TENSION

23 sts and 27 rows in 10cm (4in) over patt on 4mm (US6) needles.

BACK

Using 3¼mm (US3) needles and yarn A, cast on 104[108] sts.
Work 9cm (3½in) in K1, P1 rib.
Next row (WS) Rib 2[4], (make 1, rib 9) 11 times, make 1, rib to end. 116[120] sts.
Change to 4mm (US6) needles and beg colour patt from chart beg at 5th[1st] row, work in st st throughout, weaving contrast colours into back of work on horizontal two-colour bands and using small separate balls of yarn for motifs, twisting yarns tog on WS at colour joins to avoid holes. Cont in patt, *at the same time* inc 1 st at each end of 3rd and every foll alt row until there are 126[130] sts, and then of every foll 4th row until there are 156[162] sts. Now work straight until 78th row of chart has been completed.
Shape armholes
Cast off 3 sts at beg of next 2 rows, then 2

sts at beg of foll 2 rows. 146[152] sts. **
Now work 64 rows straight, ending with a WS row.
Shape shoulders and divide for neck
Next row Cast off 24[27] sts, patt 26 sts, including st used to cast off, turn, leaving rem sts on a spare needle and cont on these sts only for first side of neck. Work 1 row.
Cast off.
With RS of work facing return to sts on spare needle, rejoin yarn to next st, cast off 46 sts, patt to end. 50[53] sts. Cast off 24[27] sts at beg of next row. Work 1 row.
Cast off rem 26 sts.

FRONT

Work as given for back to **.
Work 50 rows straight, ending with a WS row.
Divide for neck
Next row Patt 62[65] sts, turn, leaving rem sts on a spare needle and cont on these sts only for first side of neck.
Cast off 5 sts at beg of next row, 3 sts at beg of foll alt row, 2 sts at beg of next alt row. 52[55] sts.
Work 1 row.
Now dec 1 st at neck edge on next and foll alt row. 50[53] sts.
Work 4 rows straight, ending at armhole edge.
Shape shoulder
Cast off 24[27] sts at beg of next row.
26 sts.
Work 1 row.
Cast off.
With RS of work facing, return to sts on spare needle, rejoin yarn to next st, cast off 22 sts, patt to end. 62[65] sts.
Work 1 row.
Complete second side of neck to match first side reversing shapings.

SLEEVES

Using 3¼mm (US3) needles and yarn A, cast on 48 sts.
Work 10cm (4in) in K1, P1 rib.
Next row (WS) Rib 2, (make 1, rib 4) 11 times, make 1, rib 2. 60 sts.
Change to 4mm (US6) needles and beg colour patt from chart, working between sleeve markers and beg at 5th row, *at the same time* inc 1 st at each end of 3rd and every foll alt row until there are 68 sts, then of every foll 3rd row until there are 120 sts.
Now work straight until 96[100] rows in chart patt have been completed, ending with a WS row.
Shape top
Cast off 4 sts at beg of next 2 rows, 3 sts at beg of foll 2 rows, 2 sts at beg of next 8 rows and 4 sts at beg of foll 2 rows (when 106th row of chart has been completed cont in A only). Cast off rem 82 sts.

TO MAKE UP

Join right shoulder using a backstitch seam.
Neckband
With RS of work facing, using 3¼mm (US3) needles and yarn A, K up 21 sts down left front neck, 22 sts across centre front, 21 sts up right side front neck, and 46 sts around back neck. 110 sts.
Work 6cm (2¼in) in K1, P1 rib.
Cast off evenly in rib.
Join left shoulder and neckband seam.
Fold neckband in half on to WS and catch down.
Set in sleeves.
Join side and sleeve seams.

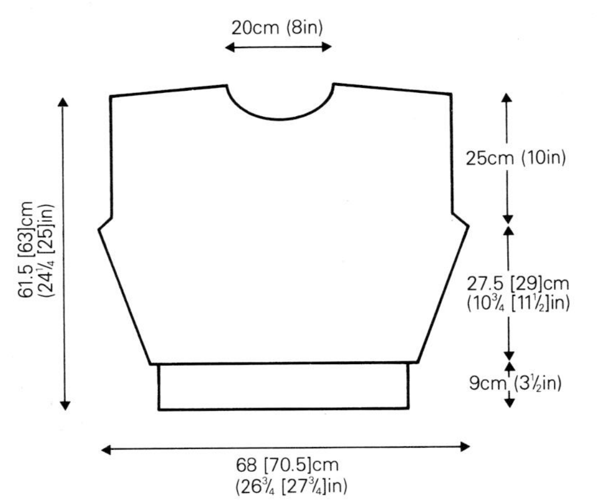

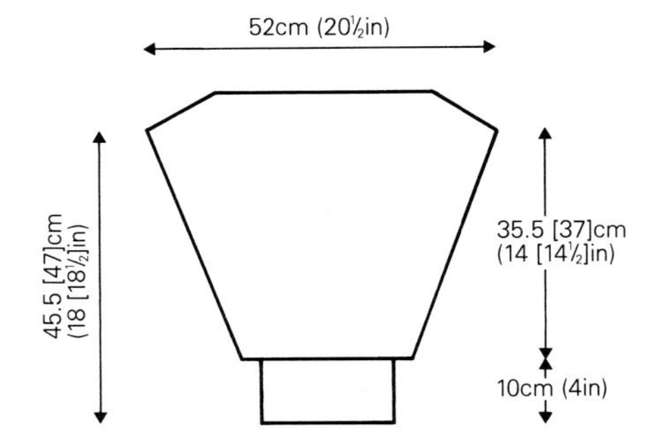

Below and right *Strong geometric shapes lend themselves well to knitting design, and Annabel Fox has always exploited this natural alliance to the full. Ethnic textiles have proved a fertile source of inspiration as in the Sioux Sweater* (right), *knitted in a rich mix of wool and cotton textures.*

MUIR AND OSBORNE

To give up interesting, salaried jobs in the arts and start a business in knitting must have seemed like madness when Sally Muir and Joanna Osborne, alias Warm and Wonderful, did just that at the end of the seventies; and they didn't even know each other. Like many successful knitwear producers, their main market is the United States which seems to have an insatiable appetite for their sweaters. It takes around 800 knitters to keep the orders flowing.

Sally and Joanna use topical fashion ideas that reflect the mood of the moment but have the extra touch of their own inspiration that makes them special. When 'witty knits' were in vogue, it was they who invented the much copied sheep sweater, favoured by Princess Diana. Later they went abstract, responding to the intangible urge that makes fashion houses all produce asymmetrics or brilliant purple at the same moment. They have the right instincts to be part of this movement, and whatever it is that inspires an idea, there is an assurance in the way they translate it into knitted form.

They make running a sizeable business all sound quite simple and straightforward, and neither makes a big deal about anything. Buyers, bank managers and burglaries are coped with – all of which have caused them problems at times – and together they design, organize and export, with an unassuming confidence that is both attractive and enviable.

Neither of them had been to art or business school. All they had at the beginning were a couple of knitting machines, Joanna's bedroom to work in and a continuous supply of warmth and wonderfulness. It has served them well.

★ ★

FLOWER SWEATER

Summer

SIZES

To fit 86[91, 96]cm (34[36, 38]in) bust

MATERIALS

300 [350, 350]g Handknit Double Knitting Cotton in navy 277 (A); 300 [300, 350]g in ecru 251 (C); 100 [100, 150]g each in charcoal 276 (D) and sky blue 264 (E); 100g in peacock 259 (G) and bayou 279 (H); 50[50, 100]g in taupe 253 (B); 50g in amethyst 278 (F)

Equivalent yarn double knitting

1 pair each 3¼mm (US3) and 4mm (US6) needles

TENSION

20 sts and 28 rows to 10cm (4in) over patt on 4mm (US6) needles.

SPECIAL ABBREVIATION

make bobble – with yarn A, (K1, P1, K1) into st, turn, K3, turn, P3, sl 2nd and 3rd sts over 1st st and off needle.

BACK

Using 3¼mm (US3) needles and yarn A, cast on 114[120, 126] sts.

Work 10 rows in K1, P1 rib.

Change to 4mm (US6) needles and beg colour patt from chart 1, working in st st beg with a K row (unless otherwise indicated), and using small separate balls of yarn for each colour area, twisting yarns tog on WS at colour joins to avoid holes. Work 156 rows from chart, marking each end of 117th row for sleeves, end with a WS row.

Divide for neck

Next row Patt 47[50, 53] sts, turn, leaving rem sts on a spare needle and cont on these sts only for first side of neck.

Dec 1 st at neck edge on next 15 rows. 32[35, 38] sts.

Work 6 rows straight, ending at armhole edge.

Shape shoulder

Cast off 7[10, 13] sts at beg of next row and 10 sts at beg of foll alt row. 15 sts.

Work 1 row. Cast off.

With RS of work facing, return to sts on spare needle, sl centre 20 sts on to a stitch holder, rejoin yarn to next st, patt to end of row.

Complete second side of neck to match first side, reversing shapings.

FRONT

Work as given for back.

SLEEVES

Using 3¼mm (US3) needles and thumb method of casting on, cast on 40 sts with yarn C and 10 sts with yarn A. 50 sts.

Work in K1, P1 rib as foll (twist yarns tog on WS at colour joins):

1st row (RS) Rib 10A, 40C.

2nd row Rib 40C, 10A.

Rep these 2 rows 4 times more.

Change to 4mm (US6) needles and beg colour patt from chart 2, work 110 rows, *at the same time* inc 1 st at each end of 1st and every foll 6th row until there are 88 sts.

Cast off loosely and evenly.

TO MAKE UP

Join right shoulder using a backstitch seam.

Neckband

With RS of work facing, using 3¼mm (US3) needles and yarn H, K up 120 sts evenly around neck edge.

Work 6 rows in K1, P1 rib.

Cast off loosely in rib.

Join left shoulder and neckband seam.

Set in sleeves between markers.

Join side and sleeve seams.

Right *A summer bouquet blossoms all over Muir and Osborne's Flower Sweater. It is worked in thick cotton yarn, mostly in stocking stitch, but with a sprinkling of bobbles.*

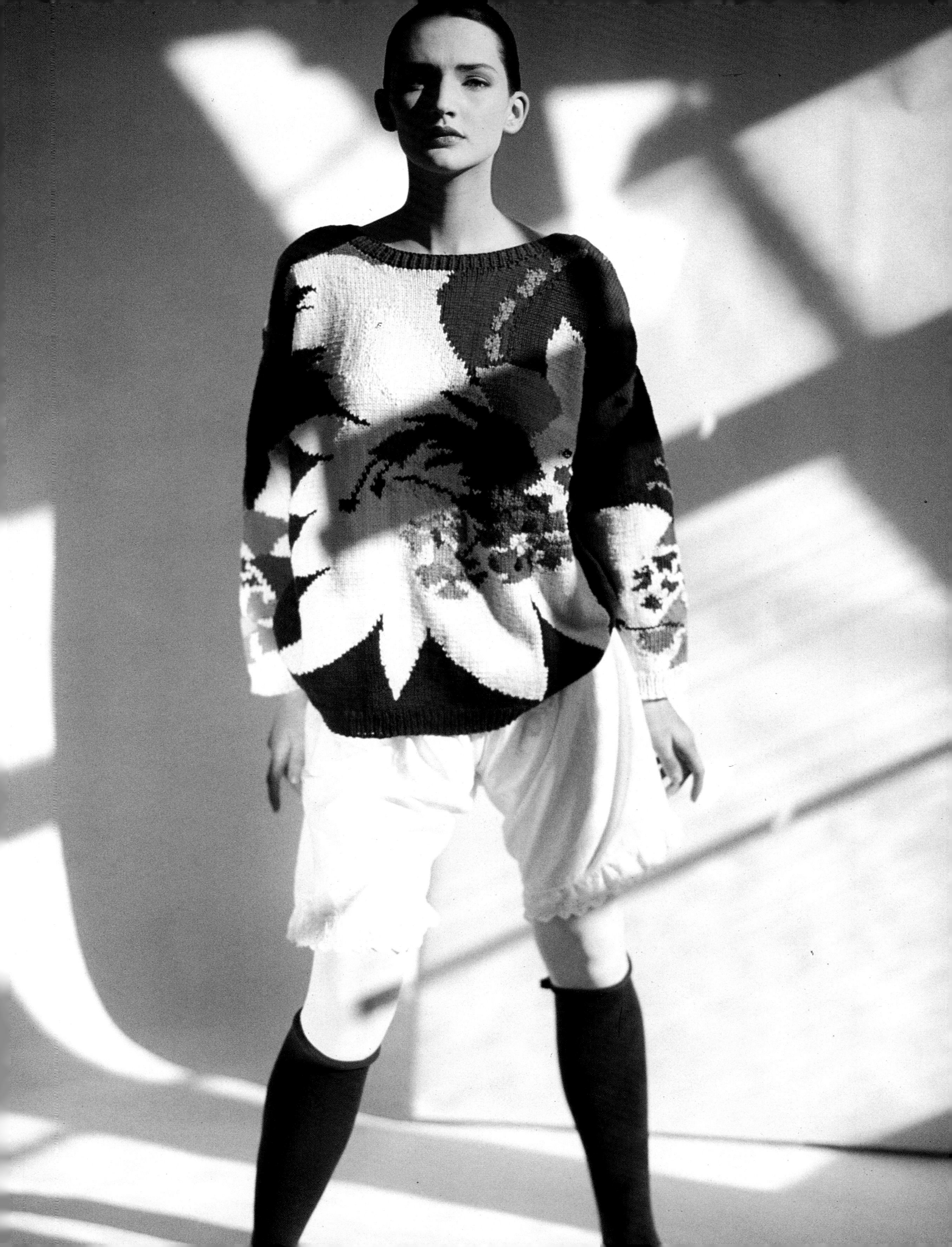

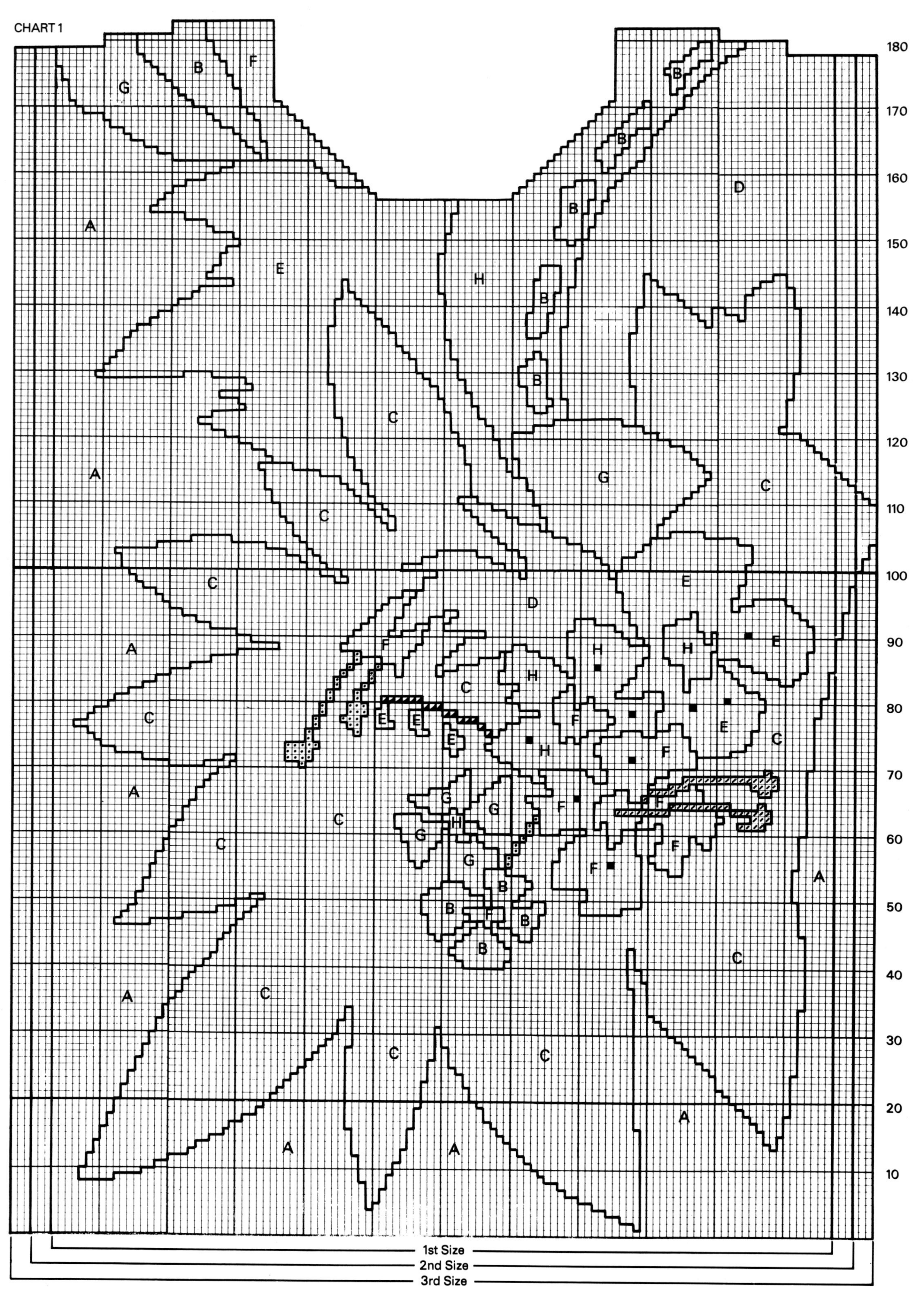
CHART 1
A
B
C
D
E
F
G
H
180
170
160
150
140
130
120
110
100
90
80
70
60
50
40
30
20
10
1st Size
2nd Size
3rd Size

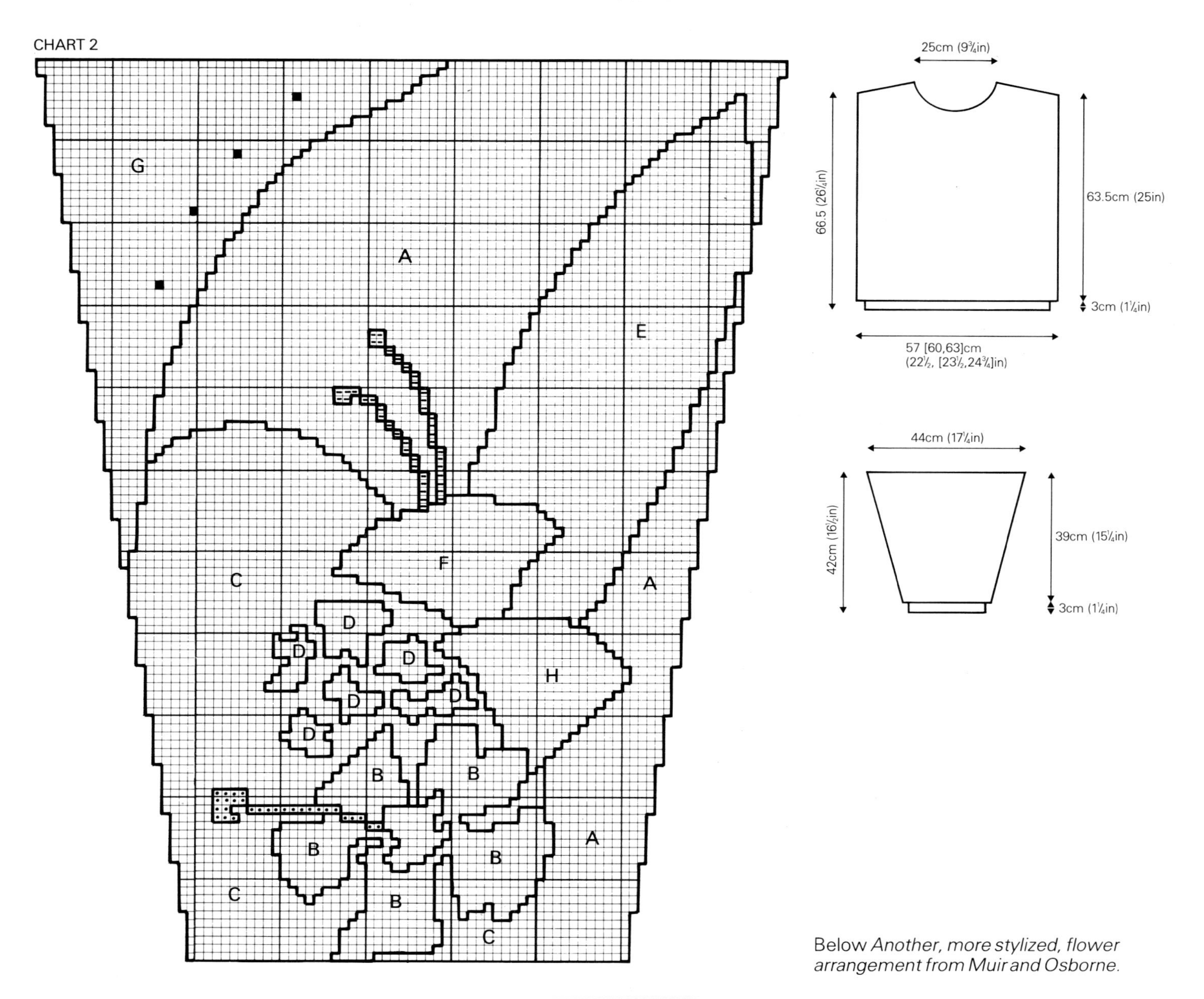

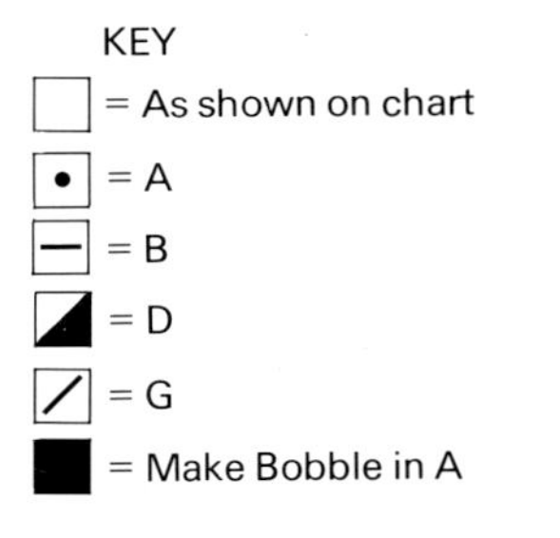

Below *Another, more stylized, flower arrangement from Muir and Osborne.*

★ ★

TARGET JACKET

Winter

SIZE
To fit one size up to 101cm (40in) bust/chest

MATERIALS
400g Bright Tweed in nautilus 727 (A); 200g each in firefly 720 (B), greystoke 724 (C) and nelson 723 (D)
100g Lightweight Double Knitting each in royal 57 (E), green 124 (F), bright purple 126 (G) and gold 13 (H)
Equivalent yarn chunky
1 pair each 5mm (US8) and 6mm (US10) needles
13 buttons

NOTE When working yarns E-H, use 2 strands together.

TENSION
14 sts and 20 rows to 10cm (4in) over patt on 6mm (US10) needles.

BACK
Using 5mm (US8) needles, cast on 93 sts as foll:
Cast-on row Cast on 10 sts in yarn E, 9G, 33A, 8B, 10C, 10B and 13C.
Now beg colour patt from chart 1, using small separate balls of yarn for each colour area and twisting yarn tog on WS at colour joins to avoid holes, work 1st-10th rows in K1, P1 rib.
Change to 6mm (US10) needles and cont in chart patt, working in st st throughout, beg with a K row, work 11th-154th rows, placing sleeve markers at each end of 95th row, and ending with a WS row.
Shape shoulders and divide for neck
Next row Cast off 11 sts, patt 24 sts including st used to cast off, turn, leaving rem sts on a spare needle and cont on these sts only for first side of neck.
Next row P2 tog, patt to end. 23 sts.
Next row Cast off 11 sts, patt to last 2 sts, K2 tog. 11 sts.
Next row P2 tog, patt to end.
Cast off rem 10 sts.
With RS of work facing, return to sts on spare needle, rejoin yarn to next st, cast off 23 sts, patt to end of row. 35 sts.
Next row Cast off 11 sts, patt to last 2 sts, P2 tog. 23 sts.
Complete second side of neck to match first side, reversing shapings.

LEFT SLEEVE
Using 5mm (US8) needles and yarn A, cast on 60 sts.
Work in K1, P1 rib, as foll:
1st row (RS) Rib to end.
2nd row Rib 2 tog, rib to last 2 sts, rib 2 tog. 58 sts.
Buttonhole row Rib 2 tog, rib 3, yo, rib 2 tog, rib to last 2 sts, rib 2 tog. 56 sts.
Cont in K1, P1 rib, work 13 rows more, *at the same time* dec 1 st at each end of every row. 30 sts.
Rib 4 rows straight.
Change to 6mm (US10) needles
P 1 row to reverse cuff.
Work 5 rows in st st, beg with a P row.
Now beg colour patt from chart 2, working in st st throughout, beg with a K row, *at the same time* inc 1 st at each end of 1st and every foll 3rd row until there are 86 sts.
Work straight until chart 2 has been completed.
Cast off loosely and evenly.

RIGHT SLEEVE
Work as given for left sleeve, working buttonhole row as foll:
Buttonhole row Rib 2 tog, rib to last 7 sts, yo, rib 2 tog, rib 3, rib 2 tog. 56 sts.
Complete as given for left sleeve.

POCKET LININGS (make 2)
Using 6mm (US10) needles and yarn A, cast on 20 sts.
Work 30 rows in st st, beg with a K row.
Leave these sts on a stitch holder.

LEFT FRONT
Using 5mm (US8) needles, cast on 44 sts as foll:
Cast-on row Cast on 10 sts in yarn C, 5B, 9C, 5B and 15C.
Now beg colour patt from chart 4 on page 108, work 1st-10th rows in K1, P1 rib.

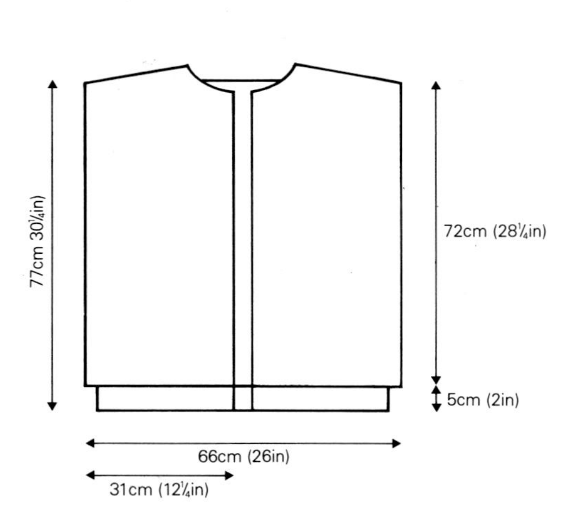

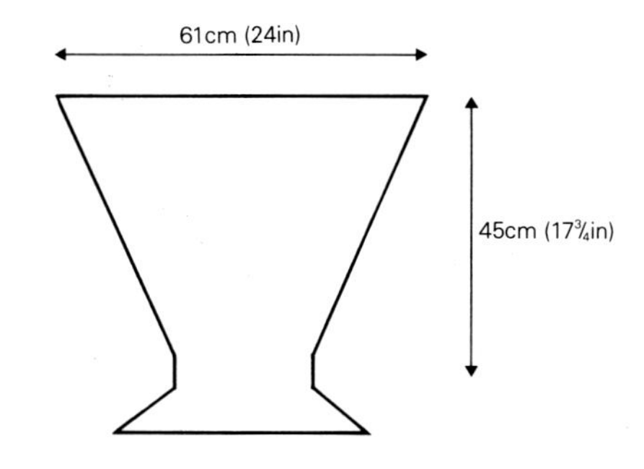

CHART 2

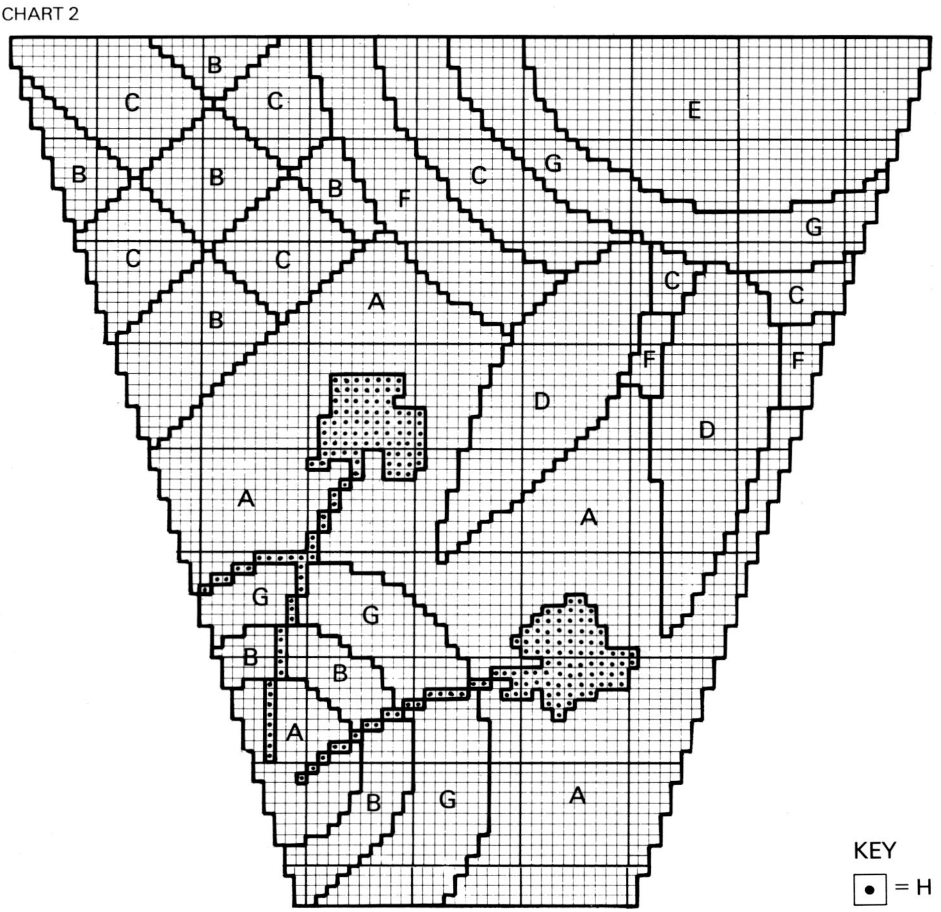

CHART 1

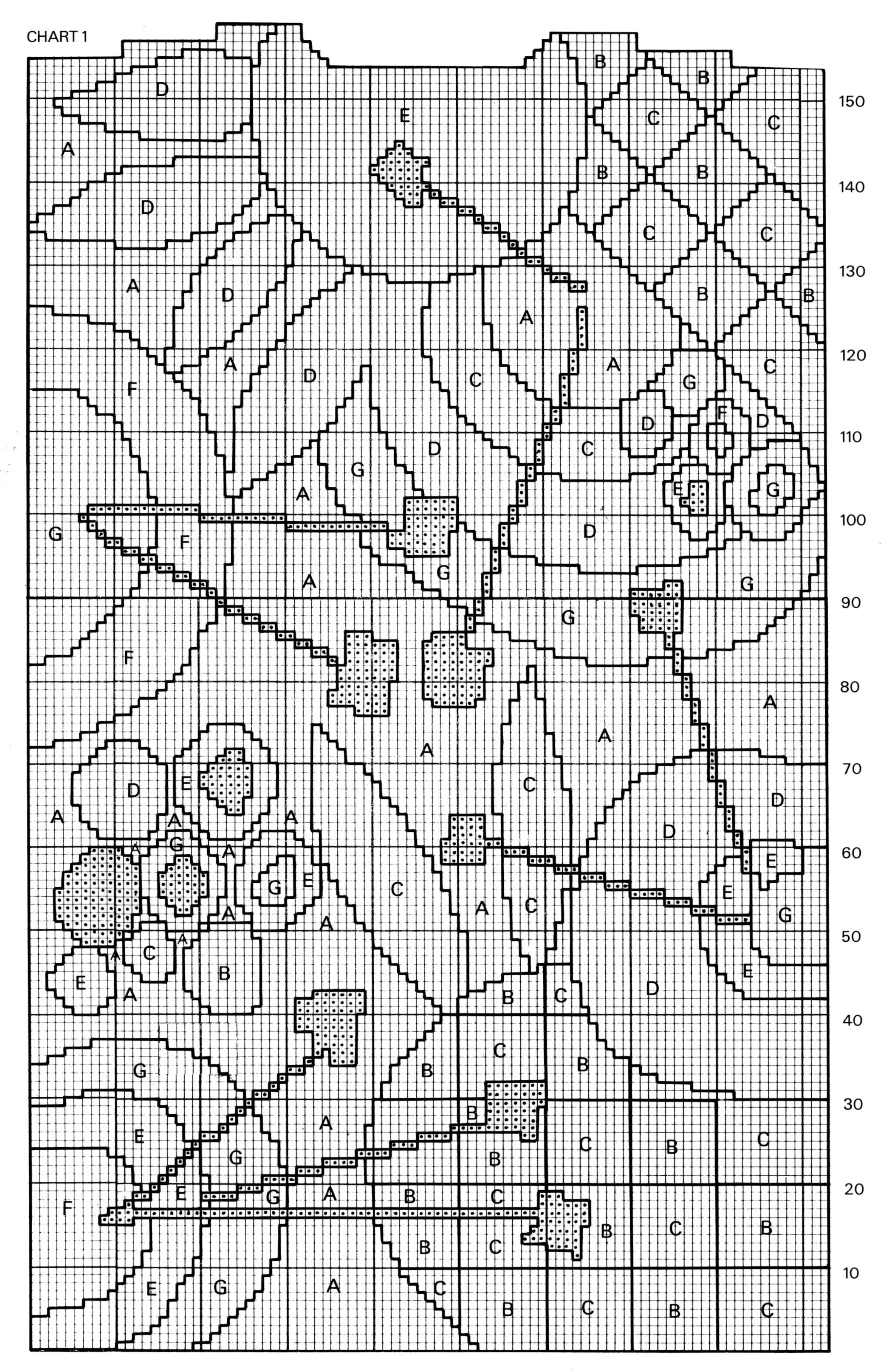

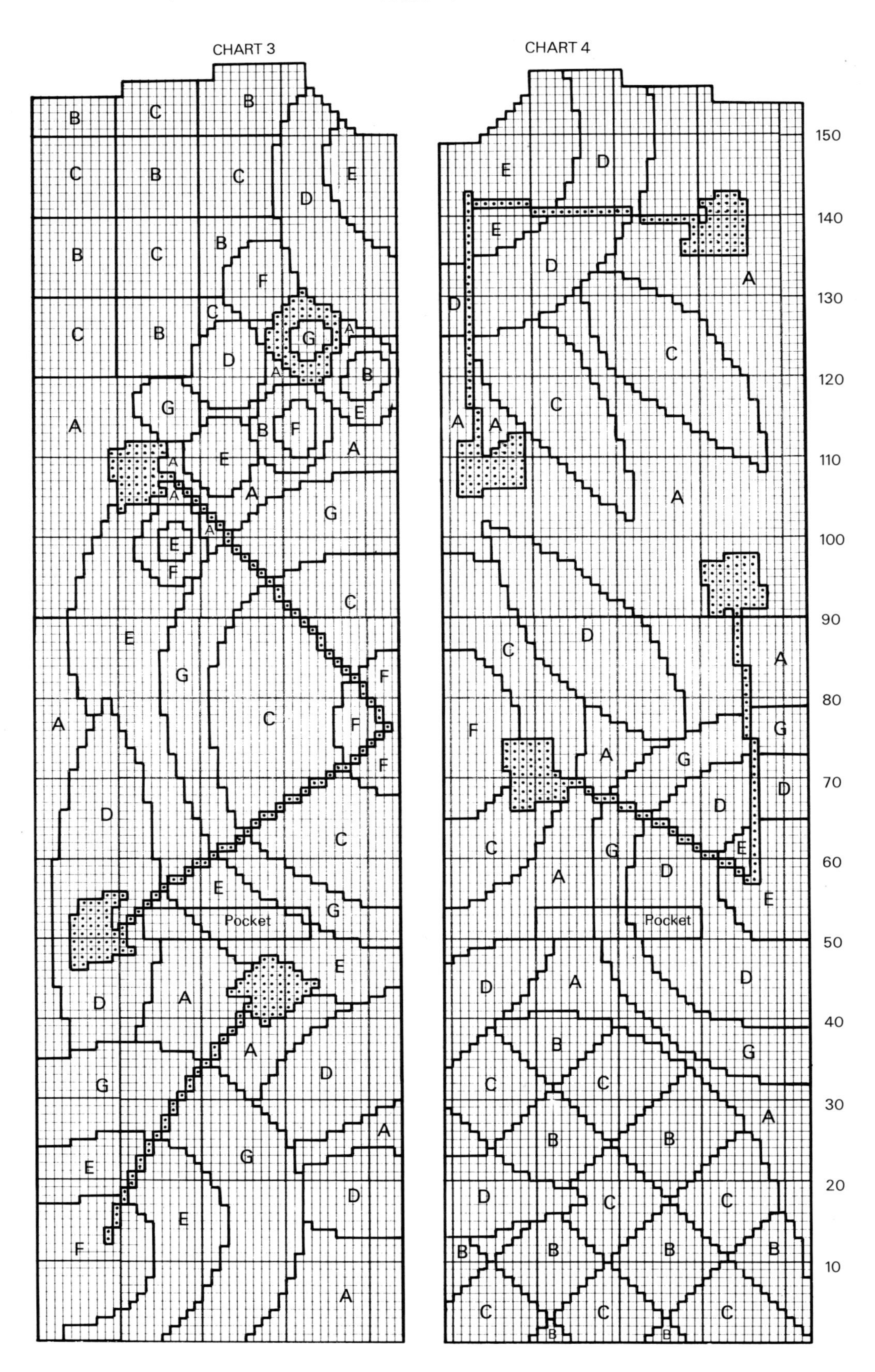

KEY

[•] = H

Change to 6mm (US10) needles and cont in chart patt, working in st st throughout, beg with a K row, work 11th-50th rows, ending with a WS row.

Place pocket lining

Next row Patt 13 sts, sl next 20 sts on to a stitch holder, patt across 20 sts of first pocket lining, patt 11 sts.

Cont in patt until 149th row of chart has been worked, placing sleeve markers at each end of 95th row, end with a RS row.

Shape neck

Cast off 5 sts at beg of next row, then dec 1 st at neck edge on next 4 rows, ending at armhole edge. 35 sts.

Shape shoulder

Next row Cast off 11 sts, patt to last 2 sts, K2 tog.

Next row P2 tog, patt to end.

Next row Cast off 11 sts, patt to end. 11 sts.

Work 1 row. Cast off.

RIGHT FRONT

Work as given for left front, working cast-on rows as foll:

Cast-on row Cast on 3 sts in F, 12E, 10G, and 19A. 44 sts.

Complete as given for left front, working from chart 3 and reversing pocket position and shapings.

TO MAKE UP

Left pocket top

With RS of work facing, using 5mm (US8) needles work in K1, P1 rib across 20 sts at left front pocket top as foll:

1st row (RS) Rib 8D, 5G, 7A.
2nd row Rib 7A, 5G, 8D.
3rd row Rib 9D, 4G, 7A.
4th row Rib 7A, 4G, 9D.
Cast off in rib in yarns as set.

Right pocket top

Work as given for left pocket top across right front pocket top as foll:

1st row (RS) Rib 12E, 8A.
2nd row Rib 7A, 13E.
3rd row Rib 1G, 13E, 6A.
4th row Rib 5A, 12E, 3G.
Cast off in rib in yarns as set.

Sew pocket linings in position on WS of fronts, and catch down pocket tops on RS.

Button band

Using 5mm (US8) needles and yarn A, cast on 6 sts.

Work in K1, P1 rib until band when slightly stretched fits up front to beg of neck shaping.

Leave these sts on a stitch holder.

Join button band on to left front opening edge.

Mark position of 9 buttons the first 2cm (¾in) from cast-on edge, the last 8cm (3in) from beg of neck shaping and the rest spaced evenly between.

Buttonhole band

Work as given for button band, making 9 buttonholes opposite button markers as foll:

Buttonhole row (RS) Rib 3, yo, rib 2 tog, rib 1.

Join on buttonhole band to right front. Join both shoulders using backstitch seams.

Set in sleeves between markers.

Join side seams and sleeve seams above foldlines.

Collar

With RS of work facing, using 5mm (US8) needles and yarn A, rib 6 sts from top of buttonhole band, K up 11 sts up right side of front neck, 30 sts around back neck, 11 sts down left front neck and rib 6 sts from top of button band. 64 sts.

Work 2 rows in K1, P1 rib, inc 1 st at each end of every row. 68 sts.

Buttonhole row Work twice into first st, rib to last 7 sts, rib 2 tog, yo, rib 4, work twice into last st. 70 sts.

Cont in rib, work 13 rows more, *at the same time* inc 1 st at each end of every row. 96 sts.

Buttonhole row Work twice into next st, rib to last 7 sts, rib 2 tog, yo, rib 4, work twice into next st. 98 sts.

Work 3 more rows in rib, inc at each end as before. 104 sts.

Cast off evenly in rib.

Sew on buttons, 9 along left front button band, 1 at left front neck, 1 each on cuffs and 1 on collar.

Right *The Target Jacket from Muir and Osborne. It is often the fine detail which makes the difference between an ordinary garment and something special. Here the designers have meticulously carried the design through the ribs and pocket tops.*

SANDY BLACK

Put on one of Sandy Black's lightweight angora coats and you immediately feel like an Erté cover design for *Vogue*. Wonderfully chic but never understated, their glamour value is high for she handles materials and ideas superbly.

Humour is frequently present in her work, and she even succeeds in knitting jokes that endure. Her fox, leopard and snake scarves of 1979 that imitate those draped animal wraps, claws and all, are still wearable and funny. Even a set of knitted cushions that together form a shoreline snapshot continue to look fresh, long after that fashion mood has passed.

Sandy Black's serious but gentle exterior gives little away, but somewhere underneath is a purposeful strength. Before graduating in maths she had already decided to make knitting her business. Few were doing such a thing in 1973, but she never doubted that she could make it work; and she did. On her own, from her studio by London's Tower Bridge she created her opportunities. Not only did she produce knitwear for London shops and then the international market, but she also became a knitwear consultant, designing for magazines and books, and preparing collections for major yarn spinners like Courtelle and Georges Picaud.

Later, when her partner Kevin Bolger joined her, she launched the Sandy Black Original Knits label for her knitting kits and yarns. Since then her reputation has continued to grow, and with it an unfailing stream of new ideas, always modern and fashionable, but never superficial.

★ ★

SCROLL GILET

Summer

SIZE

To fit one size up to 96cm (38in) bust

MATERIALS

350g Salad Days Knobbly Cotton in ecru 561 (A); 200g in cornflower 573; 100g in marine 575 (C)

Equivalent yarn four-ply

1 pair 3¾mm (US5) needles

TENSION

30 sts and 30 rows to 10cm (4in) over patt on 3¾mm (US5) needles.

SPECIAL NOTE The gilet is made up of 32 separate but identical 'tiles', each measuring 14cm (5½in) square, plus two ½-tiles which are assembled following chart 2 on page 112.

TILE (make 32)

*Using yarn B, cast on 2 sts.

Now beg colour patt from chart 1, working in st st unless otherwise indicated, weaving contrast yarns into back of work.

Work 1 row. Cont in chart patt, *at the same time* inc 1 st at each end of every row until there are 58 sts. Cont in patt, work 1 row, then dec 1 st at each end of every row until 2 sts rem. Cast off.

HALF-TILES (make 2)

Work 1st-30th rows as given for whole tile. Cast off.

TO MAKE UP

Join tiles carefully, foll chart 2 for layout and leaving 2 tiles open for armholes.

Join shoulder seams 1¼ tiles in from armhole edge on back and fronts.

With WS together, sew half-tiles to inside front neck as indicated.

Front and neck bindings

Using yarn A, cast on 20 sts.

Right *The Scroll Gilet is a cunningly constructed patchwork of patterned squares and triangles.*

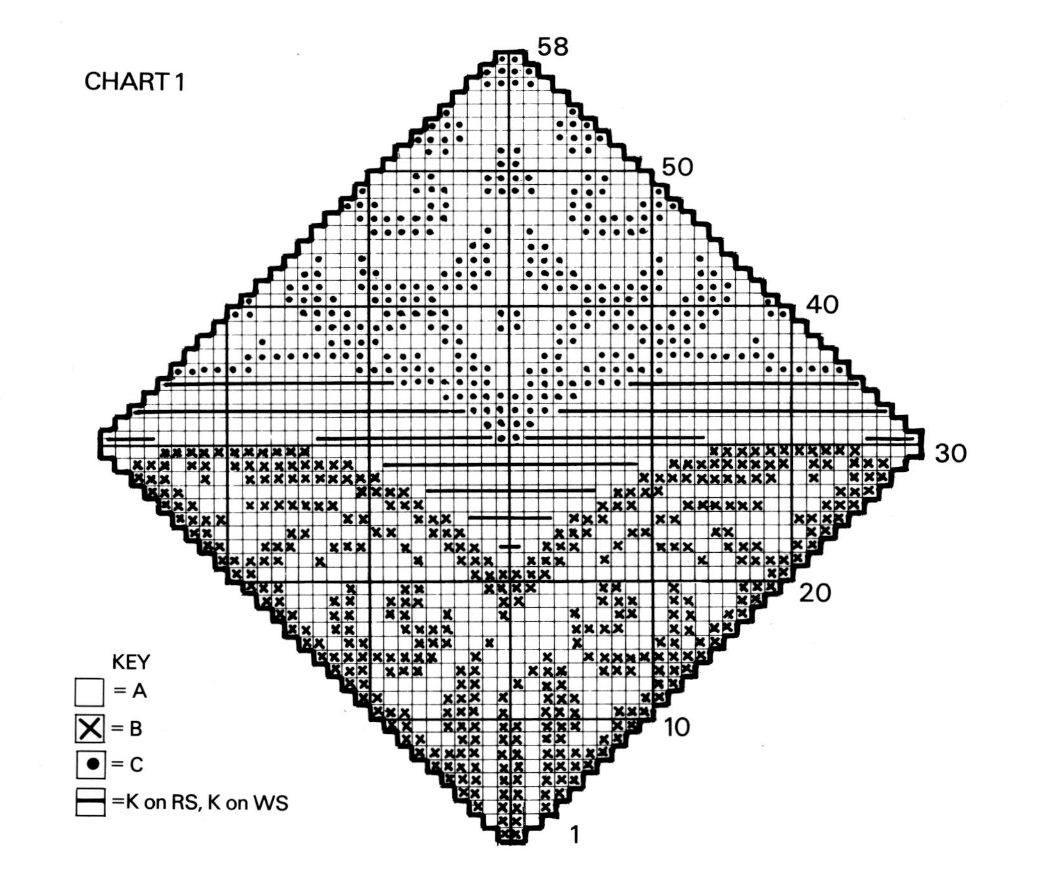

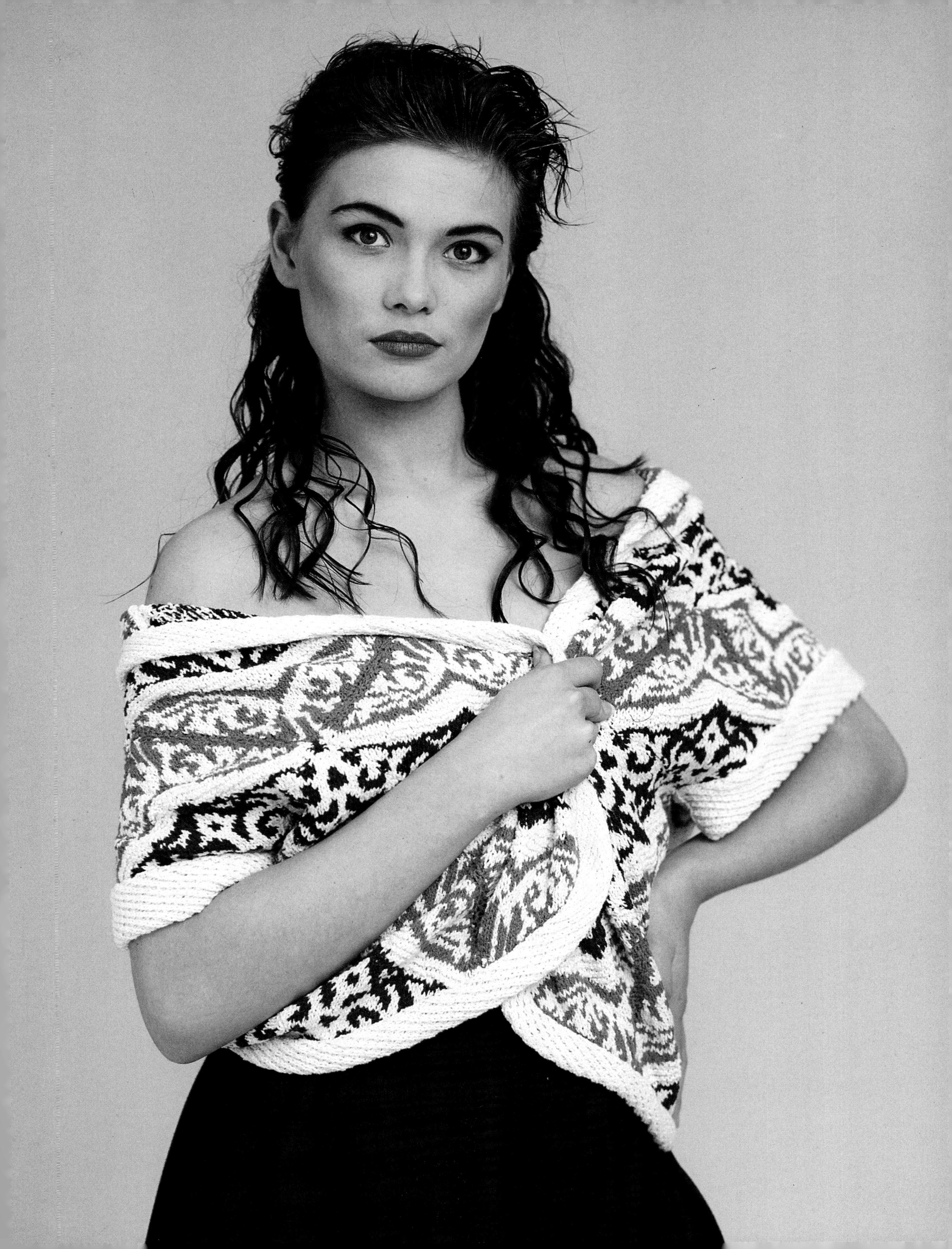

CHART 2

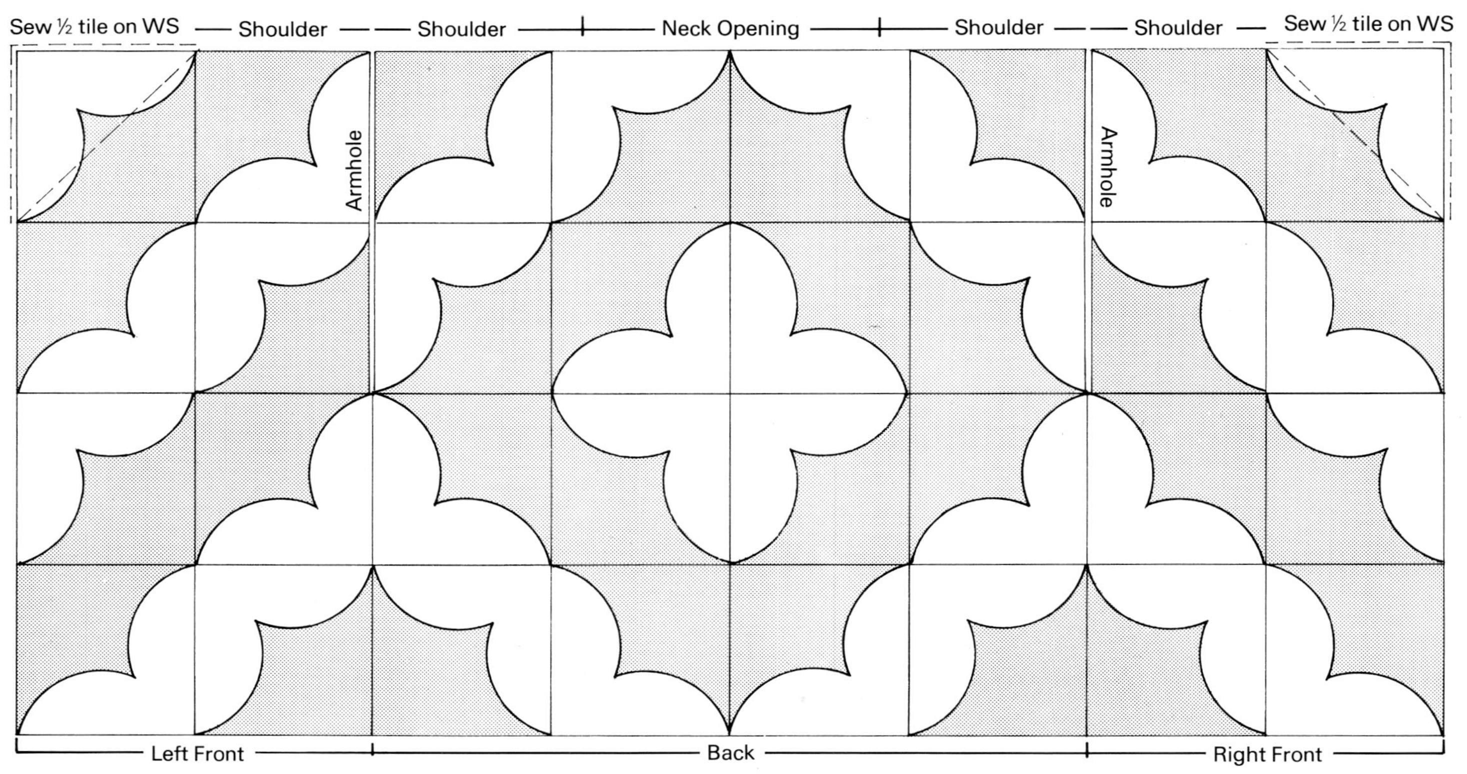

Work bias patt as foll:
1st and every alt row (WS) P to end.
2nd row *K2 tog without dropping sts from left-hand needle, then K first st again, sl both sts off needle at the same time **; rep from * to end.
4th row K1, rep from * to ** of 2nd row to last st, K1.
These 4 rows form the bias patt. Cont in patt until strip is long enough to fit around back neck, fronts and lower edge, beg and ending at a side seam. Cast off.

Arm bindings
Using yarn A, cast on 30 sts.
Work in bias patt as given for front and neck binding until strip is long enough, when slightly stretched, to fit around armhole opening.
Cast off.
With RS together, sew bindings in position with backstitch seams. Fold in half on to WS and catch down, easing bindings smoothly round corners.

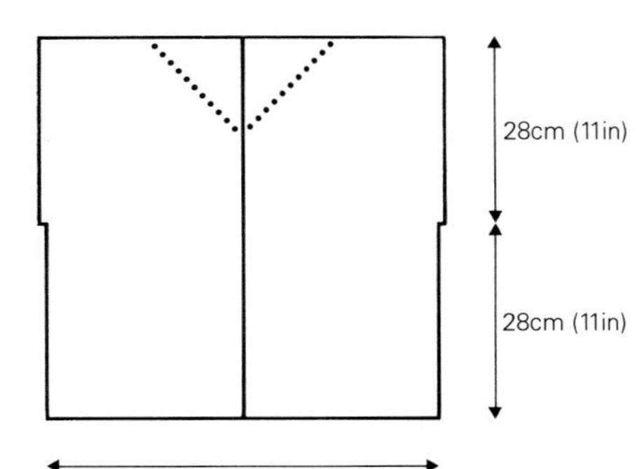

★ ★

TAPESTRY FLOWER SWEATER

Winter

SIZES
To fit 91[101]cm (36[40]in) bust

MATERIALS
800[900]g Rowanspun Tweed in one a.m. 756 (A); 100g each in cranberry 753 (B) and cedar 759 (C)
100g Cotton Chenille in periwinkle 358 (D) and forest green 362 (E)
Oddment of Lightweight Double Knitting in olive 407 (F)
Equivalent yarn Aran-weight
1 pair each 4mm (US6) and 5½mm (US9) needles

TENSION
16 sts and 23 rows to 10cm (4in) over st st on 5½mm (US9) needles.

BACK
Using 4mm (US6) needles and yarn A, cast on 90[102] sts.
Work in diagonal rib as foll:
1st row (RS) (K3, P3) to end.
2nd row (K2, P3, K1) to end.
3rd row (P2, K3, P1) to end.
4th row (P3, K3) to end.
5th row (K1, P3, K2) to end.
6th row (P1, K3, P2) to end.
These 6 rows form diagonal rib.
Cont in diagonal rib until work measures 5cm (2in) from cast-on edge ending with a WS row, inc 4 sts evenly across last rib row for 1st size only. 94[102] sts.
Change to 5½mm (US9) needles and work 6 rows in st st for 2nd size only, beg with a K row.
Now cont in st st, beg colour patt from chart on page 114 using small separate balls of yarn for each colour area, twisting yarns tog on WS at colour joins to avoid holes, work 120 rows, end with a WS row.
Shape raglan armholes
Cast off 3 sts at beg of next 2 rows, then dec 1 st at each end of every foll 5th row until 76[86] sts rem. ** Work 1 row.
Now dec 1 st at each end of next row and foll 15[17] alt rows, and then on every row until 34[36] sts rem. Cast off.

FRONT
Work as given for back to **.
Now dec 1 st at each end of every alt row until 50[54] sts rem, ending with a RS row.
Divide for neck
Next row P 2[0] tog, patt 15[19] sts, turn, leaving rem sts on a spare needle and cont on these sts only for first side of neck.
Dec 1 st at neck edge on next 8[9] rows, *at the same time* cont to shape raglan by dec 1 st at armhole edge on alt rows as before until 10[14] sts rem, then on every row until 2 sts rem. Work 2 tog.
Fasten off.
With WS of work facing, return to sts on spare needle, cast off 16 sts, patt to end.
Complete second side of neck to match first side reversing shapings.

SLEEVES
Using 4mm (US6) needles and yarn A, cast on 36 sts.
Work 4cm (1½in) in diagonal rib as given for back, inc 4 sts evenly across last row. 40 sts.
Change to 5½mm (US9) needles and work 40 rows in st st, *at the same time* inc 1 st at each end of 2nd and every foll alt row until there are 52 sts, then at each end of foll 3rd row, then at each end of every foll 5th row and 4th row alternately until there are 64 sts. Work 2 rows straight.
Now beg colour patt from chart, placing motif as foll:
Next row K13A, work first row of sleeve motif (37 sts), K14A.
Next row Inc 1 in next st, P13A, work 2nd row of sleeve motif, P to last st, inc 1. 66 sts.
Cont in patt as set, *at the same time* inc 1 st at each end of foll 5th and 4th rows alternately until there are 76 sts.
Now work straight until sleeve motif is completed, marking each end of 34th chart row for armholes. Cont in A only.
Divide for sleeve top
Next row K37, turn, leaving rem sts on a spare needle and cont on these sts only for first side of sleeve.
Work 9 rows straight.
*** Dec 1 st at inner edge on next and foll 5th row, then on 3 foll 4th rows, 9 foll alt rows, then on next 9 rows, *at the same time* dec 1 st at outer edge on next and 3 foll 6th rows, then on every foll 3rd row until 2 sts rem.
Work 2 tog and fasten off.
With RS of work facing, return to sts on spare needle, rejoin yarn, K2 tog, K to end. 38 sts.
Work 4 rows straight, dec 1 st at inner edge on next row. Work 4 rows straight.
Complete as given for first side from *** to end.

COLLAR
Using 4mm (US6) needles and yarn A, cast on 114 sts.
Work 12.5cm (4¾in) in diagonal rib as given for back.
Cast off loosely in rib.

TO MAKE UP
Embroidery
Using yarns A and E alternately, work a line of large French knots in the centre of each flower as shown on chart.
Join sleeve top seams.
Set sleeves into armholes between markers. Join side and sleeve seams.
Open collar
Oversew collar to neck edge beg and ending at centre front.
Cowl collar
Sew short ends of collar tog. Oversew collar to neck edge beg at left shoulder seam.

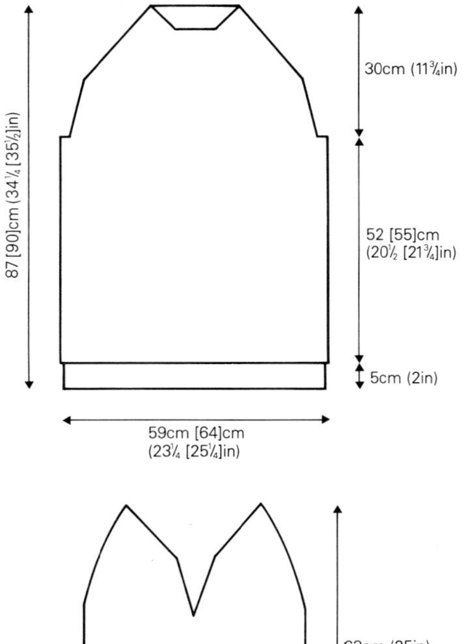

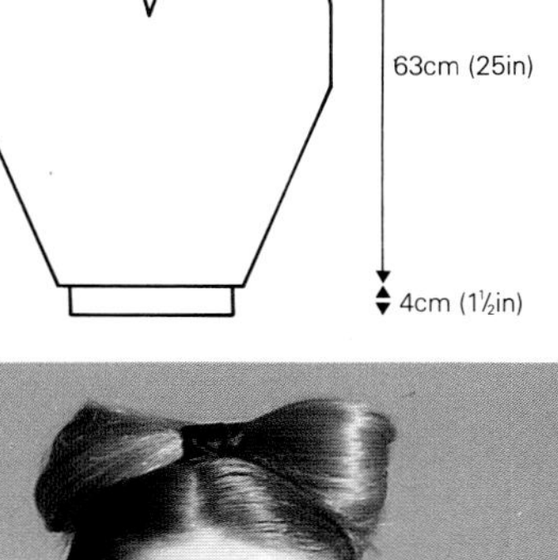

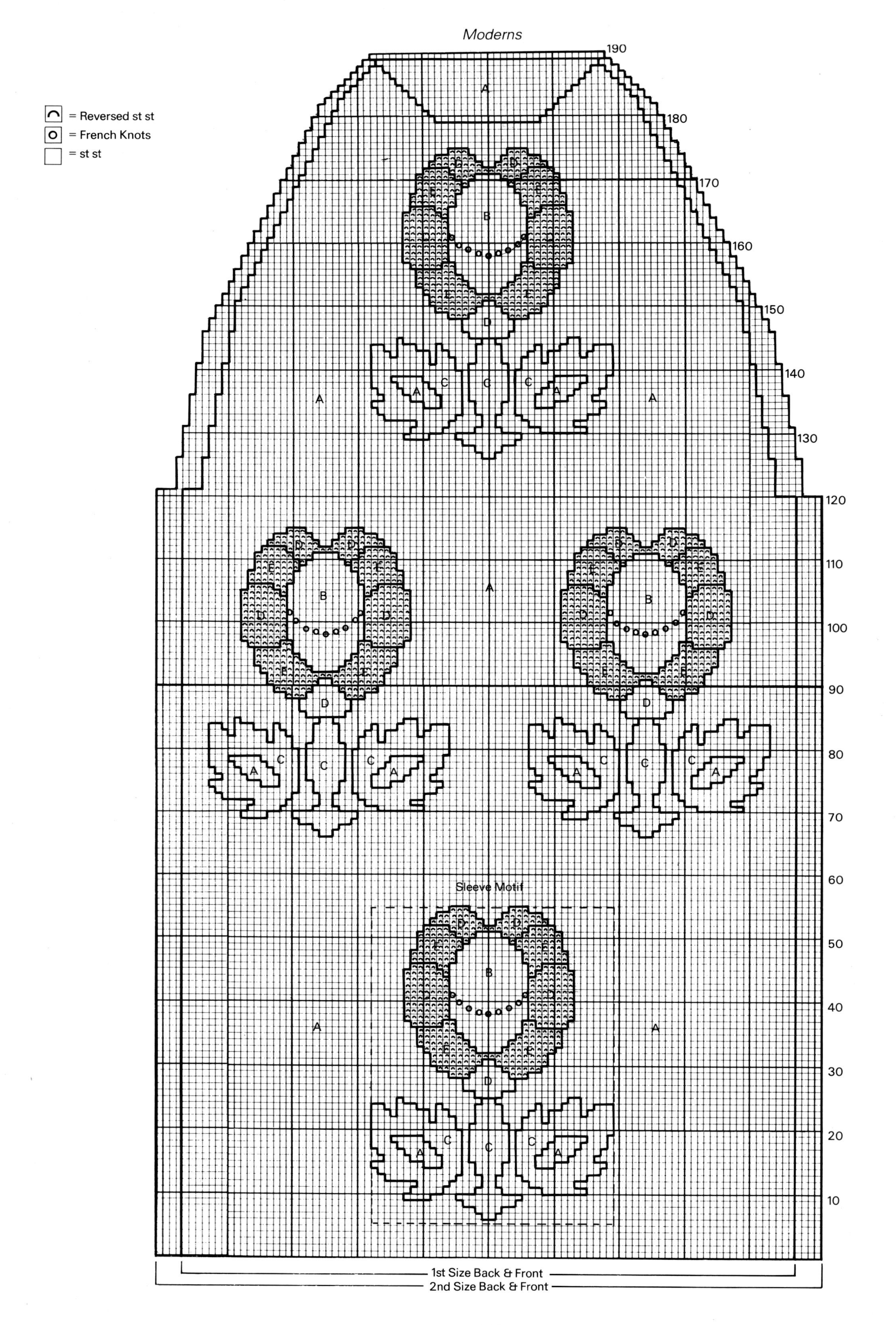
= Reversed st st
= French Knots
= st st
190
180
170
160
150
140
130
120
110
100
90
80
70
60
50
40
30
20
10
A
B
C
D
Sleeve Motif
1st Size Back & Front
2nd Size Back & Front

Sandy Black is well known for her extravagant angora coats (above), *but she also has a quieter side. The Tapestry Flower Sweater* (right) *is a rather ladylike, almost demure, garment given a touch of drama in the huge puffed sleeves. The flower centres are picked out in large French knots.*

ERIKA KNIGHT

Brighton is usually associated with trippers, old ladies and the crumbling magnificence of a once fashionable seaside resort. It is an unexpected place to find Erika Knight, a designer at the forefront of young fashion. Erika named her knitwear company 'Molto', and it is apt for a person so prodigious in her output. The flow of ideas never stops as she not only produces the designs for her own company, which keeps between 400 and 500 knitters busy, but also does four collections for Italian fashion houses every year, creates patterns for some of the British knitting wool spinners and writes about knitting too.

Erika has a true understanding of where fashion is. A new idea is unlikely to pass her by, and many of them will have orginated with her. This talent, combined with several years study of sculpture produces a confidence with shape and texture and a daring hand with colour. She can make shocking green knitting look desirable and fun on her street-fashion shapes. Somehow she might just as easily have been an originator of high-tech furniture or responsible for the retro-deco design movement. But she happened to like fashion which quickly led her to knitwear, not as a founder member of the club but as an influential figure in using knitwear for young fashion in the 1980s.

Erika, and her partner Ian Harris, a graphic designer by training, work closely on the numerous Molto projects. It is no small task she has set herself, and she talks of future ideas and hopes for the business as if there were no limit to time and energy. Others might lose sight of the joy of life in the midst of all this productivity and the responsibilities it brings, but not Erika. She remains a delight.

★

DENIM JACKET

Summer

SIZES

To fit up to 96[111]cm (38[44]in) bust

MATERIALS

1,000[1,050]g Nashville Indigo Dyed Cotton Double Knitting 225

Equivalent yarn none

1 pair each 3¼mm (US3) and 4mm (US6) needles

11 buttons

TENSION

18 sts and 26 rows to 10cm (4in) over st st on 4mm (US6) needles.

BACK

Using 3¼mm (US3) needles, cast on 112[118] sts.

Work 9cm (3½in) in K1, P1 rib.

Change to 4mm (US6) needles.

Right back panel

Next row (RS) K27[29] sts, turn, leaving rem sts on a spare needle.

Next row Cast on 2 sts, P to end. 29[31] sts.

Cont in st st on these sts only, *at the same time* inc 1 st at side edge on 7th and every foll 10th row until there are 36[38] sts.

Now work straight until work measures 39[40]cm 15¼[15¾]in) from cast-on edge, ending at side edge.

Shape armhole

Cast off 5 sts at beg of next row, then dec 1 st at armhole edge on next 3 rows, then on foll alt row. 27[29] sts.

Now work straight until work measures 56[58]cm (22[22¾]in) from cast-on edge. Cast off evenly and firmly.

Centre back panel

Return to sts on spare needle, with RS of work facing, rejoin yarn to next st, K58[60] sts, turn, leaving rem sts on spare needle.

Cont in st st, cast on 2 sts at beg of next 2 rows. 62[64] sts.

Now work straight until work measures same as right back panel from cast-on edge.

Cast off firmly and evenly.

Left back panel

Return to sts on spare needle, with RS of work facing rejoin yarn to next st. Complete to match right back panel reversing shapings.

BACK YOKE

Using 4mm (US6) needles, cast on 108[116] sts.

Work 16[17]cm (6¼[6¾]in) in st st, beg with a K row and ending with a P row.

Shape shoulders

Cont in st st, cast off 6[7] sts at beg of next 6 rows. 72[74] sts.

Divide for neck

Next row Cast off 6 sts, K15 including st used to cast off, turn, leaving rem sts on a spare needle and cont on these sts only for first side of neck. 15 sts.

Next row P2 tog, P to end. 14 sts.

Next row Cast off 6 sts, K to last 2 sts, K2 tog. 7 sts.

Next row P2 tog, P to end.

Cast off rem 6 sts.

With RS of work facing return to sts on spare needle, rejoin yarn to next st, cast off centre 30[32] sts, K to end. 21 sts.

Next row Cast off 6 sts, P to end. 15 sts.

Complete second side of neck to match first reversing shapings.

RIGHT FRONT

Using 3¼mm (US3) needles, cast on 52[56] sts.

Work 9cm (3½in) in K1, P1 rib.

Change to 4mm (US6) needles and work in st st, beg with a K row, *at the same time* inc 1 st at end of 7th row and at same edge on every foll 10th row until there are 59[63] sts.

Now work straight until work measures same as back panels to armhole, ending with a K row.

Shape armhole

Cast off 5 sts at beg of next row, then dec 1 st at armhole edge on foll 3 rows and next alt row. 50[54] sts.

Now work straight until front measures 58[60]cm (22¾[23½]in) from cast-on edge. Cast off evenly and firmly.

Right *Erika Knight's knitted version of the classic Denim Jacket.*

RIGHT FRONT YOKE

Using 4mm (US6) needles, cast on 50[54] sts.
Work 12 rows in st st, beg with a K row.
Shape front neck
Cast off 7[8] sts at beg of next row, then, dec 1 st at neck edge on foll 5 rows, and next 2 alt rows. 36[39] sts.
Now work straight until yoke measures 14[15]cm (5½[6]in) from cast-on edge, ending with a K row.
Shape shoulder
Cast off 6[7] sts, at beg of next and foll 2 alt rows, and 6 sts at beg of next 2 alt rows.
Work 1 row.
Cast off rem 6 sts.

LEFT FRONT AND YOKE

Work as given for right front and yoke, reversing shapings.

RIGHT SLEEVE

Using 3¼mm (US3) needles, cast on 66[70] sts.
Work 9cm (3½in) in K1, P1 rib.
Change to 4mm (US6) needles and work in st st.
Front sleeve panel
Next row K48[50] sts, turn, leaving rem sts on a spare needle.
Next row Cast on 2 sts, P to end. 50[52] sts.
Cont in st st, *at the same time* inc 1 st at side edge on 5th and every foll 4th row until there are 61[68] sts, then on every foll 5th row until there are 71[74] sts. Now work straight until work measures 48[49]cm (19[19¼]in) from cast-on edge, ending with P row.
Shape top
Cast off 5 sts at beg of next row, 2 sts at beg of foll 7 alt rows, then 3 sts at beg of next 5[6] alt rows and 5 sts at beg of next and foll alt row. 27 sts.
Next row (WS) Cast off 7 sts, P to end. 20 sts.
Cast off 5 sts at beg of next 2 rows.
Cast off rem 10 sts.
Back sleeve panel
With RS of work facing, return to sts on spare needle, rejoin yarn to next st, cast on 2 sts, K to end. 20[22] sts.
Cont in st st, *at the same time* inc 1 st at side edge on 5th and every foll 4th row until there are 31[38] sts, then on every foll 5th row until there are 41[44] sts.
Work straight until sleeve measures same as front sleeve panel to beg of top shaping, ending at side edge.
Shape top
Cast off 5 sts at beg of next row, 2 sts at beg of foll 7 alt rows and 3 sts at beg of next 5[6] alt rows. 7 sts.
Work 1 row.
Cast off.

LEFT SLEEVE

Work as given for right sleeve, reversing panels and all shaping.

COLLAR

Using 3¼mm (US3) needles, cast on 123 sts. Work in K1, P1 rib as foll:
1st row (RS) K1, (P1, K1) to end.
2nd row P1, (K1, P1) to end.
Rep these 2 rows once more.
Next row Rib 7, *(P1, K1, P1) into next st, rib 11; rep from * to last 8 sts, (P1, K1, P1) into next st, rib 7. 143 sts.
Next row As 2nd row.
Cont in rib until collar measures 6cm (2¼in) from cast-on edge.
Change to 4mm (US6) needles and cont in rib as set until collar measures 12cm (4½in) from cast-on edge.
Cast off loosely and evenly in rib.

POCKETS (make 2)

Using 3¼mm (US3) needles, cast on 35 sts.
Work 2 rows in K1, P1 rib, then make buttonhole on next 2 rows as foll:
1st buttonhole row Rib 16, cast off 3 sts, rib to end.
2nd buttonhole row Rib to end casting on 3 sts over those cast off in previous row.
Work 4 rows in rib.
Change to 4mm (US6) needles and work 30 rows in st st, beg with a K row.
Now shape pocket by working turning rows as foll:
Next row K to last 2 sts, turn.
Next row P to last 2 sts, turn.
Next row K to last 4 sts, turn.
Next row P to last 4 sts, turn.
Next row K to last 6 sts, turn.
Next row P to last 6 sts, turn.
Next row K to end.
Cast off.

BUTTON TABS (make 2)

Using 4mm (US6) needles, cast on 15 sts.
Work 4 rows in st st, beg with a K row. Now make buttonhole on next 2 rows as foll:
1st buttonhole row K3, cast off 3 sts, K to end.
2nd buttonhole row P to end, casting on 3 sts over those cast off in previous row.
Work 4 rows in st st.
Next row P to end to form foldline.
Work 10 rows in st st making buttonhole on 5th and 6th rows as before.
Cast off.

TO MAKE UP

With WS together, and using firm backstitch to form raised seams on RS of work, join left front to left front yoke.
In the same way, join right front to right front yoke.
Fold button tabs at foldline and pin in position on RS of left and right back panels 5cm (2in) above rib on centre back seams.
Forming raised seams as before, join right and left back panels to centre back panel.
Join back yoke to back. Join front and back sleeve panels.
Buttonband
Using 3¼mm (US3) needles, with RS of work facing, K up 163 sts evenly down left front opening edge.
Work 8 rows in K1, P1 rib.
Cast off evenly and firmly in rib.
Buttonhole band
Work as given for buttonband making 7 buttonholes on 4th and 5th rows as foll:
4th row Rib 5, (cast off 3 sts, rib 22 including st used to cast off) 6 times, cast off 3 sts, rib to end.
5th row Rib to end, casting on 3 sts over those cast off in previous row.
Wash garment pieces as instructed on ball band (they will shrink slightly).
With RS together, join shoulders using backstitch seams; join side and sleeve seams.
Set in sleeves using a raised seam, and placing back sleeve panel to back of jacket.
Sew pockets on to RS of fronts approx 15cm (6in) below yoke seams.
Sew on collar, joining cast-on edge of collar to neck edge.
Sew on 7 buttons to front button band, and 1 each on pockets and button tabs.

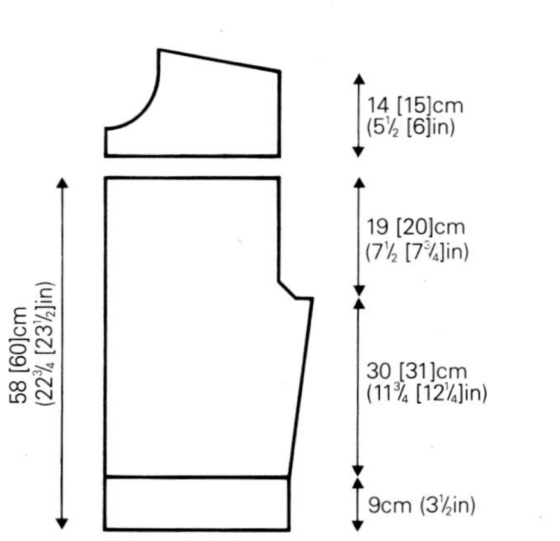

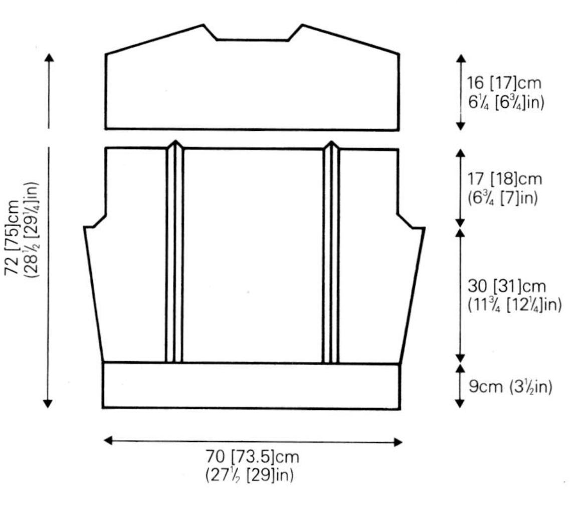

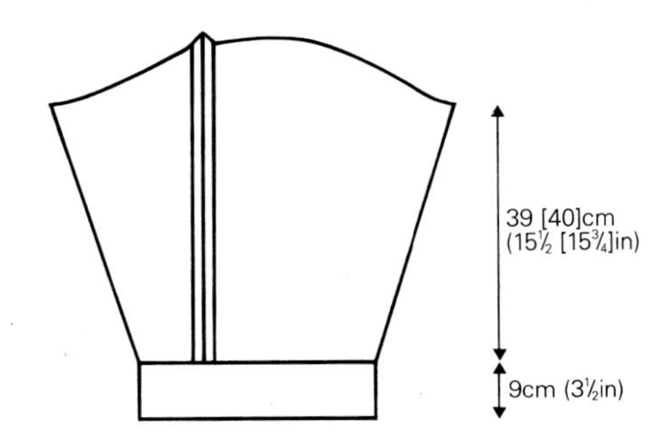

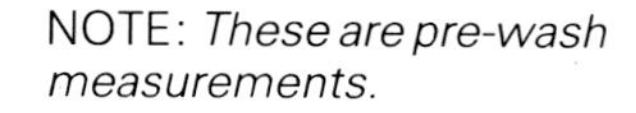
NOTE: *These are pre-wash measurements.*

★ ★

TYROLEAN JACKET

Winter

SIZES

To fit 91-97[101-107]cm (36-38[40-42]in) bust/chest

MATERIALS

500[550]g Lightweight Double Knitting each in black 62 (A) and sky 55 (B); 200[250]g in white 1 (C)
Equivalent yarn double knitting
1 pair each 3¾mm (US5), 4mm (US6) and 5½mm (US9) needles
4mm (US6) circular needle
6 buttons

NOTE When working main pieces, use 2 strands of yarn. When working borders use 1 strand of yarn.

TENSION

22 sts and 26 rows to 10cm (4in) over Fair Isle patt on 4mm (US6) needles using yarn singly.
16 sts and 18 rows to 10cm (4in) over Fair Isle patt on 5½mm (US9) needles using yarn double.

BACK

Using 3¾mm (US5) needles and yarn A singly, cast on 130[142] sts.
Work 16 rows in st st, beg with a K row.
Change to yarn B and K 2 rows to form foldline.
Change to 4mm (US6) needles and beg diamond border patt.
1st row (RS) K to end in B.
2nd row P to end in B.
3rd row K(1A, 5B) to last 4 sts, 1A, 3B.
4th row P2B, (3A, 3B) to last 2 sts, 2A.
5th row As 3rd row.
6th row P to end in B.
7th row K to end in B.
8th row P(1A, 5B) to last 4 sts, 1A, 3B.
9th row K2B, (3A, 3B) to last 2 sts, 2A.
10th row As 8th row.
11th-15th rows As 1st-5th rows.
Next row With B, (P2 tog) 2[3] times, (P2, P2 tog) 31[33] times, P2 tog 1[2] times. 96[104] sts.
Change 5½mm (US9) needles and yarns A and C double. Work in seed st as foll:
1st row (RS) K to end in A.
2nd row P to end in A.
3rd row K(3A, 1C) to end.
4th row P to end in A.
5th row K to end in A.
6th row P(2A, 1C, 1A) to end.
Rep 1st-6th rows until back measures 41[43]cm (16[17]in) from foldline, ending with a WS row.
Now beg colour patt from chart on page 120, working in st st throughout, (but twist yarns tog on WS from 34th row onwards) and weaving contrast yarns into back of work, foll colour sequence table for changes in contrast colours, work 56[58] rows placing sleeve markers at each end of 2nd patt row.
Shape shoulders and divide for neck
Next row Cast off 8[9] sts, patt 20[23] sts including st used to cast off, turn, leaving rem sts on a spare needle and cont on these sts only for first side of neck.
Next row P2 tog, patt to end.
Next row Cast off 8[10] sts, patt to last 2 sts, K2 tog. 10[11] sts.
Next row P2 tog, patt to end.
Cast off rem 9[10] sts.
With RS of work facing, return to sts on spare needle, rejoin yarn to next st, cast off centre 40 sts, patt to end. 28[32] sts.
Next row Cast off 8[9] sts, patt to last 2 sts, P2 tog.
Complete second side of neck to match first side reversing shapings.

POCKET LININGS (make 2)

Using 5½mm (US9) needles and yarn A double, cast on 26 sts.
Work 14cm (5½in) in seed st as for back, but working 1st and last sts of each row in A. Leave these sts on a stitch holder.

RIGHT FRONT

Using 3¾mm (US5) needles and yarn A singly, cast on 58[64] sts.
Work 16 rows in st st beg with a K row.
Change to yarn B and K 2 rows to form foldline.
Change to 4mm (US6) needles and work 15 rows in diamond border patt as for back.
Next row (P2 tog) once[twice], (P2, P2 tog) 14[15] times. 43[47] sts.
Change to 5½mm (US9) needles and yarns A and C double, work in seed st as foll:
1st, 2nd, 4th and 5th rows As for back.
3rd row (K3A, 1C) to last 3 sts, 3A.
6th row P1A, 1C, 1A, (2A, 1C, 1A) to end.
Rep these 6 rows until work measures 14cm (5½in) from top of border, ending with a WS row.
Place pocket lining
Next row Patt 7[9] sts, sl next 26 sts on to a stitch holder, patt across 26 sts of first pocket lining, patt 10[12].
Cont in seed st as set until front matches back to beg of chart patt, ending with a WS row.
Now work 38[40] rows in chart patt foll colour sequence table for changes in contrast colours.
Shape neck
Keeping chart patt correct, cast off 9 sts at beg of next row, then dec 1 st at neck edge on foll 5 rows. 29[33] sts.
Work 1 row, then dec 1 st at neck edge on next and foll 3 alt rows. 25[29] sts.
Now work straight until front matches back to shoulder, ending at armhole edge.
Shape shoulder
Cast off 8[9] sts at beg of next row, and 8[10] sts at beg of foll alt row.
Work 1 row.
Cast off rem 9[10] sts.

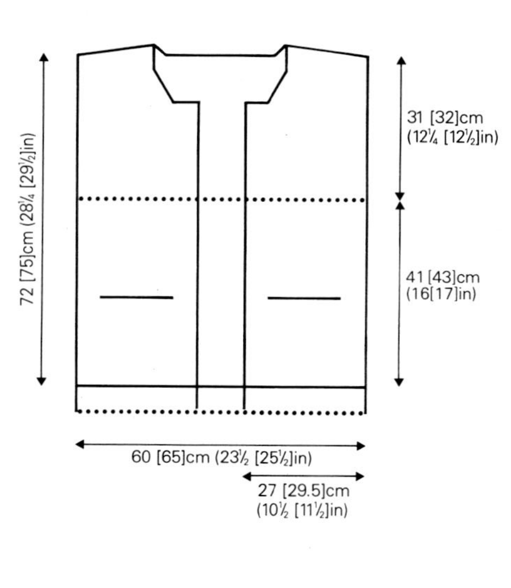

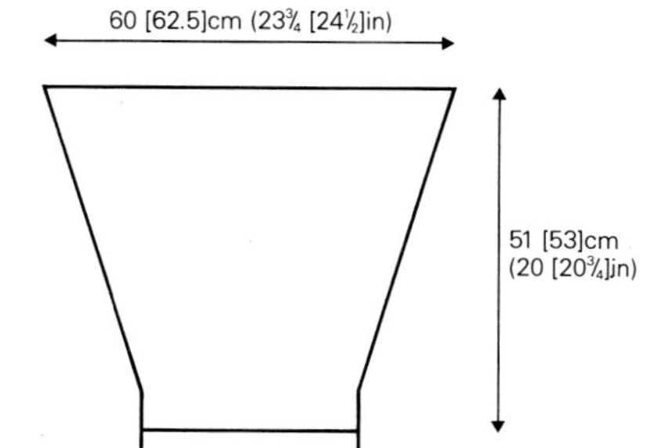

Right *Traditional Tyrolean shapes and patterns translated into modern terms by Erika Knight.*

LEFT FRONT

Work as given for right front, reversing shapings and positon of pocket.

SLEEVES

Using 3¾mm (US5) needles and yarn A singly, cast on 70[76] sts.
Work 16 rows in st st, beg with a K row.
Change to yarn B and K 2 rows for foldline.
Change to 4mm (US6) needles and work 15 rows in diamond border patt as for back.
Next row With B, (P2 tog) once[twice], (P2, P2 tog) to end. 52[56] sts.
Change to 5½mm (US9) needles and yarns double work in chart patt beg with 32nd row (cont in seed st when zigzag is completed), *at the same time* inc 1 st at each end of 4th and every foll 3rd row until there are 96[100] sts, working incs into patt.
Now work straight until sleeve measures 51[53]cm (20[20¾]in) from foldline, ending with a WS row.
Cast off loosely and evenly.

TO MAKE UP

Pocket tops

With RS of work facing, using 3¾mm (US5) needles and yarn B singly, work across 26 sts at pocket top as foll:
1st row K1, *K into front and back of first st, K2; rep from * to last st, K into front and back of last st. 35 sts.
2nd row P to end in B.
3rd row K to end in A.
4th row P2B, (1A, 5B) to last 3 sts, 1A, 2B.
5th row K1B, (3A, 3B) to last 4 sts, 3A, 1B.
6th row As 4th row.
7th row K to end in B.
8th row P to end in B.
9th-10th rows K to end for foldline.
Change to yarn A and work 10 rows in st st, beg with a K row.
Cast off.
Fold pocket tops on to WS and slipstitch down.
Sew pocket linings in position on WS.

Buttonband

With RS of work facing, using 4mm (US6) circular needle and yarn B singly, K up 142[148] sts evenly down left front edge to foldline. Work in rows.
Next row P to end in B.
Now work 15 rows in diamond border patt as for back.
Next row P to end in B.
K 2 rows in B for foldline.
Change to 3¾mm (US5) needles and yarn A singly.
Work 18 rows in st st, beg with a K row.
Cast off loosely and evenly.

Buttonhole band

Work as for button band, making 5 buttonholes on 7th and 8th rows of diamond patt as foll:
1st buttonhole row (RS) Patt 11[13] sts, (cast off 3 sts, patt 27[28] sts including st used to cast off) 4 times, cast off 3 sts, patt to end.
2nd buttonhole row Patt to end, casting on 3 sts over those cast off in previous row.
Complete as for button band, rep 2 buttonhole rows on 7th-8th rows of st st in A.
Fold front bands on to WS and slipstitch down.
Join shoulders using backstitch seams.

Collar

With RS of work facing, using 4mm (US6) needles and yarn B singly, K up 14 sts across top of buttonhole band, 36 sts up right side front neck, 47 sts across back neck, 37 sts down left side front neck and 14 sts across button band. 148 sts.
Next row P to end in B.
Work 15 rows in diamond border patt as for back, *at the same time* make a buttonhole on 7th and 8th rows as foll:
1st buttonhole row Patt 7 sts, cast off 3 sts, patt to end.
2nd buttonhole row Patt to end, casting on 3 sts over those cast off in previous row.
Next row P to end in B.
K 2 rows in B for foldline.
Change to 3¾mm (US5) needles and yarn A. Work 18 rows in st st, rep 1st and 2nd buttonhole rows on 7th and 8th rows as before.
Fold collar on to WS and slipstitch down.
Set in sleeves between markers.
Join side and sleeve seams.
Fold cuffs and hems along foldlines and stitch down.
Sew on buttons.

Right *Erika Knight's Tyrolean Jacket.*

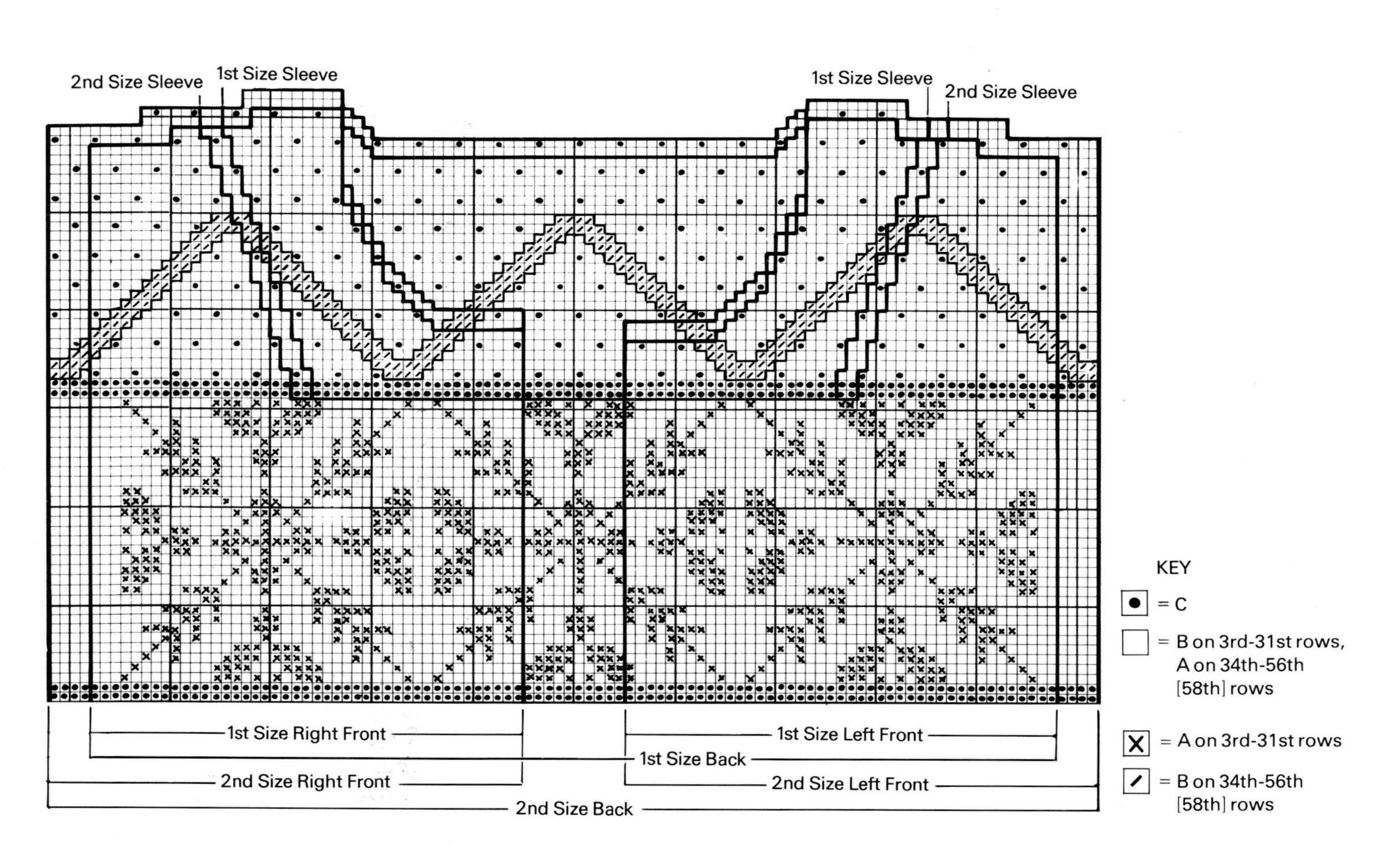

ARTWORK

From Picasso, Miró, the Impressionists and other painters – fake signatures and all – came the inspiration for Artwork's first knitwear collection in 1978. More sophisticated than the 'witty knits' they preceded, they were pioneers in the creation of the pictorial knitwear look that has lasted, in its various manifestations, for almost a decade.

Jane Foster was working in the costume department at the BBC, and Patrick Gottelier was engaged in an engineering project for Marks and Spencer when they met someone wanting Fair Isle sweaters for a shop. Jane and Patrick undertook the commission themselves. The shop went bust but the fashion retailer, Whistles, bought the order. They sold quickly, and Artwork was formed to cope with the demand.

The annual theme has remained an important element of the Artwork style. Spanish cowboy, nautical, Canadian and Eskimo idioms have all been featured, but it was the English Garden collection in 1984 with its urns and trellises overprinted on the sweaters that won them particular favour overseas.

They have a sometimes irreverent approach to yarn, superimposing silkscreened patterns on the finished work, but sometimes it is the yarn itself that dictates the use, like the 'stone-washed denim' sweaters of 1986. Though knitwear always takes the lead, they work for the total look, designing not only skirts and trousers to create the outfit, but also hats, sunglasses and other accessories.

Jane takes the design initiative, helped by Patrick who also controls the business. From Fair Isle to fashion house, Artwork has grown, put down its roots in a lovely old Bermondsey building, and matured. For the future almost anything seems possible. In their hands you feel that knitwear, like the art they once mimicked, is unlikely to die.

★ ★

GUERNSEY

Summer

SIZE
To fit one size up to 96cm (38in) bust/chest

MATERIALS
1,050g Nashville Indigo Dyed Cotton Double Knitting 225
1 pair each 3¼mm (US3) and 3¾mm (US5) needles
Equivalent yarn none
Cable needle

TENSION
20 sts and 28 rows to 10cm (4in) over st st on 3¾mm (US5) needles.

SPECIAL ABBREVIATIONS
C6F (cable 6 front) – sl next 3 sts on to a cable needle and hold at front of work, K3, then K3 from cable needle
C6B (cable 6 back) – sl next 3 sts on to cable needle and hold at back of work, K3, then K3 from cable needle.

BACK
Using 3¼mm (US3) needles, cast on 121 sts. Work in patterned rib as foll:
1st row (RS) K3, *K1 tbl, P2, K4; rep from * ending last rep K3.
2nd row P3, *K2, P1 tbl, P4; rep from * ending last rep P3.
3rd row K3, *sl next st on to cable needle and hold at front of work, P1, then K1 tbl from cable needle, P1, K4; rep from * ending last rep K3.
4th row P3, *K1, P1 tbl, K1, P4; rep from * ending last rep P3.
5th row K3, *P1, sl next st on to cable needle and hold at front of work, P1, then K1 tbl from cable needle, K4; rep from * ending last rep K3.
6th row P3, *P1 tbl, K2, P4; rep from * ending last rep P3.
7th row K3, *P1, sl next st on to cable needle and hold at back of work, K1 tbl, then P1 from cable needle, K4; rep from * ending last rep K3.
8th row P3, *K1, P1 tbl, K1, P4; rep from * ending last rep P3.
9th row K3, *sl next st on to cable needle and hold at back of work, K1 tbl, then P1 from cable needle, P1, K4; rep from * ending last rep K3.
Rep 2nd-9th rows 3 times more, then 2nd row once.
Change to 3¾mm (US5) needles. **
Work in st st, beg with a K row, until back measures 45.5cm (18in) from cast-on edge, ending with a K row.
Change to 3¼mm (US3) needles.
Increase row P1, make 1, (P7, make 1) 17 times, P1. 139 sts. ***
Now work 112 rows in patt from chart 1 on page 124, thus ending with a WS row.
Shape neck
Next row Patt 62 sts, turn, leaving rem sts on a spare needle and cont on these sts only for first side of neck.
Keeping chart patt correct, cast off 6 sts at beg of next row, dec 1 st at neck edge on foll row, cast off 5 sts at beg of next row, then dec 1 st at neck edge on foll 3 rows. 47 sts.
Work 2 rows straight.
Cast off.
With RS of work facing, return to sts on spare needle, sl centre 15 sts on to a stitch holder, rejoin yarn to next st and patt to end of row. 62 sts.
Complete second side of neck to match first side reversing shaping.

FRONT
Work as given for back to **.
Now work in st st, beg with a K row, until front measures 15cm (6in) from cast-on edge, ending with a P row.
Commence patt from chart 2 on page 124 as foll:
1st row (RS) K60, patt across 1st row of chart 2, K to end of row.
2nd row P8, patt across 2nd row of chart 2, P to end.
These 2 rows establish the position of chart 2. Cont in patt until chart 2 is completed.
Now cont in st st until front matches back to ***. Work in patt from chart 1 as given for back until 100 rows of chart 1 have been completed, thus ending with a WS row.
Shape neck
Next row Patt 64 sts, turn, leaving rem sts on a spare needle and cont on these sts only for first side of neck.

Cast off 3 sts at beg of next row, dec 1 st at neck edge on foll row, cast off 2 sts at beg of next row and dec 1 st at neck edge on foll 8 rows. Work 1 row. Now dec 1 st at neck edge on next and foll 2 alt rows. 47 sts. Work 3 rows straight.
With RS facing, return to sts on spare needle, sl centre 11 sts on to a stitch holder, rejoin yarn to next st and patt to end of row.
Complete second side of neck to match first side reversing shapings.

SLEEVES

Using 3¼mm (US3) needles, cast on 44 sts.
Work 18 rows in patterned rib as given for back, ending with a WS row.
Change to 3¾mm (US5) needles and work in st st, beg with a K row, *at the same time* inc 1 st at each end of next and every foll 3rd row until there are 92 sts, ending with a K row.
Change to 3¼mm (US3) needles.
Increase row P4, make 1, (P6, make 1) 14 times, P4. 107 sts.
Now commence patt from chart 1, working between sleeve markers, *at the same time* inc 1 st at each end of 3rd row and every foll alt row until there are 139 sts, working incs into patt as shown on chart.
Now work straight until 58 rows in all have been worked from chart 1.
Cast off loosely and evenly.

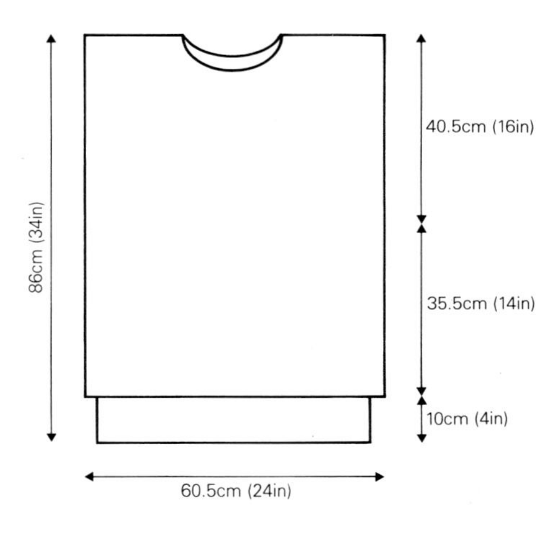

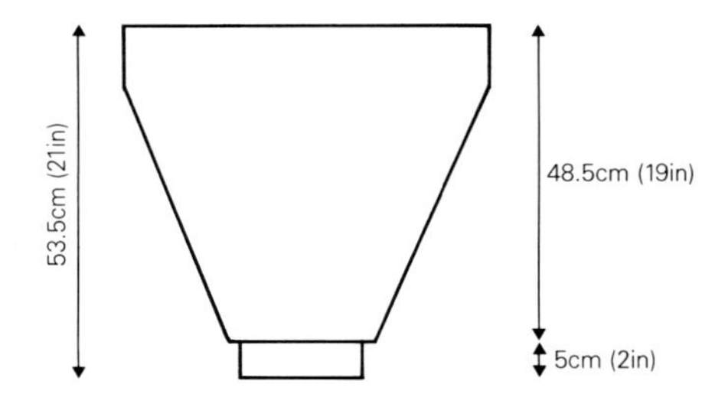

Note: These are pre-wash measurements

Right *A Guernsey with the Artwork touch, and, on the front, literally the Artwork signature. The easy classic shape is worked in an intricate collection of cables and seed stitches in a denim-style cotton yarn which is designed to fade with washing.*

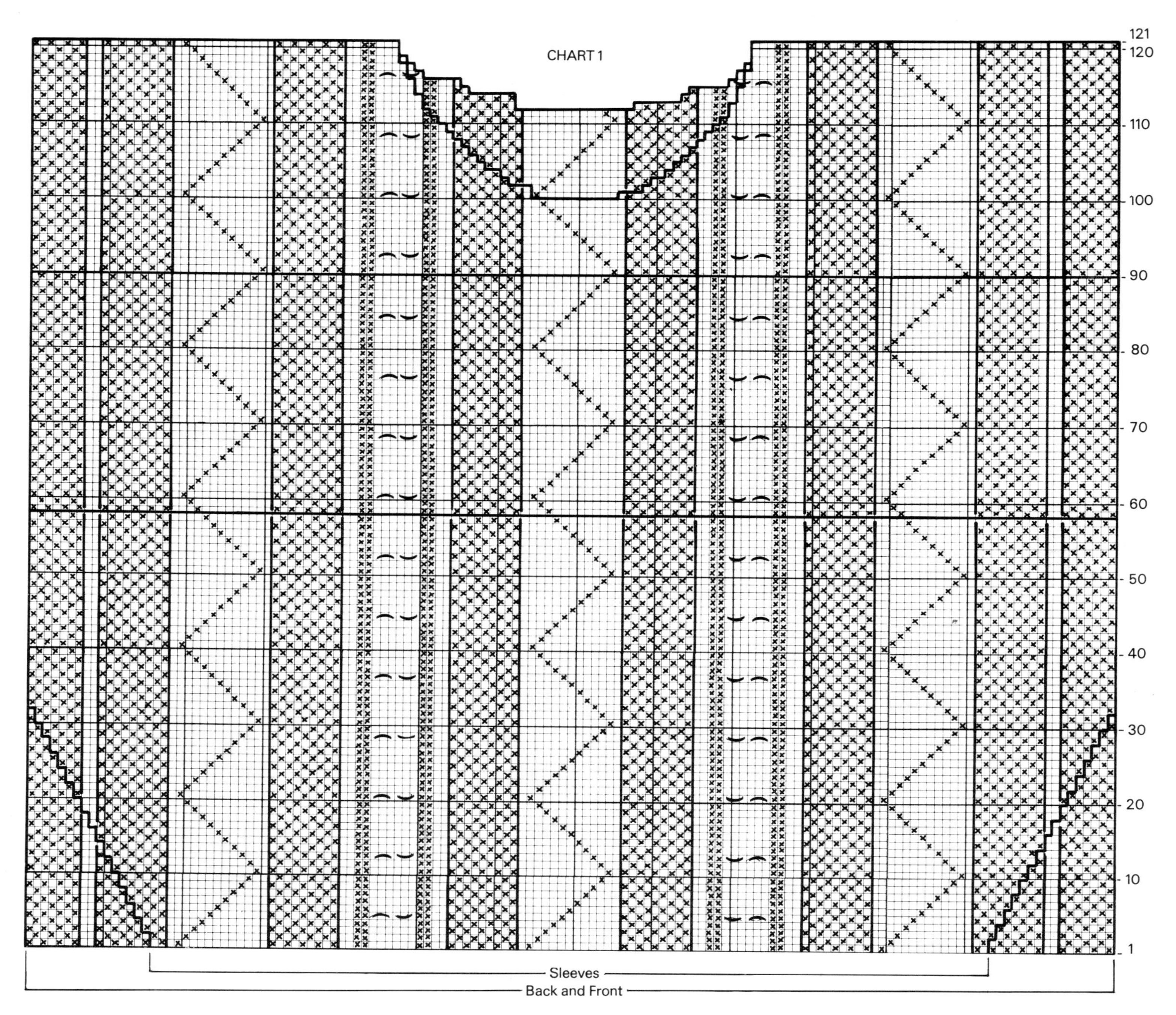

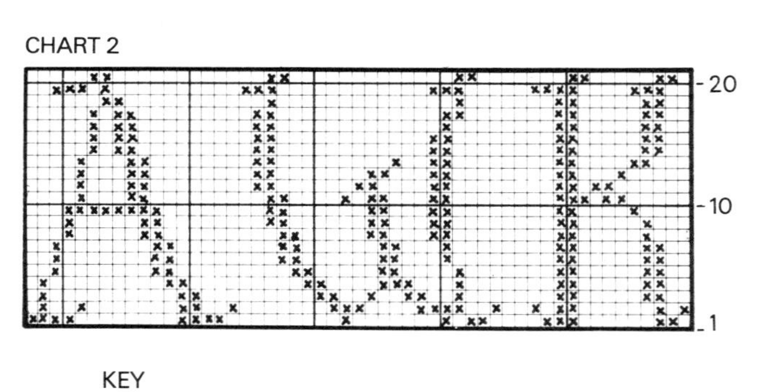

KEY

□ = K on RS rows, P on WS rows

☒ = P on RS rows, K on WS rows

= C6F

= C6B

TO MAKE UP

Join right shoulder using a backstitch seam.

Neckband

With RS of work facing, using 3¼mm (US3) needles, K up 22 sts down left side of front neck, K 11 sts from stitch holder at centre front, K up 22 sts up right side of front neck, K up 15 sts down right back neck, K 15 sts from stitch holder at centre back and K up 15 sts up left back neck. 100 sts.

Beg with 2nd row, work 17 rows in patterned rib as given for back.

Cast off loosely and evenly.

Join left shoulder and neckband seam.

Wash garment as instructed on ball band.

Fold neckband in half on to WS and slipstitch loosely in place.

Set in sleeves.

Join side and sleeve seams.

★ ★

PATCHWORK SWEATER

Winter

SIZES

To fit 91[106]cm (36[40]in) bust/chest

MATERIALS

600[650]g Lightweight Double Knitting in cream 1 (B); 500[550]g in black 62 (a); 50g in red 42 (C)

Equivalent yarn Aran-weight

1 pair each 4½mm (US7) and 6mm (US10) needles

NOTE Use yarn double.

TENSION

16 sts and 22 rows to 10cm (4in) over st st on 6mm (US10) needles.

BACK

Using 4½mm (US7) needles and yarn A, cast on 82 sts.

Work in twisted rib as foll:

Next row (K1 tbl, P1) to end.

Rep this row until rib measures 7.5cm (3in) from cast-on edge.

Next row Rib 2, make 1, (rib 6[4], make 1)

CHART 1

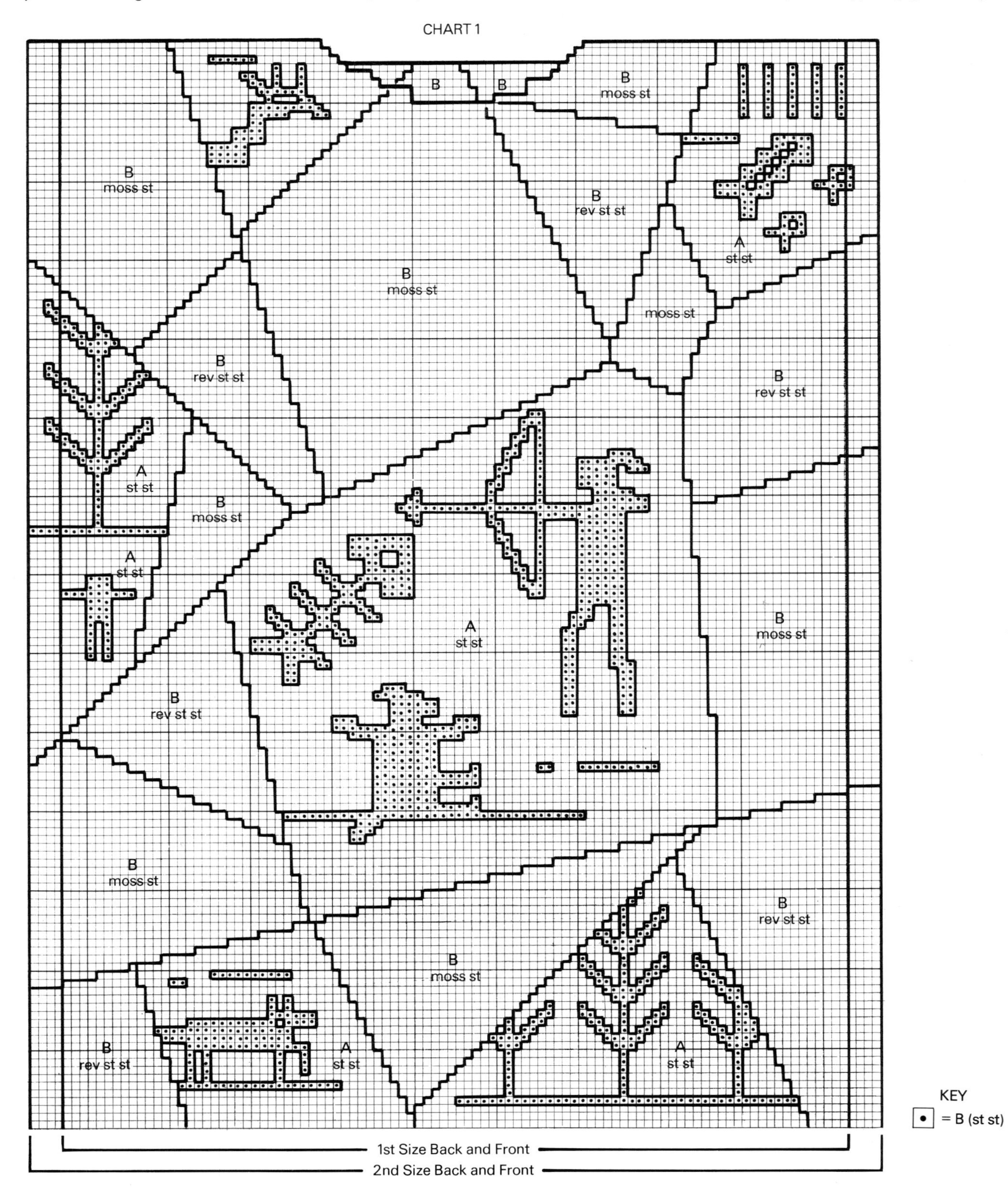

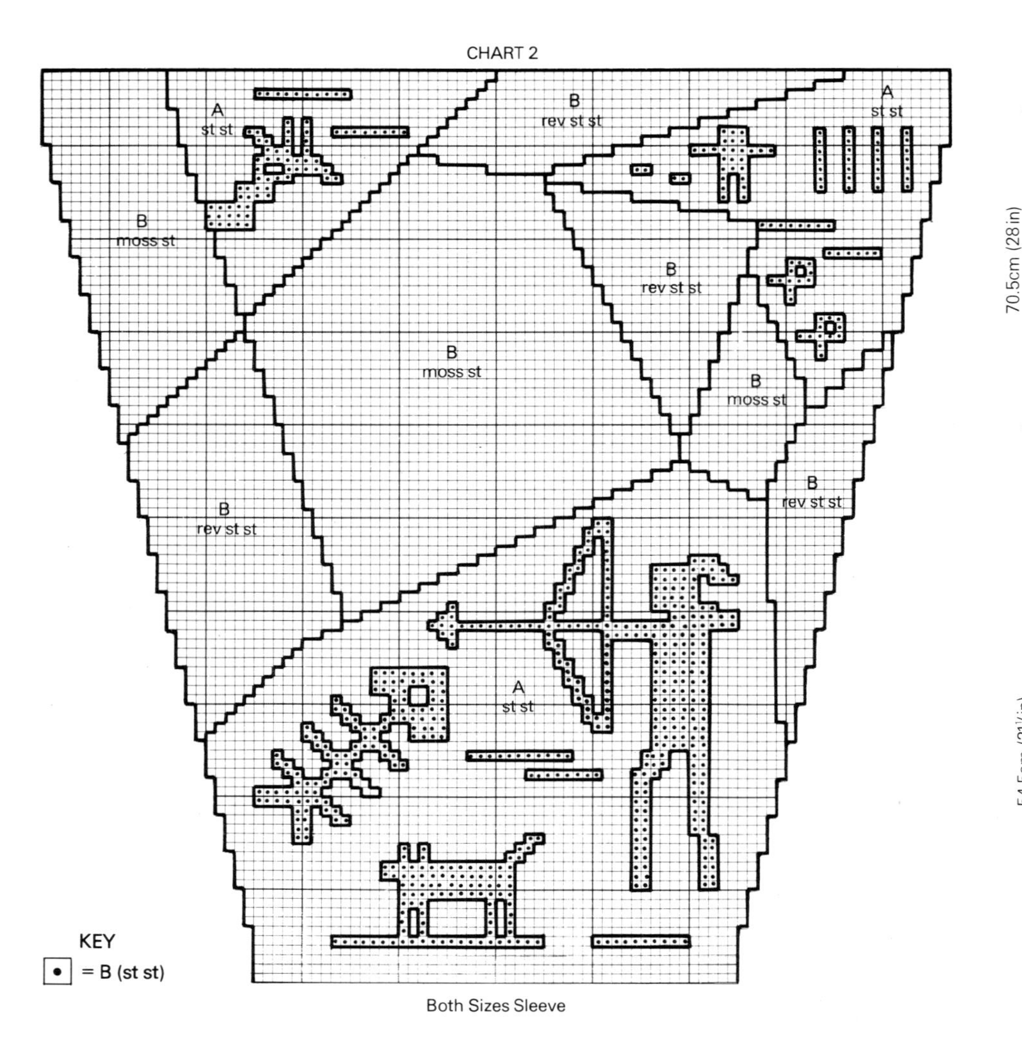

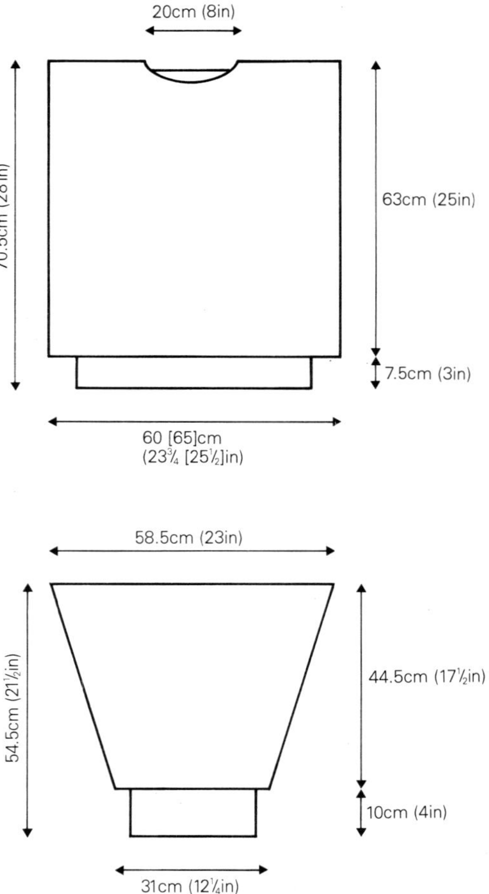

to last 2[4] sts, rib 2[(rib 1, make 1) twice, rib 2]. 96[104] sts.
Change to 6mm (US10) needles and beg colour patt from chart 1 on page 125, working reversed st st (P on RS rows, K on WS rows) and moss st (K1, P1 on RS rows, K1, P1 on WS rows) as indicated on chart and using small separate balls of yarn for each colour area, twisting yarns tog on WS at colour joins to avoid holes. **
Cont in patt until 135 rows in chart patt have been worked, ending with a RS row.

Divide for neck

Next row Patt 34[38] sts, turn, leaving rem sts on a spare needle and cont on these sts only for first side of neck.
Dec 1 st at neck edge on next 2 rows. 32[36] sts.
Cast off.
With WS of work facing, return to sts on spare needle, sl centre 28 sts on to a stitch holder, rejoin yarn to next st, patt to end. 34[38] sts.
Complete second side of neck to match first side, reversing shapings.

FRONT

Work as given for back to **.
Cont in patt until 130 rows in chart patt have been worked, ending with a WS row.

Divide for neck

Next row Patt 43[47] sts, turn, leaving rem sts on a spare needle and cont on these sts only for first side of neck.
Cast off 4 sts at beg of next row and 3 sts at beg of foll alt row.
Now dec 1 st at neck edge on next 4 rows.
Cast off rem 32[36] sts.
With RS of work facing, return to sts on spare needle, sl centre 10 sts on to a stitch holder, rejoin yarn to next st, patt to end. 43[47] sts.
Work 1 row.
Complete second side of neck to match first side, reversing shapings.
Cast off.

SLEEVES

Using 4½mm (US7) needles and yarn A, cast on 44 sts.
Work 10cm (4in) in twisted rib as given for back.
Next row Rib 5, make 1, (rib 7, make 1) 5 times, rib 4. 50 sts.
Change to 6mm (US10) needles and beg colour patt from chart 2, *at the same time* inc 1 st at each end of 7th and every foll 4th row until there are 94 sts.
Work 7 rows straight.
Cast off loosely and evenly.

TO MAKE UP

Join right shoulder using a backstitch seam.

Neckband

With RS of work facing, using 4½mm (US7) needles and yarn A, K up 16 sts down left front neck, K 10 sts from front neck stitch holder, K up 16 sts up right front neck, 3 sts down right back neck, K 28 sts from back neck stitch holder and K up 3 sts up left back neck. 76 sts.
Work 5cm (2in) in twisted rib as given for back.
Cast off loosely and evenly in rib.

Embroidery

Using yarn C, work large cross stitches along all joins between 'patches' of st st, reversed st st and moss st on back, front and sleeves, centring the stitches on the joining lines.
Join left shoulder and neckband seam.
Place markers 28cm (11in) down from shoulder seams on back and front. Set in sleeves between markers.
Fold neckband in half on to WS and catch down.
Join side and sleeve seams.
Work cross stitches in C around neckband base and along all seam lines.

Right *Artwork's Patchwork Sweater – irregular patches of moss stitch, stocking stitch and reversed stocking stitch with scattered motifs, finished with bold cross-stitched 'joins'.*

CHRISTOPHER FISCHER

Christopher Fischer was first attracted to the knitwear business while still a teenager because he thought knitting would be 'nice and clean to deal with'. Then he forgot all about it and did a degree in law and accountancy. The interest was reawakened when he visited a Spanish knitwear factory with his father in 1975. He liked what he saw and soon discovered that they were only selling this unusual work in Barcelona. Immediately he set out to find a wider European market, having first got the factory to adjust some of the designs to his specifications. Then he bought a car and set off with his samples to knock on doors around Germany, Holland and Belgium. It was a success, and soon he had an office in Brussels and an address book full of customers.

A search for Fair Isle sweaters brought him back to Britain where eventually he set up a business to design and produce as well as market knitwear. The Christopher Fischer company has grown fast since the start in 1983 and now has a small factory in Scotland where his knitwear is hand-framed – knitted on domestic style machines – as well as a workshop in London where all the design work and the finishing are undertaken.

Chris, and his co-director Sue Warmsley, have developed a style that progresses from season to season. Adjustments to cut, colour and to yarn are all employed to achieve a modern fashion element on classic shapes, and to accommodate an unfolding portfolio of ideas rather than present a completely new approach each year. Law and accountancy have proved useful, but the pleasure comes from the shelves of clean and fresh sweaters that surround Chris's desk. His first instincts were right.

★ ★ ★

LUMBERJACK

Winter

KITS A yarn kit is available for this design. *See page 160 for details.*

SIZE

To fit one size up to 106cm (42in) bust/chest

MATERIALS

275g Fine Fleck Yarn in black 62 (A); 175g in midnight 54 (C); 150g each in oatmeal 1 (B) and silver 64 (F); 75g in royal 56 (G); 50g in green 90 (J); 25g in orange 17 (D)
25g Lightweight Double Knitting each in natural 84 (E), peony 43 (H), flame 25 (L)
Equivalent yarn double knitting
1 pair each 3¼mm (US3) and 4½mm (US7) needles
Cable needle
3 buttons

NOTE When working yarns A, B, C, D, F, G, J, use 2 strands together.

TENSION

24 sts and 26 rows to 10cm (4in) over patt on 4½mm (US7) needles.

SPECIAL ABBREVIATIONS

C6b (cable 6 back) – sl next 3 sts on to a cable needle and hold at back of work, K3, then K3 from cable needle.
Tw2b (twist 2 back) – K tbl second st on left-hand needle, then K tbl first st, sl both sts off needle at the same time.

BACK

Using 3¼mm (US3) needles and yarn G, cast on 124 sts.
Work 29 rows in K1, P1 rib as foll: 3 rows in G, 10 rows in A, 4 rows in J, 12 rows in A.
Next row With A, rib 1 (make 1, rib 11) 11 times, make 1, rib 2. 136 sts.
Change to 4½mm (US7) needles and beg colour patt from chart 1 on pages 131-32; work in st st unless otherwise indicated, weaving contrast yarns into back of work (but twist yarns tog on either side of twists and cables to avoid holes) as foll:
1st row (RS) K (1J, 1E) 6 times, (2J, 2E) 3 times, 6G, (1J, 1E) 12 times, 2H, (2J, 2E) 3 times, (1J, 1E) 6 times, 2L, (1J, 1E) 6 times, (2J, 2E) 3 times, 6J (1J, 1E) 12 times.
2nd row P(1F, 1E) 12 times, 6J, (2E, 2F) 3 times, (1F, 1E) 6 times, 2L, (1F, 1E) 6 times, (2E, 2F) 3 times, 2H, (1F, 1E) 12 times, 6G, (2E, 2F) 3 times, (1F, 1E) 6 times.
These 2 rows establish the chart patt.
Cont in patt, foll colour sequence table for changes in contrast colours, *at the same time* inc 1 st at each end of next and foll 3rd, 4th, 4th, 5th, 5th, 6th, 6th rows. 152 sts.
Now work 28 rows straight, ending with a WS row.
Shape armholes
Keeping patt correct, cast off 2 sts at beg of next 2 rows and dec 1 st at each end of foll 11 rows. 126 sts. **
Work 63 rows straight, ending with a WS row.
Shape shoulders
Cast off 43 sts at beg of next 2 rows.
Cast off rem 40 sts.

FRONT

Work as given for back to **
Work 19 rows straight, ending with a WS row.
Divide for neck
Next row Patt 60 sts, turn, leaving rem sts on a spare needle and cont on these sts only for first side of neck.
Work 26 rows straight, ending at neck edge. Cast off 7 sts at beg of next row, then dec 1 st at neck edge on foll 10 rows. 43 sts.
Now work straight until front matches back to shoulder.
Cast off.
With RS of work facing, return to sts on spare needle, cast off 6 sts, patt to end. 60 sts.
Work 27 rows straight, ending at neck edge. Complete to match first side of neck, reversing shapings.

Right *Christopher Fischer's Lumberjack – a marvellously subtle, tartany mixture of wool checks and cables.*

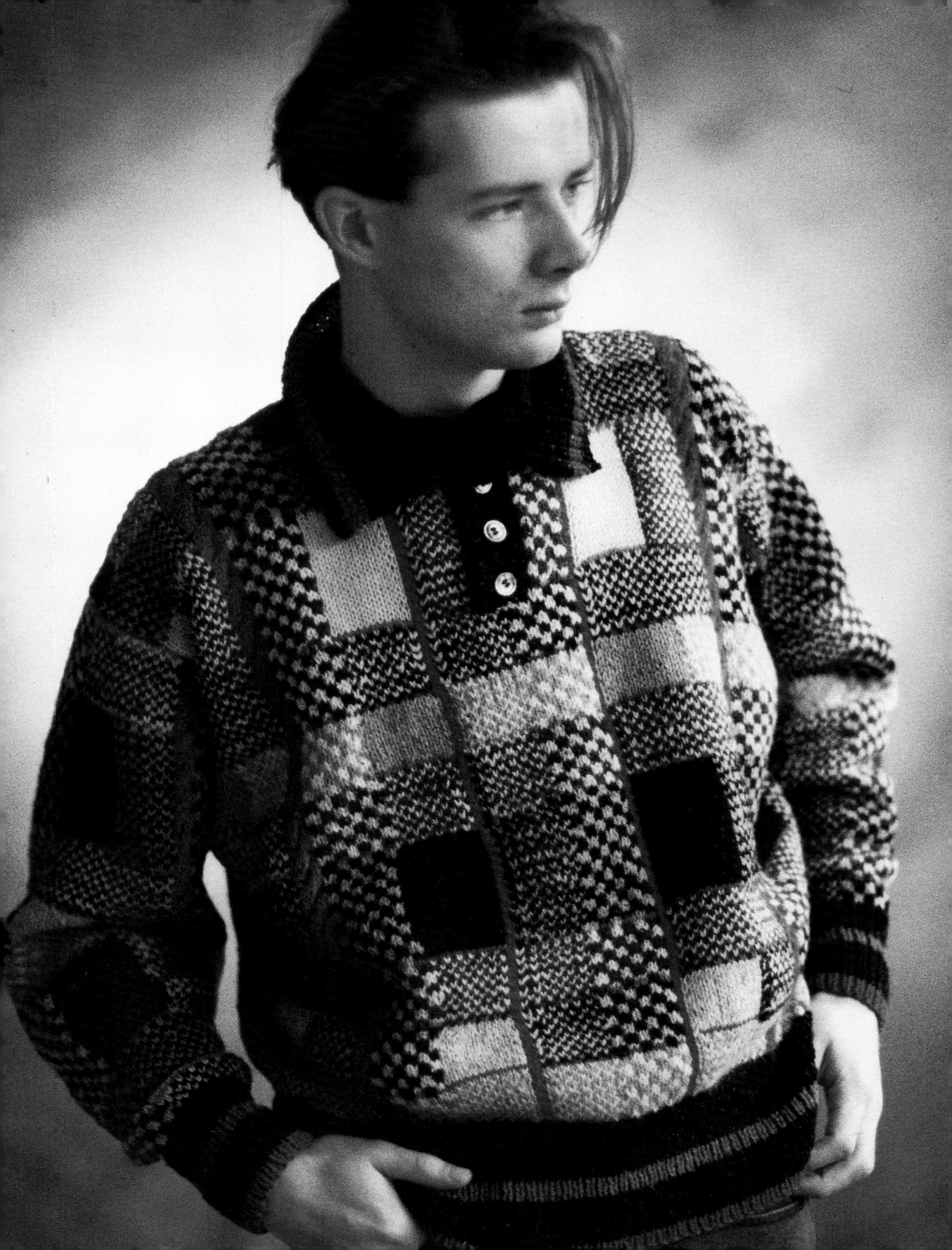

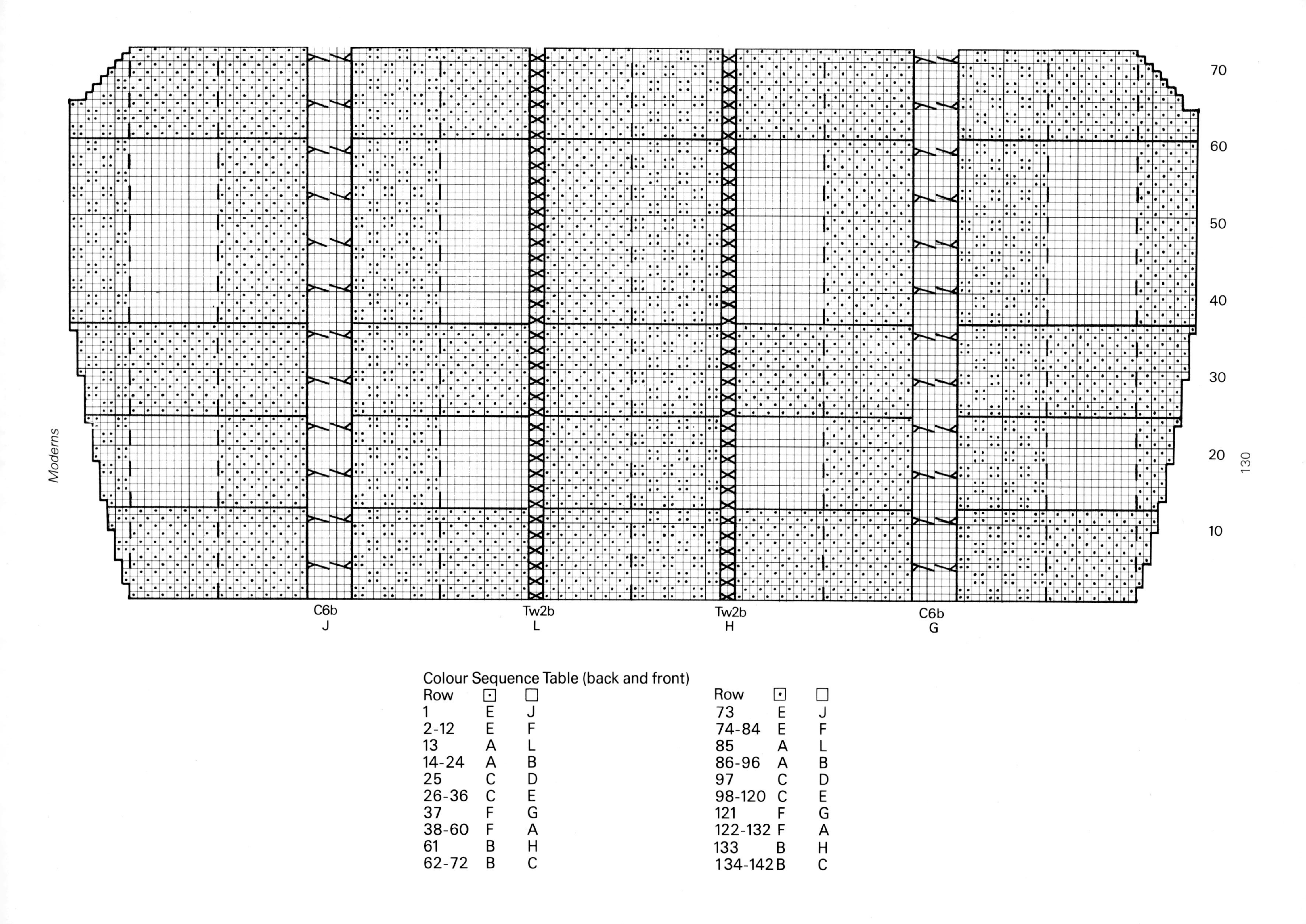

Colour Sequence Table (back and front)

Row	⊡	□
1	E	J
2-12	E	F
13	A	L
14-24	A	B
25	C	D
26-36	C	E
37	F	G
38-60	F	A
61	B	H
62-72	B	C

Row	⊡	□
73	E	J
74-84	E	F
85	A	L
86-96	A	B
97	C	D
98-120	C	E
121	F	G
122-132	F	A
133	B	H
134-142	B	C

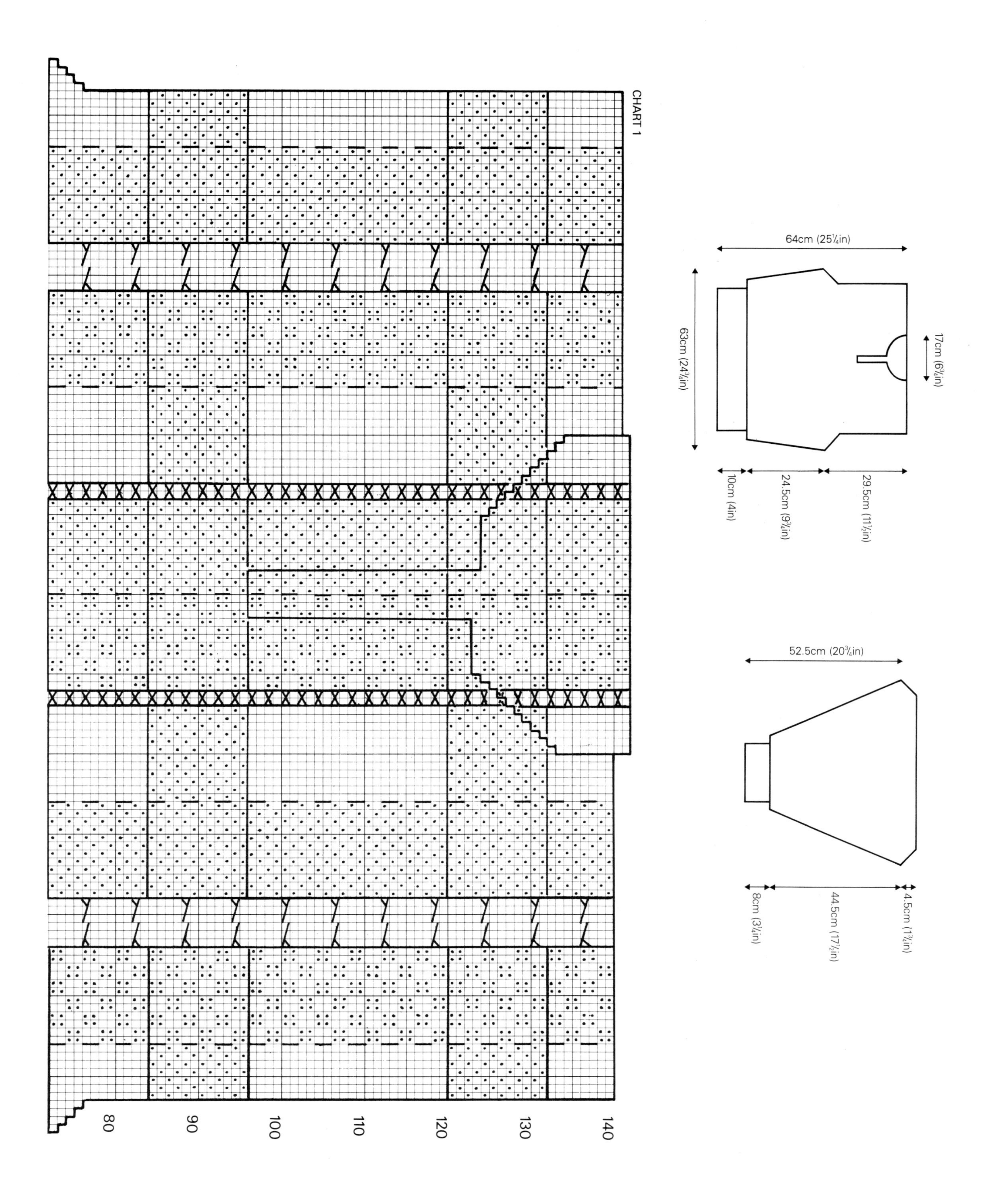
CHART 1
80
90
100
110
120
130
140
64cm (25¼in)
63cm (24¾in)
17cm (6¾in)
10cm (4in)
24.5cm (9¾in)
29.5cm (11½in)
52.5cm (20¾in)
8cm (3¼in)
44.5cm (17½in)
4.5cm (1¾in)

SLEEVES

Using 3¼mm (US3) needles and yarn G, cast on 46 sts.
Work 25 rows in K1, P1 rib as foll: 3 rows in G, 10 rows in A, 4 rows in J, 8 rows in A.
Next row With A, rib 4, (make 1, rib 3) 13 times, make 1, rib 3. 60 sts.
Change to 4½mm (US7) needles and beg colour patt from chart 2 foll colour sequence table for changes in contrast colours, *at the same time* inc 1 st at each end of 3rd and every foll alt row until there are 112 sts, then of every foll 3rd row until there are 152 sts. Work 3 rows straight, ending with a WS row.

Shape top

Cast off 2 sts at beg of next 2 rows, then dec 1 st at each end of foll 10 rows. 128 sts.
Cast off loosely and evenly.

TO MAKE UP

Button band

With RS of work facing, using 3¼mm (US3) needles and yarn A, K up 27 sts evenly up right side neck opening.
Work 11 rows in K1, P1 rib.
Cast off in rib.

Buttonhole band

On left side neck opening, work as for button band, making buttonholes on 5th and 6th rows as foll:
5th row Rib 2, (cast off 2 sts, rib 8 including st used to cast off) twice, cast off 2 sts, rib to end.
6th row Rib to end, casting on 2 sts over those cast off in previous row.
Lap buttonhole band over button band and sew ends to cast-off sts at centre front.
Join both shoulders with backstitch seams.

Collar

With RS of work facing, using 3¼mm (US3) needles and yarn A, beg halfway across button band, K up 28 sts up right side front neck, 45 sts across back neck and 28 sts down left side front neck to halfway across buttonhole band. 101 sts.
1st row K2, (P1, K1) to last st, K1.
2nd row K1, (P1, K1) to end.
Rep these 2 rows. Now work in fisherman's rib as foll:
1st row K to end.
2nd row K1, (P1, K next st in row below) to last 2 sts, P1, K1.
Rep these 2 rows 6 times more in A, 3 times more in G, then 3 times more in A.
Cast off evenly in rib.
Set in sleeves. Join side and sleeve seams.
Sew on buttons.

Colour Sequence Table (sleeves)

ROW	⊡	☐	ROW	⊡	☐
1-4	A	B	66-76	A	B
5	C	D	77	C	D
6-16	C	E	78-88	C	E
17	F	G	89	F	G
18-28	F	A	90-112	F	A
29	B	H	113	B	H
30-52	B	C	114-124	B	C
53	E	J	125	E	J
54-64	E	F	126-128	E	F
65	A	L			

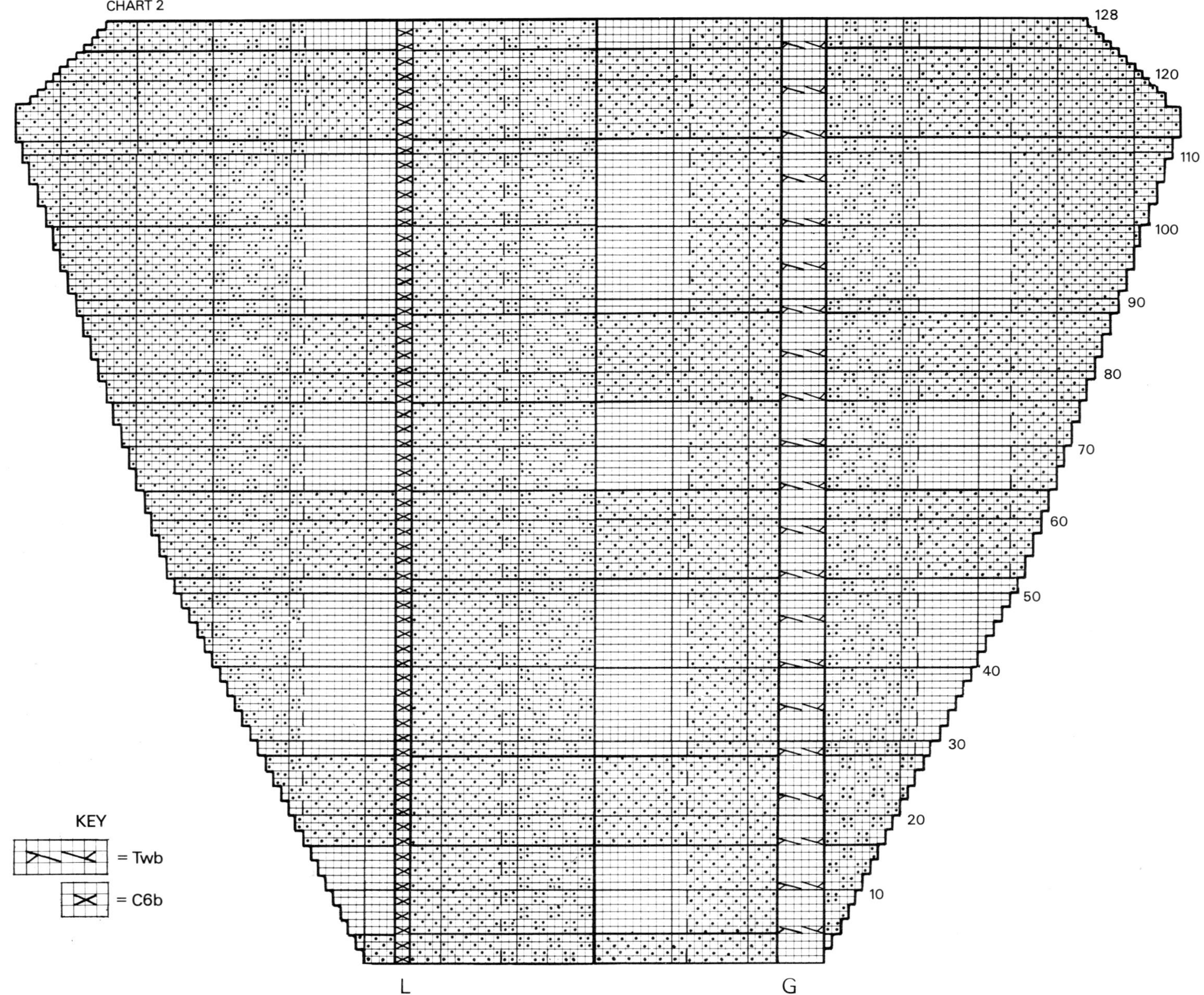

Christopher Fischer

★ ★ ★

SUN-BLEACHED

Summer

SIZE

To fit one size up to 96cm (38in) bust/chest

MATERIALS

250g Handknit Double Knitting Cotton in mint 270 (A); 150g each in sky blue 264 (D) and ecru 251 (E); 50g each in lemon 265 (F), flesh 268 (G), peacock 259 (J) and lilac 269 (L)
150g Salad Days Knobbly Cotton each in linen 562 (B) and white 560 (H)
50g Sea Breeze Soft Cotton in caramel 524 (C)
Equivalent yarn double knitting
1 pair each 3¼mm (US3) and 4½mm (US7) needles
Cable needle

NOTE When working yarns B, C, and H, use 2 strands together.

TENSION

22 sts and 22 rows to 10cm (4in) over patt on 4½mm (US7) needles.

SPECIAL ABBREVIATIONS

C6b (cable 6 back) – sl next 3 sts on to a cable needle and hold at back of work, K3, then K3 from cable needle.
Tw2b (twist 2 back) – K tbl second st on left-hand needle, then K tbl first st, sl both sts off needle at the same time.

BACK

Using 3¼mm (US3) needles and yarn A, cast on 90 sts.
Work 4cm (1½in) in K2, P2 rib.
Next row Rib 4, (make 1, rib 9) 9 times, make 1, rib 5. 100 sts.
Change to 4½mm (US7) needles and beg colour patt from chart on page 133 at 21st row, work in st st unless otherwise indicated, weaving contrast yarns into back of work (but twist yarns tog on either side of cables and twists to avoid holes) as foll:
21st row (RS) K9D, (2B, 2D) twice, 2B, 6F, (1D, 1B) 6 times, 12D, Tw2b in J, (2D, 2B) 3 times, (1D, 1B) 6 times, 6L, 14D, 2B, 3D.
22nd row P3D, 2B, 14D, 6L, (1D, 1B) 6 times, (2B, 2D) 3 times, 2J, 12D, (1D, 1B) 6 time, 6F, (2B, 2D) 3 times, 7D.
These 2 rows establish the chart patt.
Cont in patt foll colour sequence table for changes in contrast colours, *at the same time* inc 1 st at each end of foll 3rd row and of every foll 4th row until there are 132 sts, ending with a WS row.
Shape shoulders
Keeping patt correct, cast off 44 sts at beg of next 2 rows.
Cast off rem 44 sts.

FRONT

Work as given for back until front measures 14 rows less than back to shoulder, ending with a WS row.
Divide for neck
Next row Patt 58 sts, turn, leaving rem sts on a spare needle and cont on these sts only for first side of neck.
Cast off 3 sts at neck edge on next and foll alt row. 52 sts.
Dec 1 st at neck edge on next 8 rows. 44 sts.
Work 2 rows straight.
Shape shoulder
Cast off.
With RS of work facing, return to sts on spare needle, rejoin yarn to next st, cast off 16 sts, patt to end.
Work 1 row.
Complete second side of neck to match first, reversing shapings.

SLEEVES

Using 3¼mm (US3) needles and yarn A, cast on 46 sts.
Work 2.5cm (1in) in K2, P2 rib, ending with a WS row.
Next row Rib 2, (make 1, rib 14) 3 times, make 1, rib 2. 50 sts.
Change to 4½mm (US7) needles and beg colour patt from chart at 1st row foll colour sequence table for changes in contrast colours, *at the same time* inc 1 st at each end of 3rd and every foll alt row until there are 86 sts, then at each end of every foll 3rd row until there are 122 sts.
Work 5 rows straight.
Cast off loosely and evenly.

TO MAKE UP

Join right shoulder using a backstitch seam.
Neckband
With RS of work facing, using 3¼mm (US3) needles and yarn A, K up 20 sts down left side of front neck, 20 sts across centre front, 20 sts up right side front neck and 43 sts across centre back. 103 sts.
Next row (P1, K1) to last st, P1.
Next row K to end.
Next row (P1, K next st in row below) to last st, P1.
Rep last 2 rows 7 times more.
Cast off evenly in rib.
Join left shoulder and neckband seam.
Mark 28cm (11in) down from shoulders on back and front.
Set in sleeves between markers.
Join side and sleeve seams.

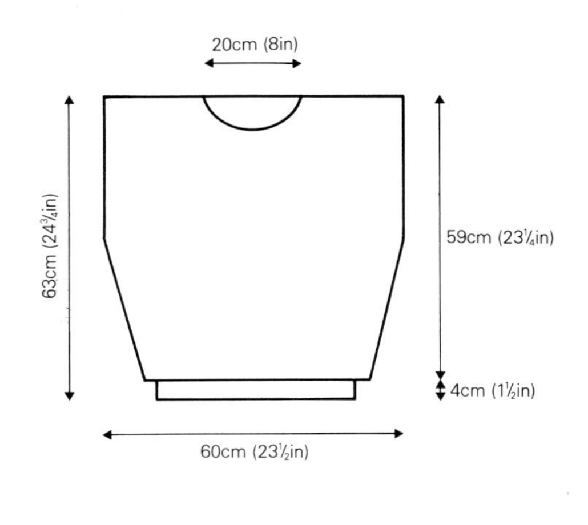

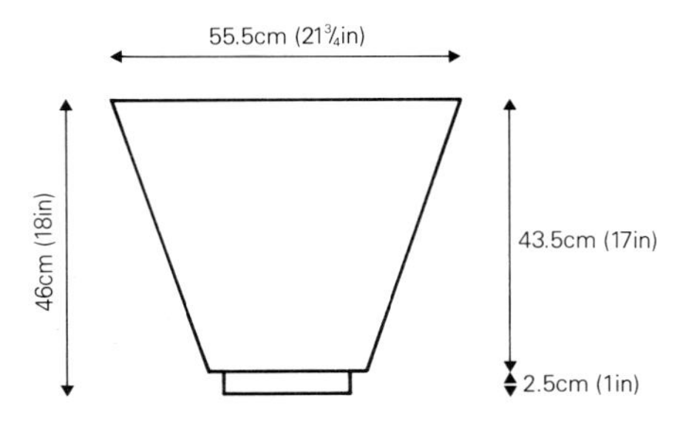

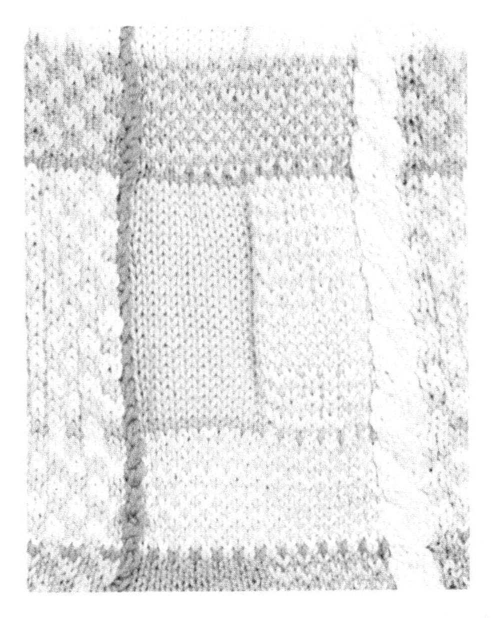

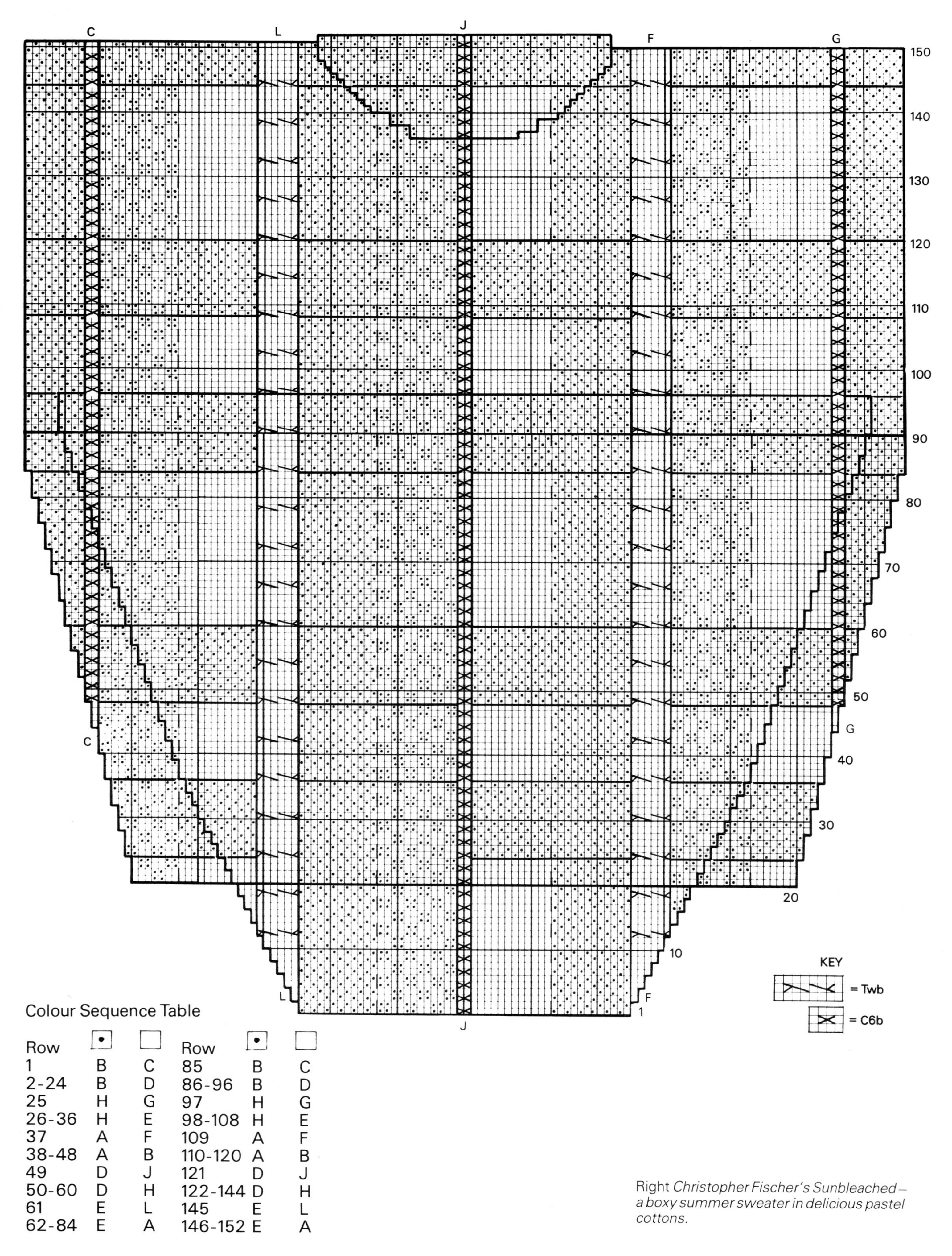

Colour Sequence Table

Row	•	☐	Row	•	☐
1	B	C	85	B	C
2-24	B	D	86-96	B	D
25	H	G	97	H	G
26-36	H	E	98-108	H	E
37	A	F	109	A	F
38-48	A	B	110-120	A	B
49	D	J	121	D	J
50-60	D	H	122-144	D	H
61	E	L	145	E	L
62-84	E	A	146-152	E	A

Right *Christopher Fischer's Sunbleached – a boxy summer sweater in delicious pastel cottons.*

SARAH DALLAS

In a steep, cobbled, back street of Colne, Lancashire, is an old industrial building where fleeces were once sorted. Slightly reminiscent of a Methodist chapel, it towers above the small terraced houses that surround it. There is no sign or number outside, but step through the anonymous door and you enter a sophisticated world of pale grey carpet and black matt furniture that sets off a striking collection of colourful and elegant knitwear. This is Sarah Dallas's showroom and studio. Wool in its raw state, and now in refined and finished form, has always been at home here.

However, the Sarah Dallas look owes little to knitting traditions – smooth surfaces and blocks and stripes of bold colours are the fabric she creates for the very modern and disarmingly simple lines and elegant cut that she employs for her outfits.

She put her first collection together in 1976 while studying textiles at the Royal College. Some of the pieces were included in the Fashion Show; an honour at a time when knitwear was still regarded as a poor relation to fashion. Her partner in life and in work, John Bolen, became involved at this point; he helped her to knit these first pieces when she got behind with her collection for graduation.

John never became the furniture designer he was trained to be, for Sarah soon needed help again. Fortunately, it has been a happy and successful collaboration where he runs the business and she designs the knitwear. When they needed outknitters, he went back north to help find them, and then they moved there to be near the production. Now their collections are knitted in a factory in Leicestershire – the clean-cut look and perfect finish required for pockets, collars and co-ordinated skirts and trousers is best achieved this way. But they stay on in Lancashire, preferring to be one step removed from the hurly burly of London fashion life. But step off the cobbles and through the unmarked door; imbibe the atmosphere of the studio, and you just might be in Milan.

★ ★

ARGYLL SWEATER

Summer

SIZE

To fit one size up to 101cm (40in) bust/chest

MATERIALS

600g Handknit Double Knitting Cotton in ecru 251 (A); 150g each in black 252 (B) scarlet 255 (C) and clover 266 (D)

Equivalent yarn double knitting

1 pair 4mm (US6) needles

TENSION

20 sts and 28 rows to 10cm (4in) over st st on 4mm (US6) needles.

BACK

Using yarn A, cast on 113 sts.

Work in K1, P1 rib as foll: 1 row in A, 6 rows in B.

Beg colour patt from chart 1 on page 138, working in st st throughout, beg with a K row, and using small separate balls of yarn for each colour area, twisting yarns tog at colour joins to avoid holes, work 1st-138th rows, then 3rd-62nd rows again.

Shape shoulders

Cast off 10 sts at beg of next 8 rows. 33 sts.

Leave these sts on a stitch holder.

FRONT

Using yarn A, cast on 113 sts.

Work in K1, P1 rib as given for back.

Beg colour patt from chart 2 on page 139, working in st st throughout beg with a K row, work 1st-90th rows, then 3rd-90th rows again, ending with a WS row.

Divide for neck

Next row Patt 48 sts, turn, leaving rem sts on a spare needle and cont on these sts only for first side of neck.

Work 1 row.

Dec 1 st at neck edge on next and foll 7 alt rows. 40 sts.

Work 3 rows straight.

Shape shoulder

Cast off 10 sts at beg of next and foll 2 alt rows.

Work 1 row.

Cast off rem 10 sts.

With RS of work facing, return to sts on spare needle, sl centre 17 sts on to a stitch holder, rejoin yarn to next st, patt to end of row.

Complete second side of neck to match first side, reversing shapings, and working 1 more row before shoulder shaping.

SLEEVES

Using yarn A, cast on 51sts.

Work in K1, P1 rib as given for back.

Beg colour patt from chart 3 on page 140, working in st st throughout, beg with a K

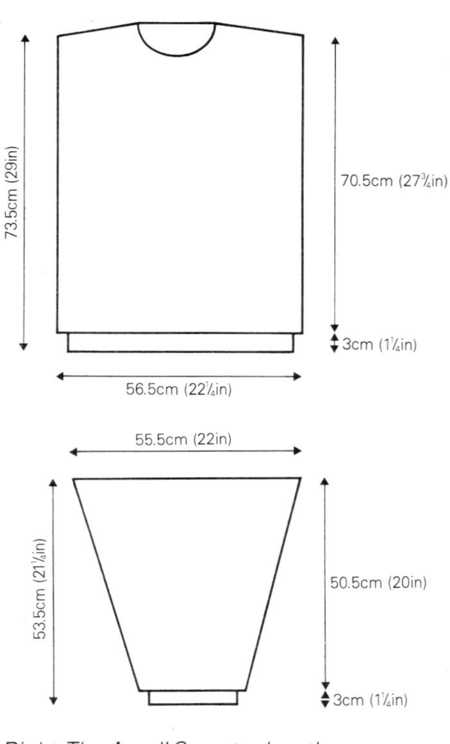

Right *The Argyll Sweater has three different diamond patterns on the back, front and sleeves.*

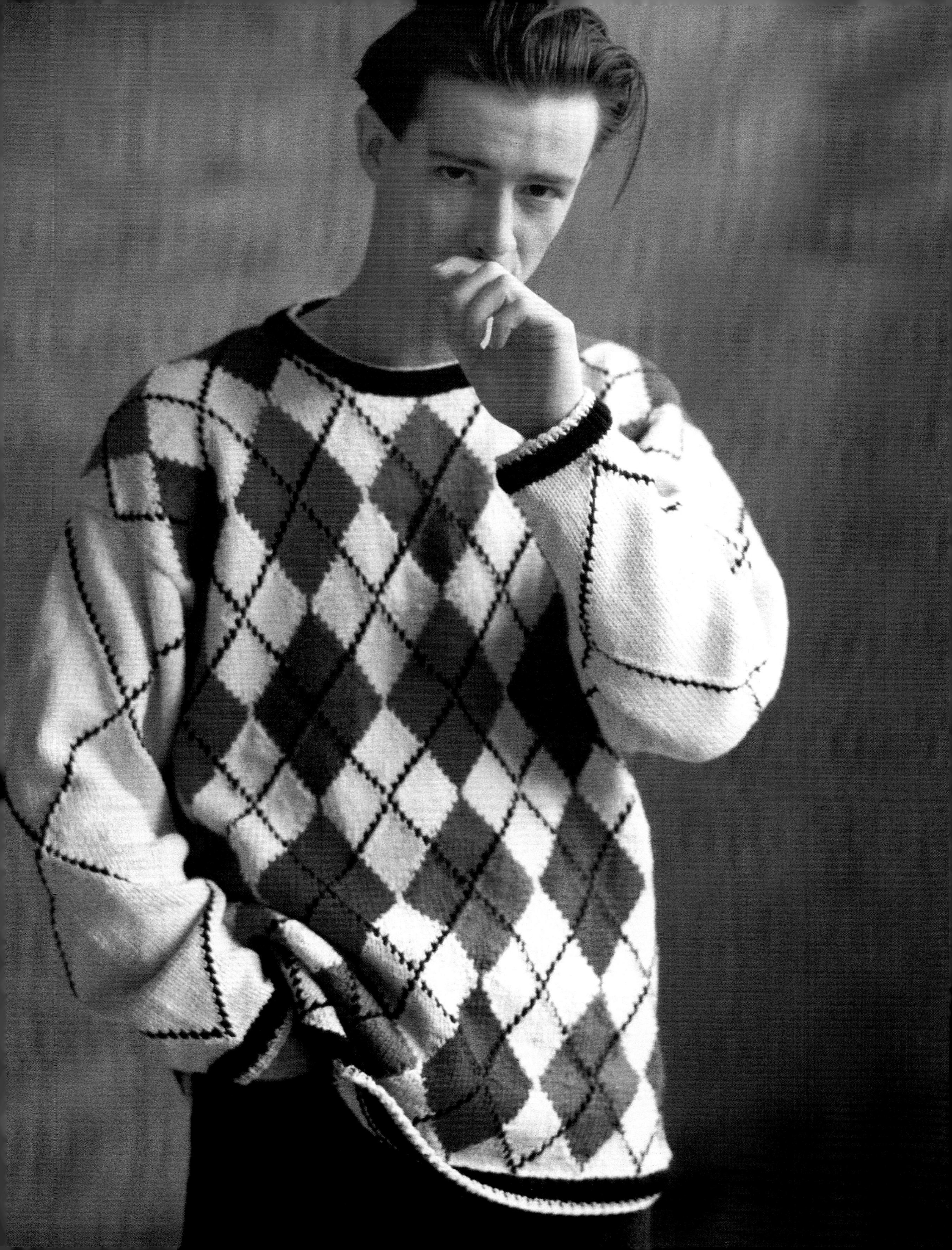

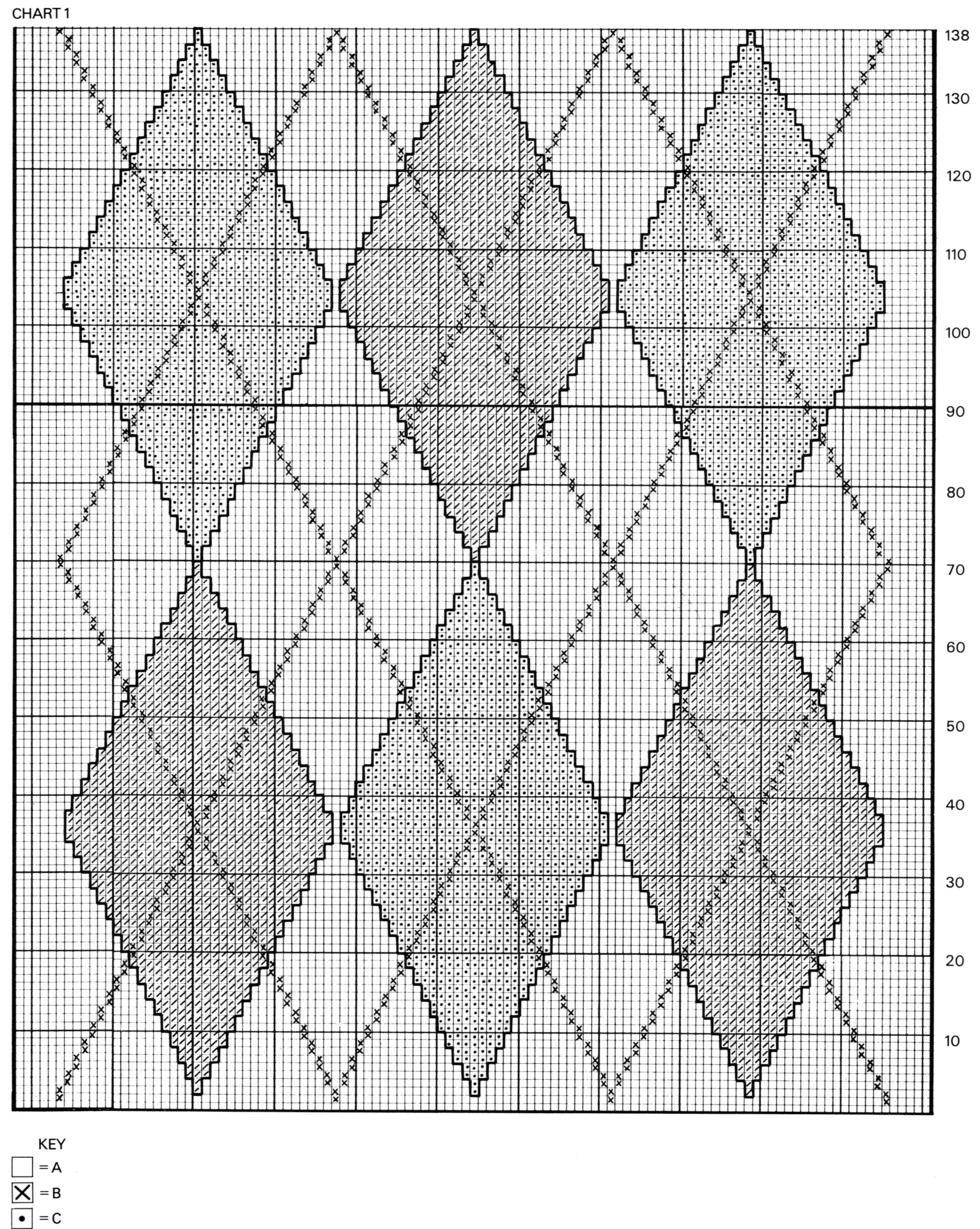
CHART 1
138
130
120
110
100
90
80
70
60
50
40
30
20
10
KEY
= A
= B
= C
= D

CHART 2

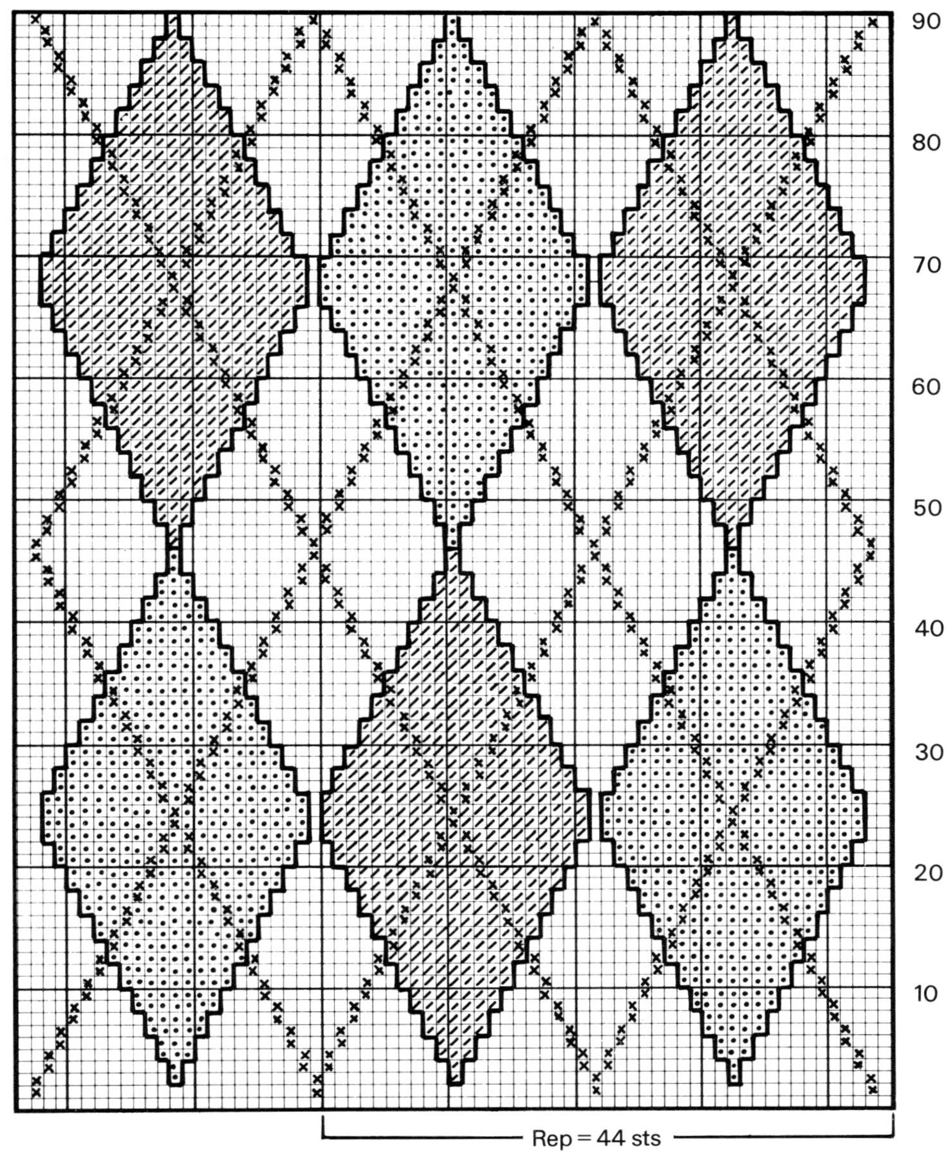

row, *at the same time* inc 1 st at each end of 7th and every foll 4th row until there are 111 sts. Now work straight until 142 rows in all have been worked in chart patt.
Cast off loosely and evenly.

TO MAKE UP

Join right shoulder using a backstitch seam.

Neckband

With RS of work facing, using yarn B, K up 14 sts down left side of neck, K 17 sts from stitch holder at front neck, K up 14 sts up right side of neck and K 33 sts from stitch holder at back neck. 78 sts.
Work 7 rows in K1, P1 rib.
Change to yarn A and cast off evenly in rib.
Join left shoulder and neckband seam.
Place markers 28cm (11in) down from shoulder seams on back and front of sweater.
Set in sleeves between markers.
Join side and sleeve seams.

Above *One of Sarah Dallas' slinky machine-knits.*

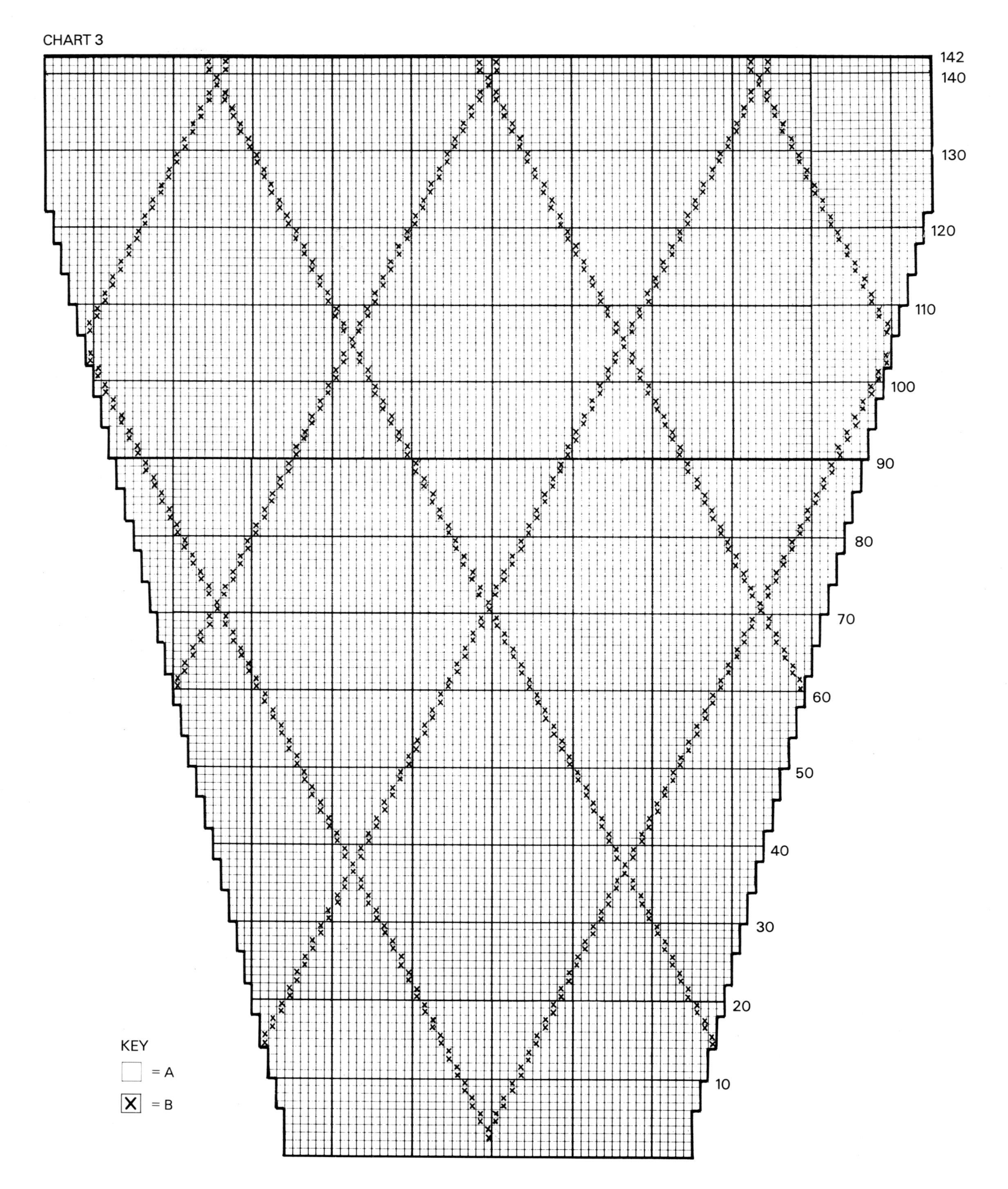

Right *Versatility is the hallmark of Sarah Dallas' work. It encompasses hand- and machine-knitting, intricate colour patterns and, as here, fine textures.*

★

ZIGZAG STRIPE SWEATER

Winter

SIZE
To fit one size up to 101cm (40in) bust/ chest

MATERIALS
275g Lightweight Double Knitting each in dark navy 97 (A) and bottle green 91 (B); 75g in yellow 12 (C); 50g in red 42 (D)
Equivalent yarn double knitting
1 pair 3¾mm (US5) needles

TENSION
23 sts and 33 rows to 10cm (4in) over st st on 3¾mm (US5) needles.

BACK
Using 3¾mm (US5) needles and yarn A, cast on 129 sts.
Work in K1, P1 rib as foll: 1 row in A, 7 rows in B.
Now beg stripe patt.
1st-2nd rows K to end in D.
3rd row K to end in A.
4th-5th rows P to end in D.
6th row P to end in A.
7th-26th rows Work in colour patt from chart between back markers working in st st throughout, beg with a K row, using small separate balls of yarn for each colour area, twisting yarns tog at colour joins to avoid holes.
27th-30th rows As 3rd-6th rows.
31st-32nd rows K to end in D.
** **33rd-55th rows** With B, work in st st, beg with a K row.
56th-57th rows P to end in C.
58th row K to end in C.
59th-81st rows With A, work in st st beg with a K row.
82nd-84th rows As 56th-58th rows. **
85th-188th rows Rep from ** to ** twice more.
189th-214th rows As 33rd-58th rows.
215th-230th rows With A, work in st st, beg with a K row.
Shape shoulders
With A, cont in st st, cast off 11 sts at beg of next 6 rows and 12 sts at beg of foll 2 rows. 39 sts.
Leave these sts on a stitch holder.

FRONT
Work as given for back until 201 rows in stripe patt have been completed, ending with a RS row.
Divide for neck
Next row Patt 57 sts, turn, leaving rem sts on a spare needle and cont on these sts only for first side of neck.
Work 1 row.
Dec 1 st at neck edge on next and foll 11 alt rows. 45 sts.
Work 5 rows straight, ending at armhole edge.
Shape shoulder
Cast off 11 sts at beg of next and foll 2 alt rows. 12 sts.
Work 1 row.
Cast off.
With WS of work facing return to sts on spare needle, sl centre 15 sts on to a stitch holder, rejoin yarn to next st, patt to end. 57 sts.
Complete second side of neck to match first side, reversing shapings and working 1 less row before shoulder shaping.

SLEEVES
Using 3¾mm (US5) needles and yarn A, cast on 57 sts.
Work in K1, P1 rib as given for back.
Now work in stripe patt as for back working chart between sleeve markers, *at the same time* inc 1 st at each end of 5th and every foll 4th row until there are 127 sts.
Now work straight until 160 rows in all have been completed in stripe patt.
Cast off loosely and evenly.

TO MAKE UP
Join right shoulder using a backstitch seam.
Neckband
With RS of work facing, using 3¾mm (US5) needles and yarn B, K up 18 sts down left side of neck, K 15 sts from stitch holder at front neck, K up 18 sts up right side of back neck and K 39 sts from stitch holder at back neck. 90 sts.
Work 8 rows in K1, P1 rib.
Change to yarn A.

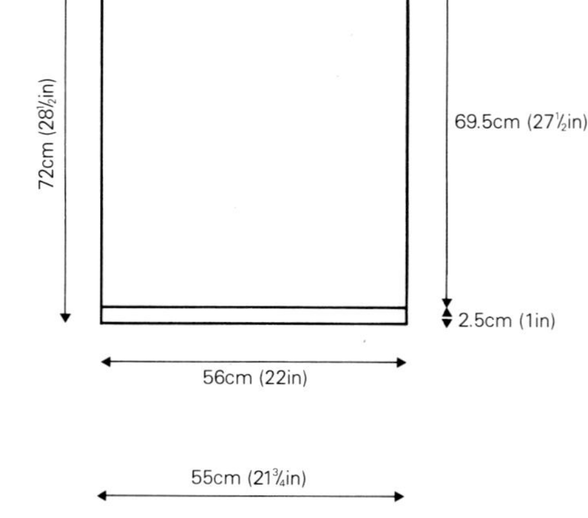

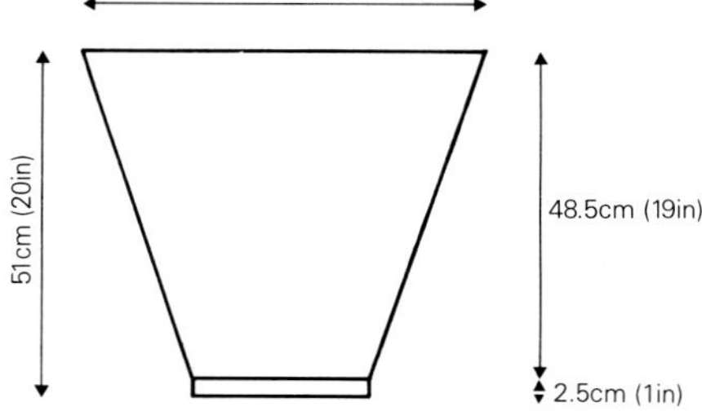

Cast off evenly in rib.
Join left shoulder and neckband seam.
Place markers 27.5cm (10¾in) below shoulder seams on back and front.
Set in sleeves between markers.
Join side and sleeve seams.

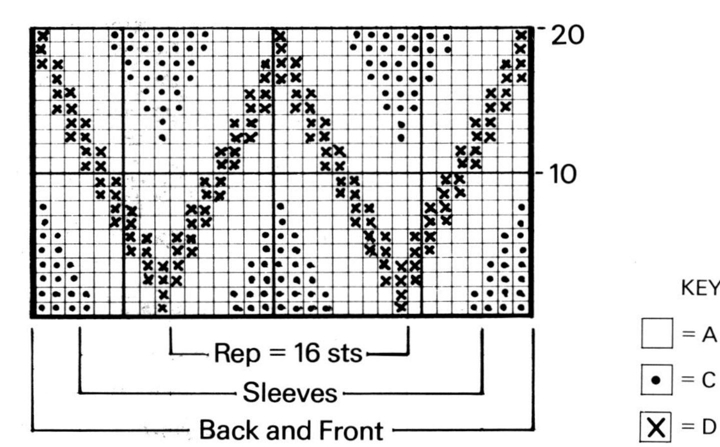

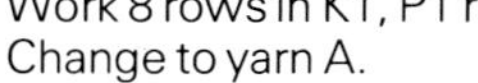

KEY

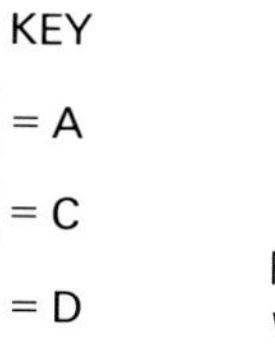

Right *Sarah Dallas' Zigzag Stripe Sweater is very easy and quick to knit.*

ANGELA KING

Angela King's enthusiasm for knitting is infectious. She has the common touch, and her message comes across loud and clear in the books, magazines and newspapers that she fills with ideas for stylish knits. Big needles, quick results and instant fashion may be her trademark, but underlying this is a boundless versatility. Like someone who can play anything you ask on the piano and instantly catch the mood, she can look at a magazine and know just what those particular readers will want next month. Fulfilling the need makes her an ideal magazine knitting designer, a role she won through her engaging personality – her enormous smile and direct remarks make an irresistible combination – and kept through her talent. Originally inspired by French wool shops that she frequented during an extended stay in France as a teenager, she has hardly put her needles down since. The French buy yarns first, and then think about knitting something to suit it. The method not only gave her confidence, but is fundamental to her approach. Whether she is using silk or string, she starts with the materials and designs a pattern to make good use of its particular qualities resulting in fully integrated ideas that work well for her clients. Whilst being a popular designer, there is no hint that she is compromising her style. She does not set out to change the world but to teach, encourage and enthuse people to get knitting and make something they will want to wear.

From her sitting room in Hampstead she creates a following through her ideas and patterns. Angela is a born communicator, and it is not surprising that her books about knitting have been successful for it is difficult to be idle once you have dipped in. She can create designs that really are easy to achieve, and those abandoned knitting projects at the back of the cupboard are unlikely to have come from the Angela King portfolio.

★ ★ ★

ARABESQUE SWEATER

Summer

SIZES

To fit 86-91[96-101]cm (34-36[38-40]in) bust

MATERIALS

650[700]g Mercerised Cotton in natural 301

Equivalent yarn four-ply

1 pair each 2¾mm (US1) and 3mm (US2) needles

TENSION

1 patt rep (over 22 sts and 14 rows) measures 7.5cm (3in) wide by 3.6cm (1¼in) deep on 3mm (US2) needles.

SPECIAL NOTE

Work cluster lace patt as foll:

1st row (RS) K1, *yo, (K1, P3) 5 times, K1, yo, K1; rep from * to end.

2nd row P3, *(K3, P1) 4 times, K3, P5; rep from * ending last rep P3.

3rd row K1, *yo, K1, yo, (K1, P3) 5 times, (K1, yo) twice, K1; rep from * to end.

4th row P5, *(K3, P1) 4 times, K3, P9; rep from * ending last rep P5.

5th row K1, *yo, K1, yo, sl 1, K1, psso, yo, (K1, P2 tog, P1) 5 times, K1, yo, K2 tog, yo, K1, yo, K1; rep from * to end.

6th row P7, *(K2, P1) 4 times, K2, P13; rep from * ending last rep P7.

7th row K1, *K1, (yo, sl 1, K1, psso) twice, yo, (K1, P2) 5 times, K1, yo, (K2 tog, yo) twice, K2; rep from * to end.

8th row P8, *(K2, P1) 4 times, K2, P15; rep from * ending last rep P8.

9th row K2, *(yo, K2 tog) twice, yo, K1, yo, (K1, P2 tog) 5 times, (K1, yo) twice, (sl 1, K1, psso, yo) twice, K3; rep from * ending last rep K2.

10th row P10, *(K1, P1) 4 times, K1, P19; rep from * ending last rep P10.

11th row Sl 1, K1, psso, *(yo, K2 tog) 3 times, K1, yo, (K1, P1) 5 times, K1, yo, K1, (sl 1, K1, psso, yo) 3 times, sl 2, K1, p2sso; rep from * ending last rep K2 tog instead of sl 2, K1, p2sso.

12th row As 10th row.

13th row K1, * (K2 tog, yo) twice, K2 tog, K2, yo, (sl 1, K1, psso) twice, sl 1, K2 tog, psso, (k2 tog) twice, yo, K2, sl 1, K1, psso, (yo, sl 1, K1, psso) twice, K1; rep from *

14th row Ytf, sl 2 sts on to right-hand needle, yb, sl 2 sts on to left-hand needle, ytf, sl 2 on to right-hand needle) to cluster 2 sts, *P7, cluster 5 sts (sl 5 sts instead of 2), P7, cluster 3 sts (sl 3 sts instead of 2); rep from * ending last rep cluster 2 sts instead of cluster 3.

These 14 rows form the patt rep.

BACK

Using 2¾mm (US1) needles, cast on 139[149] sts.

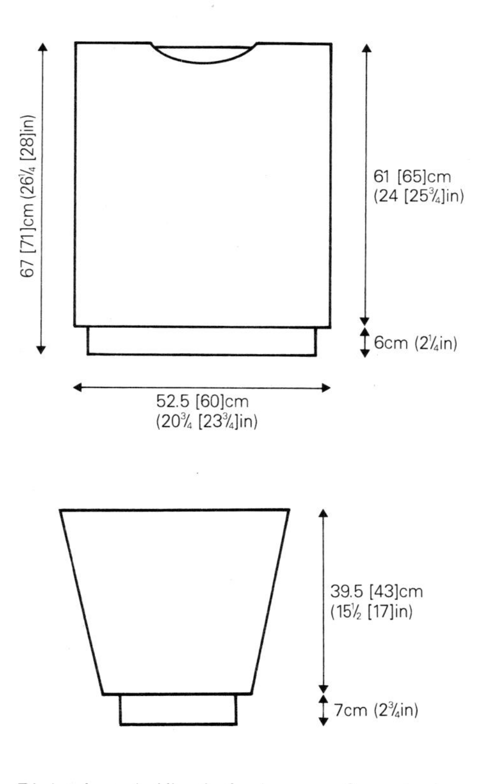

Right *Angela King's Arabesque Sweater is worked in fine cotton in an intricate but beautiful lacy stitch.*

Work 6cm (2¼in) in K1, P1 rib.
Next row (WS) Rib 2[3], (make 1, rib 9) 15[17] times, make 1, rib to end. 155[177] sts.
Change to 3mm (US2) needles and work in cluster lace patt as above. **Work 1st-14th rows 16[17] times, then 1st-6th rows again, ending with a WS row. 190[217] sts.
Divide for neck
Next row Patt 61[73] sts, K2 tog, turn, leaving rem sts on a spare needle and cont on these sts only for first side of neck. 62[74] sts.
Keeping patt correct, dec 1 st at neck edge on foll alt rows [next 7 rows]. 45[56] sts rem on 13th[14th] patt row (when calculating decs for neck shaping take account of incs and decs worked as part of cluster lace patt).
Now work straight until 17th[18th] patt row has been completed.
Cast off.
With RS of work facing return to sts on spare needle, sl centre 64[67] sts on to a stitch holder, rejoin yarn to next st K2 tog, patt to end. 62[74] sts.
Complete second side of neck to match first reversing shapings.

FRONT
Work as given for back to **.
Work 1st-14th rows 14[15] times, ending with a WS row.
Divide for neck
Next row Patt 53[64] sts, K2 tog, turn, leaving rem sts on a spare needle and cont on these sts only for first side of neck.
Keeping patt correct, dec 1 st at neck edge on next 9 rows (58[72] sts rem on 10th patt row).
Now work straight until front matches back to cast-off edge. (45[56] sts rem on 14th patt row).
Cast off.
With RS of work facing, return to sts on spare needle, sl centre 45 sts on to a stitch holder, rejoin yarn to next st, K2 tog, patt to end. 54[55] sts.
Complete second side of neck to match first side, reversing shapings.

SLEEVES
Using 2¾mm (US1) needles, cast on 69[77] sts.
Work 7cm (2¾in) in K1, P1 rib.
Next row (WS) Rib 6[5], (make 1, rib 3[6]) to last 6 sts, make 1, rib 6. 89 sts.
Change to 3mm (US2) needles and work 1st-14th patt rows twice.
Now cont in patt, *at the same time* inc 1 st at each end of next and every foll 4th row until there are 149[159] sts, working the extra sts P3, K1 rib.
Work straight until 11[12] patt reps have been completed.
Cast off loosely and evenly.

TO MAKE UP
Join right shoulder using a backstitch seam.
Neckband
With RS of work facing, using 2¾mm (US1) needles K up 43 sts down left side front neck, work (K2 tog, K1) 15 times across stitch holder at front neck, K up 43 sts up right front neck, 12 sts down right back neck, work K5[1], (K2 tog, K2) 13[16] times, K2 tog, K5 [0] across stitch holder at back neck, and K up 12 sts up left back neck. 190 sts.
Work 11 rows in K1, P1 rib.
Cast off evenly in rib.
Join left shoulder and neckband seam.
Set in sleeves.
Join side and sleeve seams.

Above *Angela King is particularly known for her wonderfully wearable loose sweater shapes.*

★ ★

WHITE KNIGHT

Winter

SIZES

Sweater
To fit 86[91, 96]cm (34[36, 38]in) bust
Skirt
To fit 86[91]cm (36[38]in) hips

MATERIALS

Sweater
600[600, 650]g Designer Double Knitting in white 1 (A); 250[250, 300]g in black 62 (B)
Hood
100g each in white 1 (A) and black 62 (B)
Skirt
400[450]g in white 1
Equivalent yarn double knitting
1 pair each 3¾mm (US5), 4mm (US6) and 4½mm (US7) needles
1 each 4mm (US6) and 4½mm (US7) circular needles
4cm (1½in) wide elastic, length of waist measurement

TENSION

Sweater and hood
22 sts and 24 rows to 10cm (4in) over patt on 4½mm (US7) needles.
Skirt
25 sts and 26 rows to 10cm (4in) over K2, P2 rib (when slightly stretched) on 4mm (US6) needles.

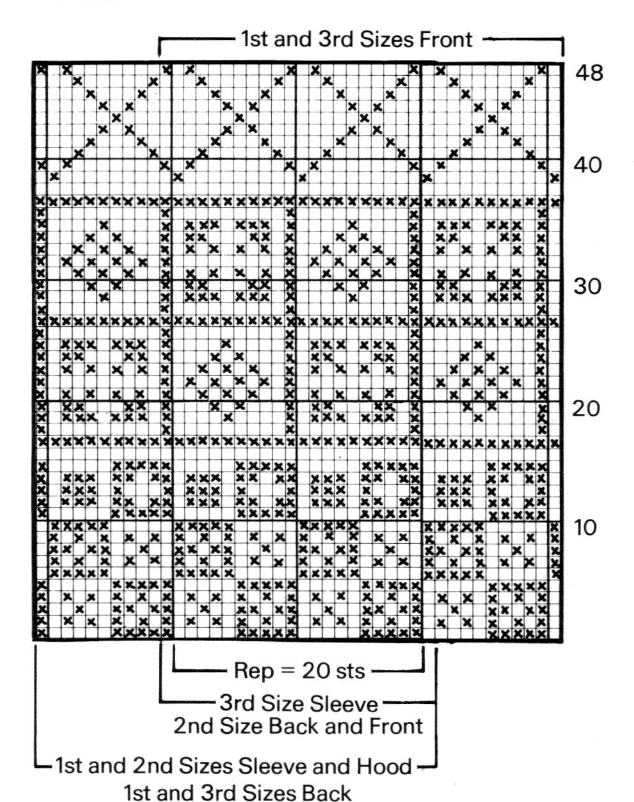

KEY
□ = A
☒ = B

SWEATER

BACK

Using 3¾mm (US5) needles and yarn A, cast on 110[118, 126] sts.
Work 7cm (2¾in) in K2, P2 rib.
Next row (WS) Rib 38[26, 18], (make 1, rib 36[23, 18]) 2[4, 6] times. 112[122, 132] sts.
Change to 4½mm (US7) needles and work 4 rows in st st, beg with a K row. **
Now beg colour patt from chart, work in st st throughout, beg with a K row, weaving contrast yarns into WS and working between back markers, patt 1st-38th rows, then rep 39th-48th rows until back measures 79[80, 81]cm (31[31½, 31¾]in) from cast-on edge ending with a WS row.
Shape shoulders
Cast off 15[18, 20] sts at beg of next 2 rows, and 18[20, 23] sts at beg of foll 2 rows. Leave rem 46 sts on a stitch holder.

FRONT

Work as given for back to **.
Now work in chart patt working between front markers, patt 1st-38th rows, then rep 39th-48th rows until front measures 18 rows less than back to shoulder, ending with a WS row.
Divide for neck
Next row Patt 44[49, 54] sts, turn, leaving rem sts on a spare needle and cont on these sts only for first side of neck.
Dec 1 st at neck edge on every row until 33[38, 43] sts rem.

Right *Angela King's White Knight outfit.*

Work 6 rows, ending at armhole edge.
Shape shoulder
Cast off 15[18, 20] sts at beg of next row.
Work 1 row. Cast off rem 18[20, 23] sts.
With RS of work facing, return to sts on spare needle, sl centre 24 sts on to a stitch holder, rejoin yarn to next st, patt to end.
44[49, 54] sts.
Complete second side of neck to match first reversing shapings, working 1 more row before shoulder shaping.

SLEEVES

Using 3¾mm (US5) needles and yarn A, cast on 62[62, 70] sts.
Work 7cm (2¾in) in K2, P2 rib.
Next row (WS) Rib 4[4, 2], (make 1, rib 6) 9[9, 11] times, make 1, rib 4[4, 2]. 72[72, 82] sts.
Change to 4½mm (US7) needles and work in chart patt between sleeve markers, patt 1st-38th rows, then rep 39th-48th rows, *at the same time* inc 1 st at each end of 11th[11th, 3rd] row and every foll 5th[5th, 7th] row until there are 106[106, 110] sts, working the incs into patt.
Now work straight until sleeve measures 48cm (18¾in) from cast-on edge.
Cast off loosely and evenly.

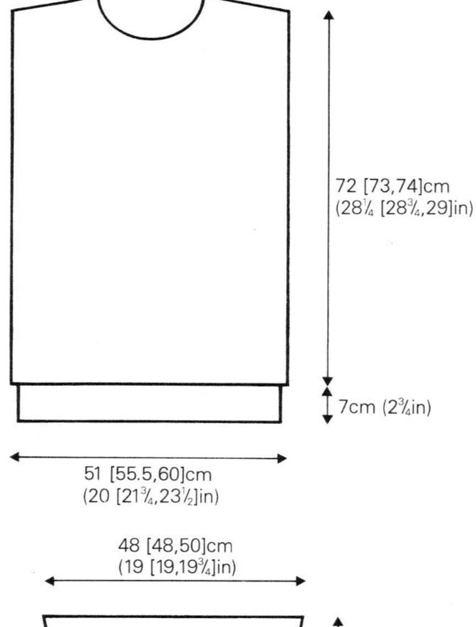

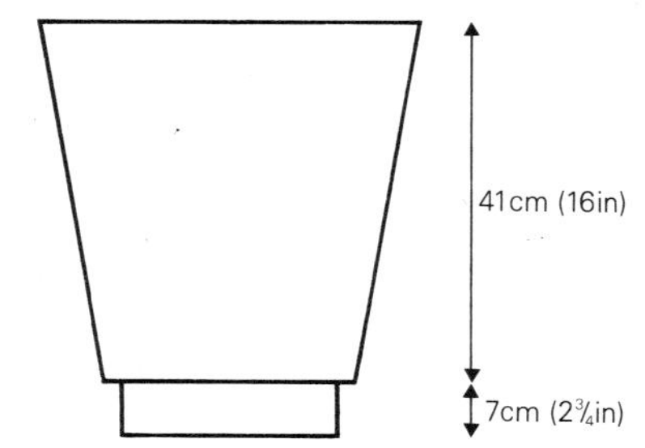

HOOD (one piece)

Using 4½mm (US7) needles and yarn B, cast on 150 sts.
K 2 rows.
Next row (WS) K1, (make 1, K7) 21 times, K2. 172 sts.
Now work in chart patt, working between markers, rep 1st-38th rows until hood measures 46cm (18in) from cast-on edge, ending with a RS row.
Next row With yarn B, P1, (P2 tog, P6) 21 times, P2 tog, P1. 150 sts.
K 3 rows. Cast off evenly.

SKIRT (one piece)

Using 4½mm (US7) circular needle and yarn A, cast on 214[230] sts. Work in rows.
Work 66[69] cm (26[27]in) in K2, P2 rib.
Change to 4mm (US6) circular needle and cont in rib until skirt measures 72[75]cm (28¼[29½]in) from cast-on edge.
P 1 row for foldline.
Waistband
Work 4cm (1½in) in K2, P2 rib.
Cast off evenly in rib.

TO MAKE UP

Sweater
Join right shoulder using a backstitch seam.
Collar
With RS of work facing, using 3¾mm (US5) needles and yarn A, K up 22 sts down left front neck, K 24 sts from centre front stitch holder, K up 22 sts up right front neck and K 46 sts from back stitch holder.
114 sts.
Work 18cm (7in) in K2, P2 rib.
Cast off evenly in rib.
Join left shoulder and collar seam.
Fold collar in half on to WS and slipstitch to neck edge.
Place markers 24[24, 25]cm (9½[9½, 9¾]in) down from shoulder seams on back and front.
Set in sleeves between markers.
Join side and sleeve seams.
Hood
With row ends tog, join side seam.
Fold a 5cm (2in) hem on to WS at cast-on edge and slipstitch down.
Skirt
With row ends tog, join side seam.
Join elastic into circle, overlapping approx 2.5cm (1in) and stitch firmly.
Place elastic inside skirt waist below foldline.
Fold waistband on to WS over elastic and catch down with herringbone stitch.

Right *The White Knight sweater and skirt. This simple, stark elegance is also seen in another Angela King design* (above).

BODYMAP

Stevie Stewart had her first market stall when she was 15 years old selling anything that might make some money. It was mainly fashion accessories, but her first step into selling clothes was to stock her stall with dyed army surplus pyjamas. That was in 1981. Since then, with the help of her partner Dave Hulah, Bodymap has gone a long way.

Stevie and Dave met at college. They say they started Bodymap because they couldn't think of anything else to do. While other graduates were still searching the job columns, they were meeting the British Prime Minister and being received by Princess Diana in recognition of their contribution to the worldwide standing of British fashion. They admit to being a little surprised at the speed at which they have made things happen, but don't quite acknowledge it as success. There has been little time to think about such things.

In five years they have built an international business with concessions in Japanese stores supported by manufacturing in Korea, collections for Italian fashion houses, and agreements with a US company to sell Bodymap throughout America. Along the way they went into liquidation, unable to cope with volume production and its attendant financing problems, but only a few weeks later they had rebuilt the company on more stable foundations, and were back in business.

Their 'costumes' defy tradition, often combining contradictory styles within one garment. The influence of Tudor dress may creep into the most modern piece of clothing imaginable. They use knitting as a fabric, ruching it, tucking and cutting and mixing it with other materials. It is intriguing to think of outknitters in rural cottages working on some of these clothes. But some of their knitwear is curiously, though perhaps unwittingly, retrospective. The little cropped cardigans of 1986 were close to the twin-sets of the fifties, so scorned by sixties trendies. This small person who hasn't had time to lose her puppyfat might easily have invented knitting herself if others had not got there first. With hard work, help from Dave, fashion flair and an amazing instinct for the market, Stevie has made Bodymap a household name.

★

RUCHED PANEL CARDIGAN

Summer

SIZE

To fit one size up to 101cm (40in) bust

MATERIALS

600g Handknit Double Knitting Cotton in white 263 (A)
300g Sea Breeze Soft Cotton in black 526 (B)
Equivalent yarn double knitting and four-ply
1 pair each 3¾mm (US5), 4½mm (US7) and 5mm (US8) needles
7 buttons

TENSION

19 sts and 30 rows to 10cm (4in) over garter st on 4½mm (US7) needles using yarn A.

SPECIAL ABBREVIATIONS

3 from 1 – K into front, back and front again of next st to make 3 sts from 1.

BACK

Using 3¾mm (US5) needles and yarn A, cast on 114 sts.
Work 11 rows in garter st (K every row).
Change to 4½mm (US7) needles and beg patt, using separate balls of yarn for each colour block and twisting yarns tog on WS at colour joins to avoid holes, as foll:
1st row (RS) K18A, with yarn B (3 from 1) 24 times, K30A, with yarn B (3 from 1) 24 times, K18A.
2nd row K18A, P72B, K30A, P72B, K18A.
3rd row K18A, 72B, 30A, 72B, 18A.
4th-40th rows Rep 2nd-3rd rows 18 times more, then 2nd row again.
41st row With A, K18, (K3 tog) 24 times, K30, (K3 tog) 24 times, K18.
42nd-46th rows With A, work in garter st.
These 46 rows form the patt rep.
Rep 1st-46th rows once more, then 1st-6th rows again.
Shape armholes
Keeping patt correct, cast off 6 sts at beg of next 2 rows, then dec 1 st at each end of next and foll 5 alt rows. 90 sts. Work 69 rows straight, ending with a 42nd patt row.
Shape shoulders
Cont in garter st, cast off 7 sts at beg of next 4 rows, and 8 sts at beg of foll 4 rows. 30 sts.
Leave these sts on a spare needle.

POCKET LININGS (make 2)

Using 4½mm (US7) needles and yarn A, cast on 24 sts. Beg with a K row, work 40 rows in st st.
Leave these sts on a stitch holder.

LEFT FRONT

Using 3¾mm (US5) needles and yarn A, cast on 60 sts.
Work 11 rows in garter st.
Change to 4½mm (US7) needles and beg patt as foll:
1st row (RS) K18A, with yarn B (3 from 1) 24 times, K18A.
This row sets the position of the colour blocks. Cont in patt as given for back until 44th patt row has been completed.
Place pocket lining
Next row With yarn A, K18, cast off 24 sts, K to end.
Next row With yarn A, K18, K across 24 sts of first pocket lining, K to end.
Cont in patt, work 52 rows, ending at armhole edge.
Shape armhole
Keeping patt correct, cast off 6 sts at beg of next row.
Work 1 row.
Dec 1 st at beg of next and foll 5 alt rows. 48 sts.
Work 58 rows in patt, thus ending with a 31st patt row.

Right *The Ruched Panel Cardigan is a clever combination of double knitting and four-ply yarns.*

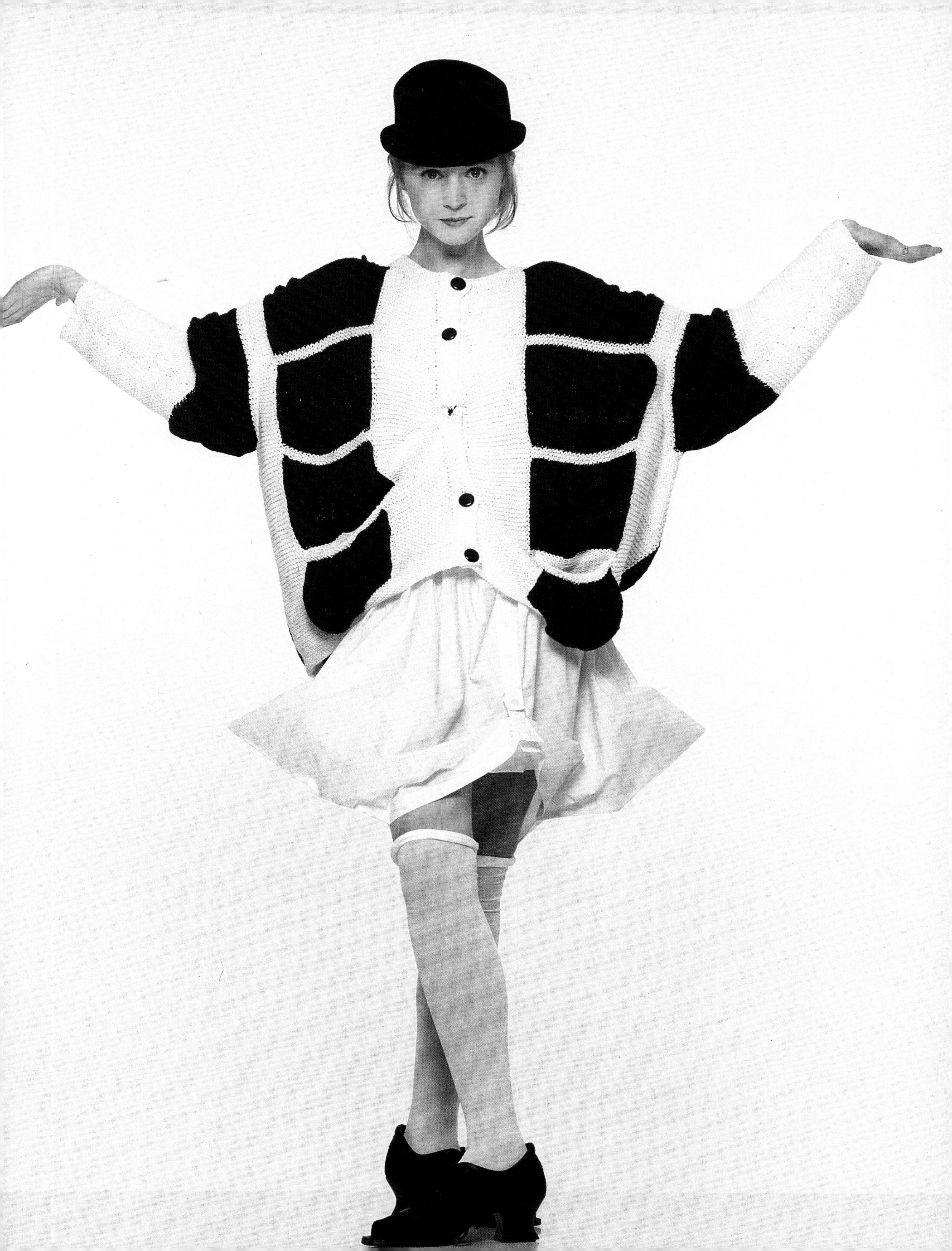

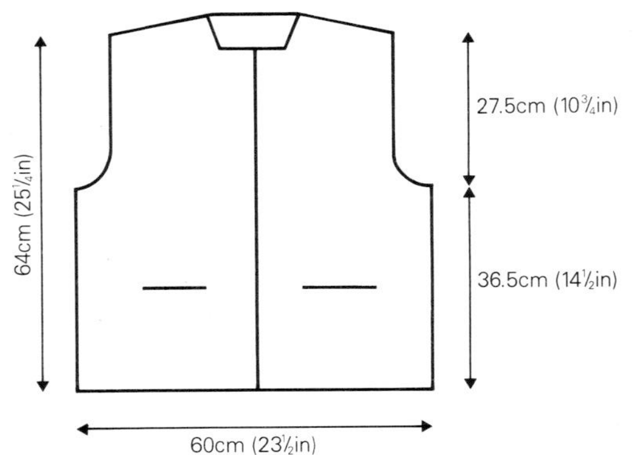

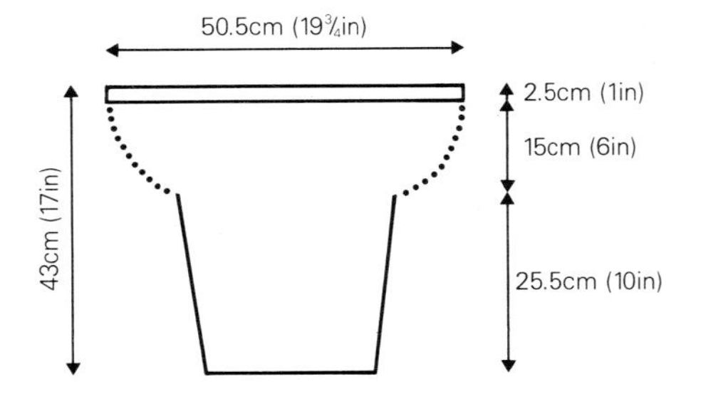

Shape neck
Cast off 12 sts at beg of next row, then dec 1 st at neck edge on foll 6 rows. 30 sts.
Work 4 rows straight, ending at armhole edge.
Shape shoulder
Cast off 7 sts at beg of next and foll alt row and 8 sts at beg of next alt row.
Work 1 row.
Cast off rem 8 sts.

RIGHT FRONT
Work as given for left front, reversing shapings.

SLEEVES
Using 3¾mm (US5) needles and yarn A, cast on 48 sts.
Work 11 rows in garter st.
Change to 4½mm (US7) needles and cont in garter st, *at the same time* inc 1 st at each end of next and every foll 10th row until there are 64 sts.
Work straight until sleeve measures 25.5cm (10in) from cast-on edge, ending with a WS row.
Change to yarn B.
Next row (3 from 1) to end. 192 sts.
Work 39 rows in st st, beg with a P row.
Change to yarn A and 5mm (US8) needles.
Next row (K2 tog) to end. 96 sts.
Work 5 rows in garter st.
Cast off very loosely.

TO MAKE UP
Join both shoulders using backstitch seams.
Neckband
With RS of work facing, using 3¾mm (US5) needles and yarn A, K up 12 sts from cast-off sts at right front neck, K up 12 sts to shoulder, K 30 sts across back neck stitch holder, K up 12 sts down left side front neck and K up 12 sts from cast-off sts at left front neck. 78 sts.
Work 11 rows in garter st.
Cast off.
Buttonhole band
With RS of work facing, using 3¾mm (US5) needles and yarn A, K up 108 sts evenly along right front edge and K up 6 sts from neckband. 114 sts.
Work 5 rows in garter st.
Buttonhole row K2, (cast off 2 sts, K16 including st used to cast off) 6 times, cast off 2 sts, K to end.
Next row K to end, casting on 2 sts over those cast off in previous row.
Work 4 rows in garter st.
Cast off.
Buttonband
Work to match buttonhole band, omitting buttonholes.
Set in sleeves joining last 5 rows of sleeve to cast-off sts at underarm. Join side and sleeve seams.
Sew pocket linings to WS of fronts.
Sew on buttons.

Above *The Bodymap approach to shapes is always a revelation. This is their version of the two-piece suit.*

★

POLO NECK DRESS

Winter

SIZE
To fit one size up to 91cm (36in) bust

MATERIALS
1,700g Lightweight Double Knitting Wool in black 62
Equivalent yarn Aran-weight
1 pair each 5mm (US8) and 6mm (US10) needles
Set of four double-pointed 5mm (US8) needles

NOTE Use yarn double.

TENSION
16 sts and 22 rows to 10cm (4in) over reversed st st on 6mm (US10) needles.

BACK
Using 5mm (US8) needles, cast on 78 sts. Work in K2, P2 rib as foll:
1st row (K2, P2) to last 2 sts, K2.
2nd row K1, P1, (K2, P2) to last 4 sts, K2, P1, K1.
Rep these 2 rows 48 times more. **
Change to 6mm (US10) needles.
Work 100 rows in reversed st st (P on RS rows, K on WS rows), beg with a P row.
***__Shape armholes__
Cont in reversed st st, cast off 5 sts at beg of next 2 rows. Now dec 1 st at each end of next and foll 2 alt rows. 62 sts.
Work 13 rows straight, ending with a WS row. ****
Now work 28 rows in K2, P2 rib as for welt, ending with a WS row.
Shape shoulders
Keeping rib correct, cast off 7 sts at beg of next 4 rows and 6 sts at beg of foll 2 rows. 22 sts.
Leave these sts on a stitch holder.

FRONT
Work as given for back to **.
Change to 6mm (US10) needles and beg patt from chart 1, work 1st-31st rows, then rep 2nd-31st rows twice more, then 2nd-10th rows again, thus ending with a WS row.
Shape armholes
Work as given for back from *** to ****, foll chart 2 for patt.
Now work 20 rows in K2, P2 rib as given for back, ending with a WS row.
Divide for neck
Next row Rib 24, turn, leaving rem sts on a spare needle and cont on these sts only for first side of neck.
Dec 1 st at neck edge on next and foll 3 alt rows, ending at armhole edge. 20 sts.
Shape shoulder
Cast off 7 sts at beg of next and foll alt row. Work 1 row. Cast off rem 6 sts.
With RS of work facing, return to sts on spare needle, sl centre 14 sts on to a stitch holder, rejoin yarn to next st, patt to end. 24 sts. Complete second side of neck to match first, reversing shapings.

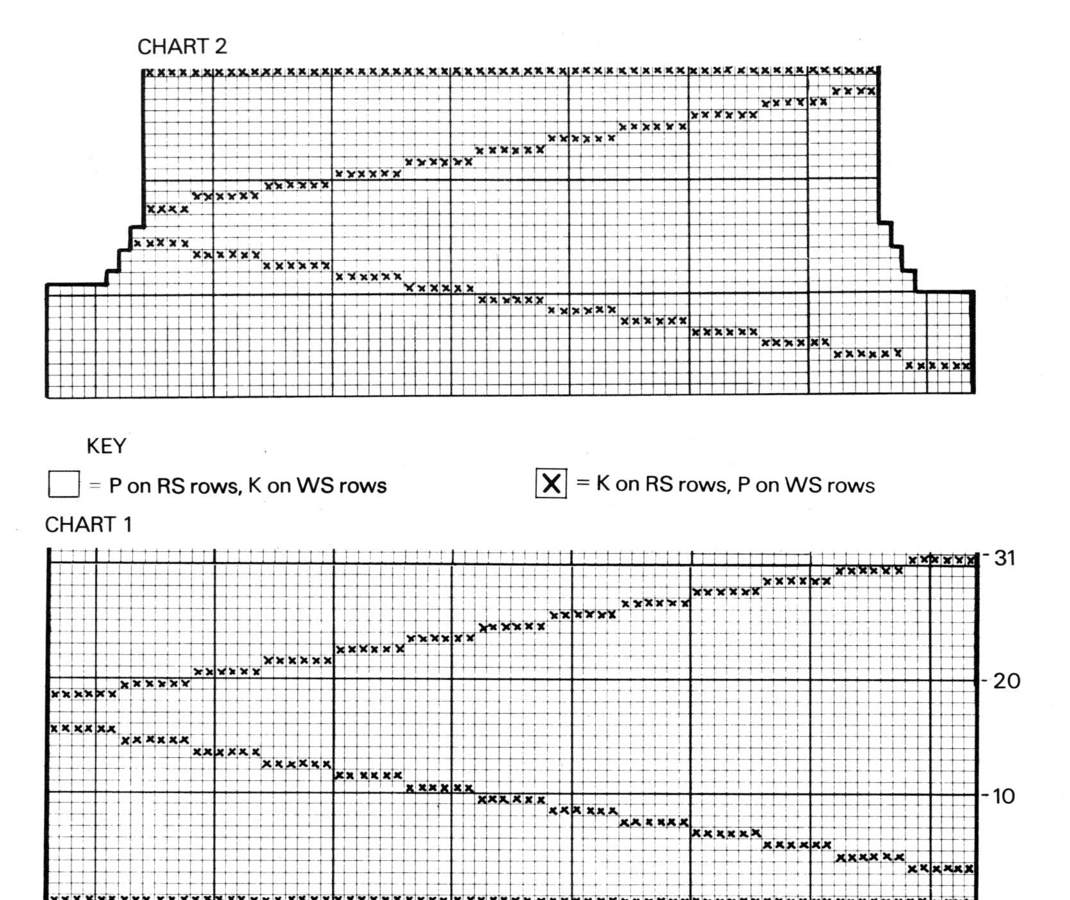

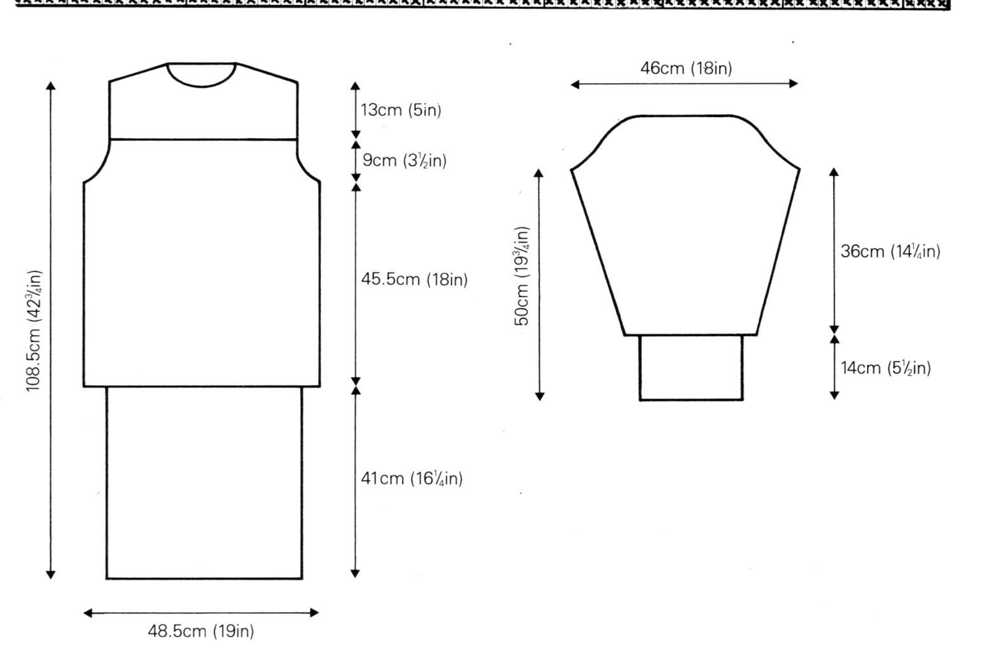

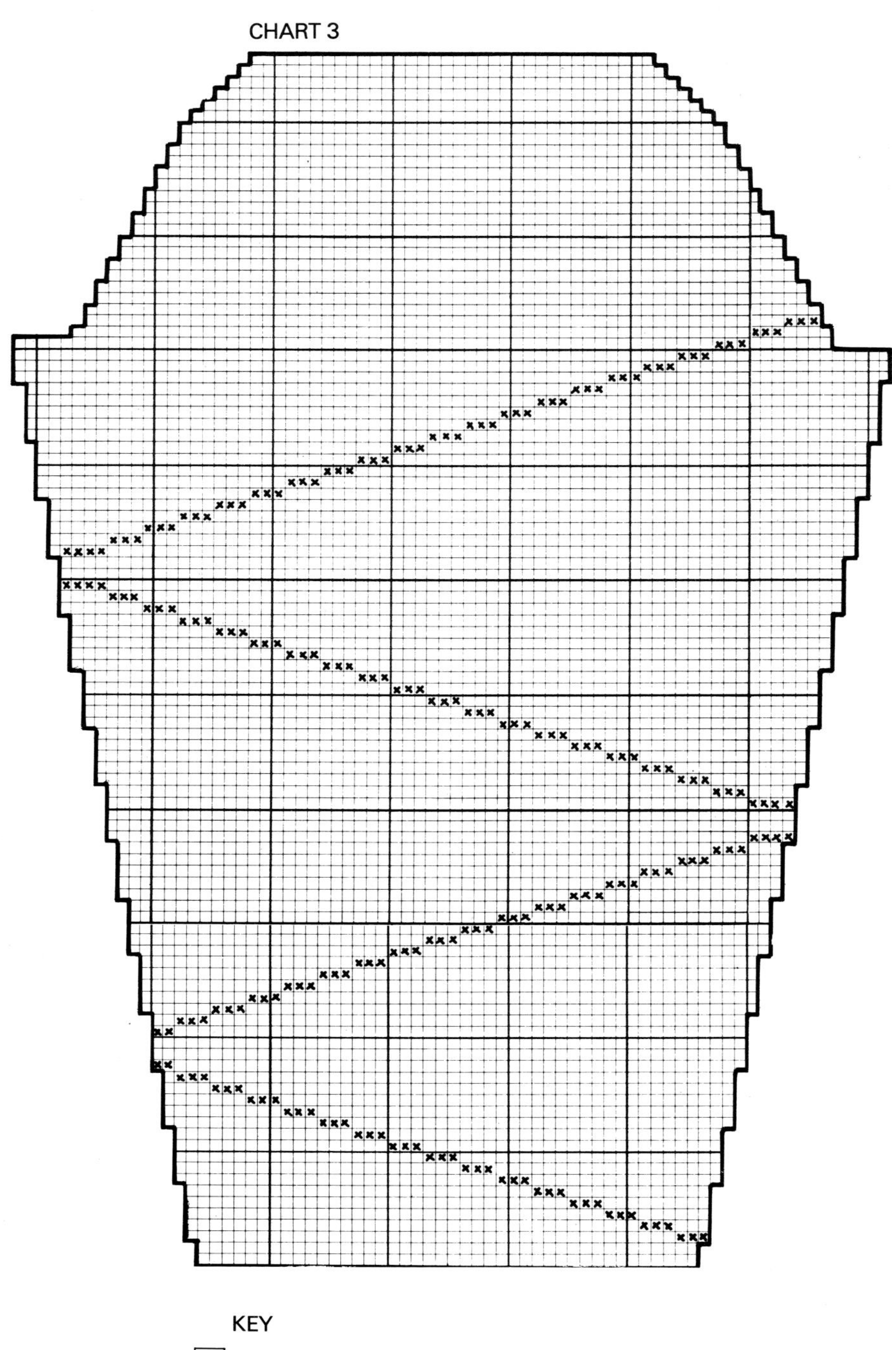

KEY

☐ = P on RS rows, K on WS rows

☒ = K on RS rows, P on WS rows

SLEEVES

Using 5mm (US8) needles, cast on 42 sts.
Work 34 rows in K2, P2 rib as given for back.
Change to 6mm (US10) needles and beg patt from chart 3, *at the same time* inc 1 st at each end of 3rd and every foll 5th row until there are 74 sts.
Work 2 rows straight, ending with a WS row.

Shape top

Keeping chart patt correct, cast off 5 sts at beg of next 2 rows, then dec 1 st at each end of next and every foll alt row until 44 sts rem (cont in reversed st st when chart patt is completed).
Dec 1 st at each end of every row until 34 sts rem.
Cast off.

FRILLS

Front

Using 6mm (US10) needles, with RS of work facing, K up 78 sts along 1st row of chart patt (1 st for every K st on chart).
***Next row** Inc 1 st in every st. 156 sts.
Work 10 rows in garter st (K every row).
Cast off loosely.*
Make 9 more frills in the same way, K up 1 st for each K st on chart and rep from * to *.

Sleeve

Work as given for front frills, make 4 frills, K up 47 sts for first frill, 54 sts for second frill and so on.

TO MAKE UP

Join both shoulders using backstitch seams.

Collar

With RS of work facing, using double-pointed 5mm (US8) needles, rib 22 sts across back neck stitch holder, K up 14 sts down left front neck, rib 14 sts from front neck stitch holder, K up 14 sts up right front neck. 64 sts.
Work 20cm (8in) in K2, P2 rib in rounds.
Cast off evenly in rib.
Join side and sleeve seams.
Set in sleeves.

Right *Bodymap's Frilled Dress – tiers of garter-stitch frills knitted on to a long slinky polo-necked little black sweater dress.*

READING THE PATTERNS

STAR RATINGS
The patterns have all been graded with one, two or three stars according to their degree of difficulty.

★

Easy straightforward knitting, suitable for beginners

★★

More difficult, suitable for average knitters with a little experience

★★★

Challenging and/or time consuming, for the more experienced knitter

SIZES
The instructions are given first for the smallest size, with those for larger sizes following in square brackets. Where there is only one set of instructions, it applies to all sizes. Some of the patterns are given for one size only. The 'to fit' measurement includes varying amounts of ease, depending on the styling of the garment (whether it is intended to be tight-fitting or baggy). Actual garment measurements are shown on the measurement diagrams.

MATERIALS
All the yarns specified are Rowan yarns, and both shade names and numbers are given. In some cases yarns are combined and knitted as one yarn. The weight described as the 'equivalent yarn' refers to overall weight of yarn for that particular garment and this is the weight that should be used if you are substituting a single yarn for combined yarns.

The quantities given are for Rowan yarns only. If you substitute a different yarn the amounts may vary, especially if the substitute yarn is of a different fibre composition from the original.

Some yarns are available in the shops in minimum quantities of 50g. This means that, in the case of certain patterns (for example, Kaffe Fassett's Windows Coat), you will be buying much larger amounts of some yarns than will be needed. However, yarn kits are available for a number of garments and these will provide yarn amounts much closer to those actually used. If a yarn kit is available, this is indicated in the pattern, and a complete list of kits will be found on page 160.

Both UK and US needle sizes are given. There is also a needle conversion chart with old UK sizes on page 159. In many cases, even if they are not specified, it may be helpful to use circular needles, especially where the number of stitches or the size of the garment makes it impractical to use single-pointed needles.

TENSION
The tension measurement is given in metric and standard measurements. Since they are not exactly equivalent, there will be a slight difference in the measurements produced. It is very important to work *either* to metric *or* to standard measurements, and not move to and fro between the two.

It is also essential to obtain the correct tension for each garment. This is the single most important factor which makes the difference between a successful garment and a disastrous one. It governs the shape and size of a garment, so any variation, however small, can completely distort the finished look. Many different designers appear in this book and it is *their* tension which must be matched. This is the tension which is specified on each pattern. It is essential to knit up a tension square and match your tension to that given in the pattern, before beginning to knit the garment.

MAKING A TENSION SQUARE
Using the yarn specified for the garment (if there are several weights, use one which matches the 'equivalent yarn') and the recommended needle size in the tension measurement, knit up a tension square slightly larger than the 10cm (4in) given in the tension measurement, in the stitch pattern specified. Place the tension square on a flat surface and measure it as follows:

1 Place a ruler horizontally on the square, lining it up along the bottom of a row of stitches. Place a pin at zero, and another at the 10cm (4in) mark. Count the stitches between the pins, including half-stitches if any.

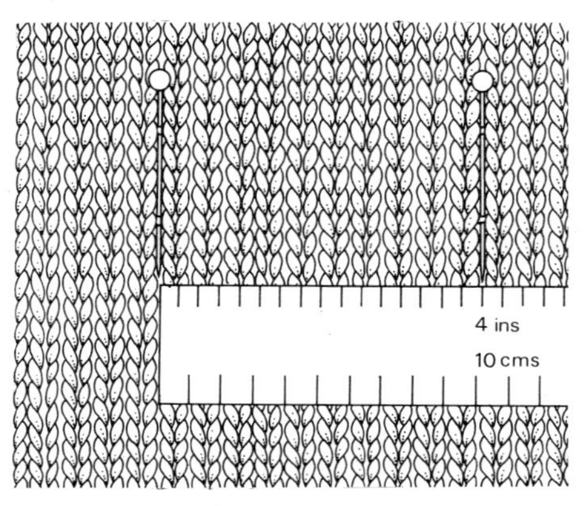

2 Place a ruler vertically on the square lining it up along one side of a column of stitches. Place a pin at the zero mark and another at the 10cm (4in) mark. Count the rows between the pins including half-rows if any.

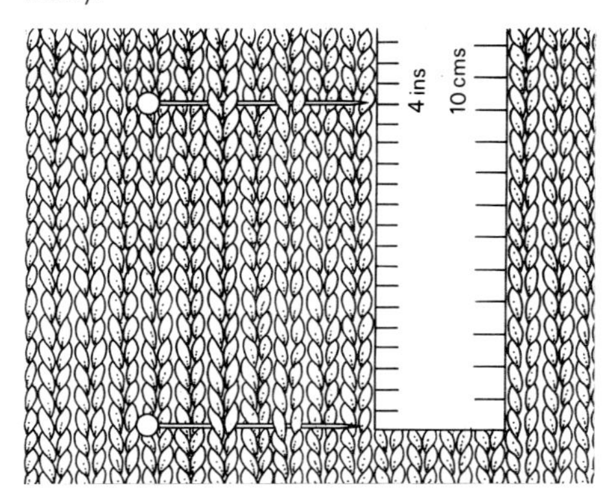

ADJUSTING YOUR TENSION
If the number of stitches or rows is greater than that given in the tension measurement, your knitting is too tight and the garment will be too small. Knit up another tension square using larger needles. If the number of stitches or rows is less than that given in the tension measurement, your knitting is too loose and the garment will be too big. Knit up another tension square using smaller needles. Carry on changing the needle size until your tension matches exactly that of the pattern. If you do have to use a different needle size to the one given, you will also have to make a similar adjustment for any other needle sizes given, for example, for ribs, neckbands, hems and so on.

CHARTS
Many of the patterns in this book are knitted from charts. Some of the charts show the whole of a garment; others show only a pattern repeat. Each square on the chart represents one stitch and each row of squares one row. With every chart there is a key which tells you which colour or which stitch to work for each square. Unless otherwise indicated in the pattern, work all charts reading right-side rows from right to left and wrong-side rows from left to right. Where a pattern repeat only is shown, the stitches must be worked several times across the row, and the rows repeated as specified in the pattern or alongside the chart.

KNITTING WITH COLOUR
There are two main methods of working colour into a knitted fabric: intarsia (block or motif knitting) and Fair Isle type knitting. The first method produces a single thickness fabric and is generally used where a colour is required only in a particular area of a fabric. The Fair Isle method is used when a colour is repeated several times across a row. The yarns are handled quite differently for each method.

INTARSIA
Use separate lengths of yarn about 60-100cm (2-3 feet) long, or small balls, for each area of colour. Link each colour to the next by twisting them together on the wrong side at the colour joins, thus avoiding holes between the colours. This is particularly important when working vertical joins. As each block of colour is completed, darn in the ends along the colour joins, or knit them into the back of the work.

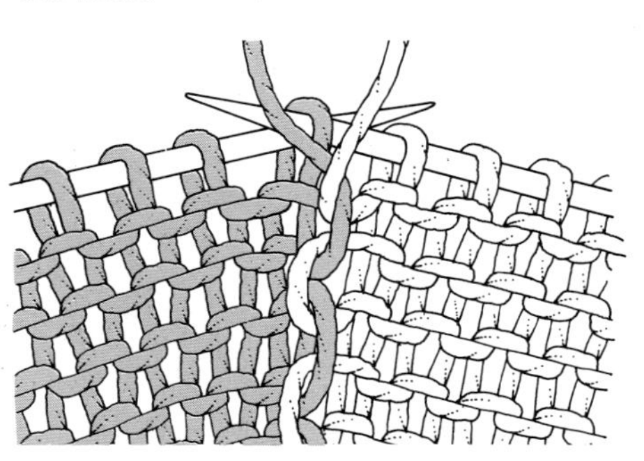

Twisting yarns to avoid gaps.

FAIR ISLE

In this method two or more colours are repeated across the row, and the yarns not being used at a particular moment are carried across the back of the work in various ways. If three or fewer stitches have to be spanned, float or 'strand' the yarns loosely across the back. If more than two colours are used, treat all the floating yarns as one yarn and spread the stitches out to the correct width to keep the knitting elastic. If more than three stitches have to be spanned, weave the floating yarns under and over the colour you are working, so that they are caught at the back of the work.

It cannot be stressed too much that floating yarns must be carried very loosely otherwise the knitting will pucker and the finished work will be much too narrow.

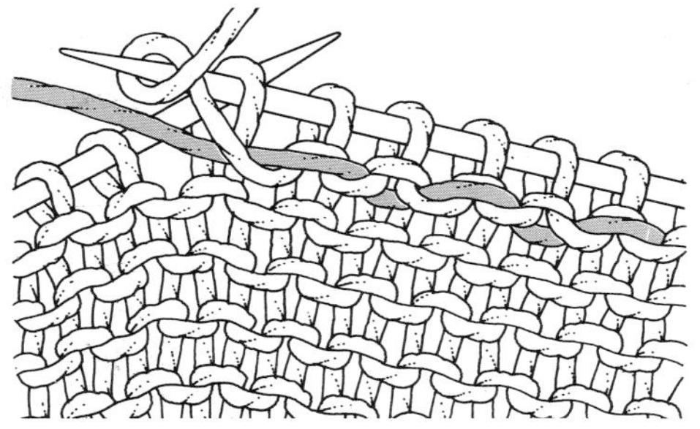

Weaving yarns across the back.

Above *A striking example of the intarsia method from Sandy Black.*

Below *A beautiful Kaffe Fassett jacket worked using Fair Isle techniques.*

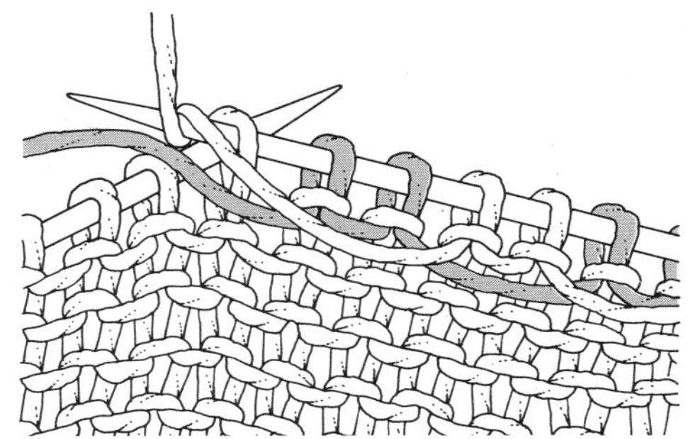

Stranding yarns in a purl row.

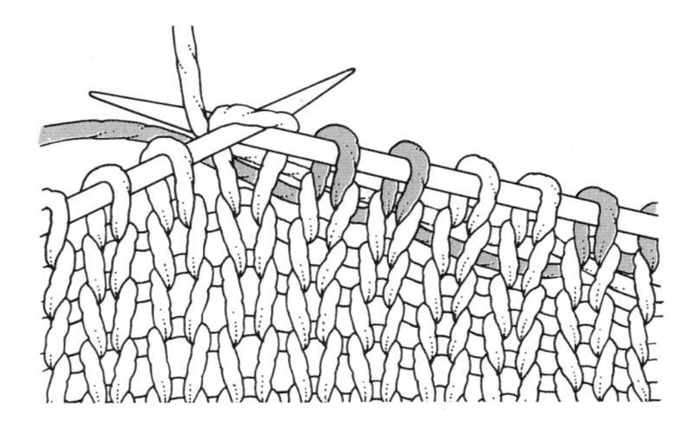

Stranding yarns in a knit row.

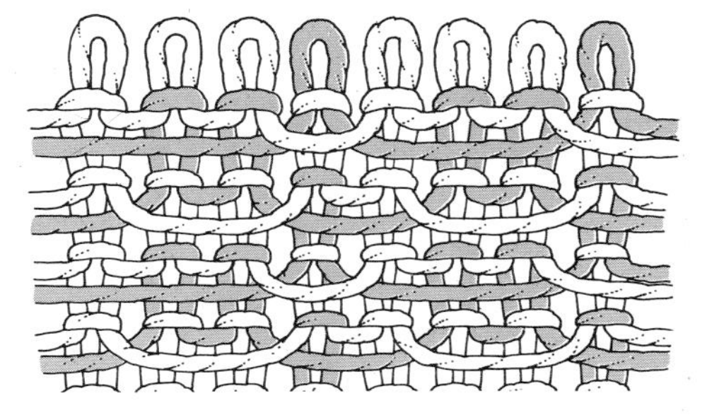

Stranding at the back of the work.

SWISS DARNING

This is a very useful technique used by one or two of the designers in this book to work odd areas of colour after the pieces of knitting are completed. It can also be used to correct mistakes by working the correct colour over a wrong one.

1 Thread a tapestry needle with the required colour (it must be the same weight as the basic yarn in the garment). Anchor the yarn at the back of the work and bring it through to the front at A. Pass the needle behind the stitch above at B to C.

2 Take the needle to the back of the work at D and bring it to the front again through the base of the next stitch to be covered at E. Carry on in this way until all the stitches are covered.

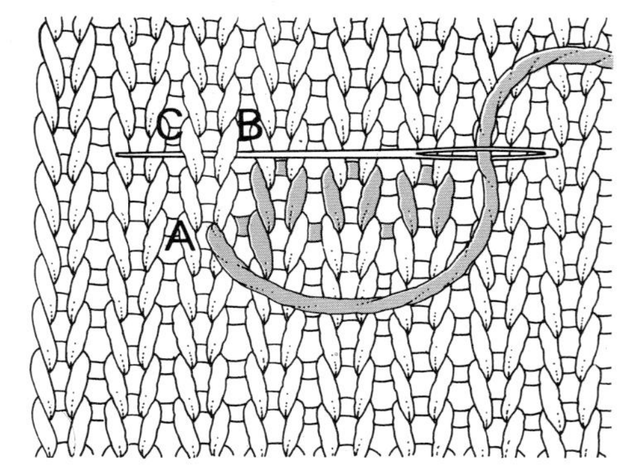

Above *Swiss darning can be used to fill in the fine detail of a garment after the main work is completed, as in the narrow trellis on Martin Kidman's sweater.*

MAKING UP

After working for hours and hours knitting a garment, it seems a great pity that many garments are spoiled because so little care is taken in the finishing. After darning in all the ends, block each piece of knitting and press gently following the instructions on the label or ball band. Wool and cotton yarns such as the ones used in this book may be pressed using a warm iron and a damp cloth, but many synthetic yarns may not be pressed at all. If you are pressing, take special care to press the edges as this will make the sewing up much easier. When stitching the pieces together match the colour patterns very carefully. After sewing up, press seams and hems. Ribbed welts and neckbands and any areas of garter stitch should not be pressed.

AFTERCARE

Follow the washing instructions shown on the ball band or label. All the yarns in this book (except Nashville) can be hand-washed (or dry-cleaned in certain solvents) only. They must not be machine-washed. Wash very carefully in hand-warm water using a very mild soap, preferably one designed for knitwear. Gently squeeze the garment in the water. Do not rub as this will cause felting. Do not leave the garment to soak. Rinse several times in clean water to remove the suds. Do not wring. Spin for a few seconds to remove excess moisture, then dry flat. Longer spinning will result in felting. Do not tumble dry.

Nashville is not a pre-shrunk or fast-dyed yarn. There will be a loss of dye so it is important, especially in the first wash, to wash separately at 60°C.

ABBREVIATIONS

alt – alternate(ly)
approx – approximately
beg – begin(ning)
cm – centimetres
cont – continu(e)(ing)
dec – decreas(e)(ing)
foll – follow(s)(ing)
g – grams
in – inch(es)
K – knit
K up – pick up and knit
make 1 – pick up horizontal loop before next stitch and knit into the back of it
mm – millimetres
P – purl
patt – pattern
psso – pass slipped stitch over
p2sso – pass 2 slipped stitches over
rem – remain(s)(ing)
rep – repeat(s)
RS – right side of work
sl – slip
st(s) – stitch(es)
st st – stocking stitch (stockinette stitch)
tbl – through back of loop(s)
tog – together
WS – wrong side of work
yb – yarn to back of work
yo – yarn round needle (yarn over)
ytf – yarn to front of work

HINTS FOR AMERICAN KNITTERS

American knitters will have few problems in working from English patterns and *vice versa*. The following tables and glossaries should prove useful.

TERMINOLOGY

UK	US
cast off	bind off
catch down	tack down
double crochet	single crochet
stocking stitch	stockinette stitch
Swiss darning	duplicate stitch
tension	gauge
yarn round needle	yarn over

All other terms are the same in both countries.

UK/US YARN EQUIVALENTS
The following table shows approximate yarn equivalents in terms of thickness. However, it is always essential to check your tension.

UK	US
4-ply	sport
double knitting	knitting worsted
Aran/medium-weight	fisherman/medium-weight
chunky	bulky

METRIC CONVERSION TABLES

Length (to the nearest ¼in) / **Weight (rounded up to the nearest ¼oz)**

cm	in	cm	in	g	oz
1	½	55	21¾	25	1
2	¾	60	23½	50	2
3	1¼	65	25½	100	3¾
4	1½	70	27½	150	5½
5	2	75	29½	200	7¼
6	2½	80	31½	250	9
7	2¾	85	33½	300	10¾
8	3	90	35½	350	12½
9	3½	95	37½	400	14¼
10	4	100	39½	450	16
11	4¼	110	43½	500	17¾
12	4¾	120	47	550	19½
13	5	130	51¼	600	21¼
14	5½	140	55	650	23
15	6	150	59	700	24¾
16	6¼	160	63	750	26½
17	6¾	170	67	800	28¼
18	7	180	70¾	850	30
19	7½	190	74¾	900	31¾
20	8	200	78¾	950	33¾
25	9¾	210	82¾	1000	35½
30	11¾	220	86½	1200	42¼
35	13¾	230	90½	1400	49¼
40	15¾	240	94½	1600	56½
45	17¾	250	98½	1800	63½
50	19¾	300	118	2000	70½

NEEDLE SIZE CONVERSION TABLE
The needle sizes given in the patterns are recommended starting points for making tension samples. The needle size actually used should be that on which the stated tension is obtained.

Metric	US	Old UK
2mm	0	14
2¼mm	1	13
2½mm		
2¾mm	2	12
3mm		
3¼mm	3	10
3½mm	4	
3¾mm	5	9
4mm	6	8
4½mm	7	7
5mm	8	6
5½mm	9	5
6mm	10	4
6½mm	10½	3
7mm		2
7½mm		1
8mm	11	0
9mm	13	00
10mm	15	000

ACKNOWLEDGMENTS

This book owes much to the help and influence of many people. First, the designers whose skills have made it possible. The consummate artistic and design flair of Kaffe Fassett is probably the single most important reason that this book evolved. He has continually made me re-evaluate and search for excellence in all matters concerning design. In the daily task of running a small business, his unique perspective on all things visual is a tonic.

Kathleen Hargreaves, Linda Clarke and their team of knitters have worked tirelessly to knit, check and write patterns. Simon Cockin, a founding director of Rowan Yarns, and my wife Kathryn have supported me throughout the months of preparation and photography.

Thanks are also due to Karen Elder who chatted to the designers and so professionally expressed their thoughts, and to all the staff of Rowan Yarns. Friends, colleagues and customers including Hugh Ehrman, Shirley Barnett, Richard Heppenstall and John Webb, photographers Tony Boase and Eamonn J. McCabe, our overseas distributors – especially Kenneth Bridgewater of Westminster Trading Corporation in the United States – have all assisted in many ways.

Many stockists of Rowan Yarns worldwide are so supportive of our efforts to bring about changes in creative knitting; shops like Ries Wools of Holborn and Creativity of New Oxford Street, Phil and Marlene at Parc Laine, Oxford, England, Jane and Pauline at Up Country in Holmfirth, West Yorkshire, England, and many many more give us so much encouragement. Gail Rebuck, my publisher, and her colleague Sarah Wallace deserve a special thank you for their clear, unflinching belief in the project without compromise.

Finally, I must thank the knitters at home who have welcomed our ideas so enthusiastically; this book, after all, is for their enjoyment.

CREDITS

The photographs were styled by Kimberley Watson and Julia Fletcher (the Classics), and by Caroline Baker, Anne Drummond and Tracey Jacob (the Moderns). Hair and make-up by Rod Smith (the Classics) and Sally Francombe (the Moderns). The models were Jo Thompson, Diana Mulbey, Rachel Davies, Emma Wollard, Rachel Mulholland, Ben Shawl, Sacha Parsons, David Convy and Petrushka (the Classics), and Mark, Emma Campbell, Nora, Will Stewart-Brown, Little Echo, Saffron Aldridge, Sara, Sibyl, Clara and Tian (the Moderns). Clothes were loaned by Dickens and Jones, Nigel Preston, Warehouse, Benedetto, Amalgamated Talent, American Classics Bodymap, Richmond/ Cornejo, Erika Knight for Molto, Joseph Tricot, Sarah Dallas, Jones, Christopher Fischer, Katherine Hamnett, Artwork, Martin Kidman, Benetton, Fenwicks.

Shoes were loaned by Richmond/ Cornejo, hosiery and socks by Mary Quant, Benetton and Funn, belts by Pure Fabricaton, gloves by Cornelia James, jewellery by Talisma, antique wraps and scarves by the Gallery of Antique Clothes and Textiles, antique lace by Lunn Antiques and hats by The Hat Shop, Warehouse, Bernstock/Spiers and Cristys.

STOCKISTS

All the patterns in this book have been specially designed for Rowan yarns and these are available from a wide range of quality yarn shops. Knitting kits can also be obtained for the following designs:

Kaffe Fassett's Windows Coat (page 12)
Zoë Hunt's Mosaic Sweater (page 24)
Carrie White's Bijar Sweater (page 34)
Jean Moss's Bellmanear Sweater (page 42)
Jamie and Jessi Seaton's Caspian Flowers (page 68)
Susan Duckworth's Venetian Tile Cardigan (oatmeal colourway) (page 74)
Martin Kidman's Horses and Flowers Sweater (adult version) (page 82)
Martin Kidman's Hunt Sweater (page 88)
Christopher Fischer's Lumberjack (page 128)

Please write to the following addresses for details of yarn stockists and knitting kits.

United Kingdom
Rowan Yarns
Green Lane Mill
Holmfirth
West Yorkshire HD7 1RW
Tel. 0484 686714/687374

United States
Westminster Trading
5 Northern Boulevard
Amherst
New Hampshire 03031
Tel. 603 886 5041

Canada
Estelle
38 Continental Place
Scarborough
Ontario M1R 2T4
Tel. 416 298 9922

Australia
Sunspun
195 Canterbury Road
Canterbury 3126
Tel. 03 830 1609

New Zealand
Creative Fashion Centre
PO Box 45083
Epuni Railway
Lower Hutt
Tel. 674 085

West Germany
Textilwerkstatt
Friedenstrasse 5
3000 Hanover 1
Tel. 49 511 818001

Holland
Handwerken zonder grenzen
Dorpstraat 9
5327 Ar Hurwenen
Tel. 31 4182 1764

Denmark
Mosekonens Vaerksted
Mosevej 13
Li Binderup
9600 Aars
Denmark
Tel. 45 8656065

Sweden
Faroprodukter
Tysta Gatan 11
115 24 Stockholm
Tel. 08 672202

Cyprus
Litsa Christofides
18 Parnithos Street
Nicosia
Cyprus
Tel. 357 472933